Independence in Latin America

JOE R. AND TERESA LOZANO LONG SERIES IN
LATIN AMERICAN AND LATINO ART AND CULTURE

Independence in Latin America

CONTRASTS AND COMPARISONS
THIRD EDITION

By Richard Graham

University of Texas Press   *Austin*

Requests for permission to reproduce material from this work should be
sent to:
   Permissions
   University of Texas Press
   P.O. Box 7819
   Austin, TX 78713-7819
   http://utpress.utexas.edu/about/book-permissions

♾ The paper used in this book meets the minimum requirements of
ANSI/NISO Z39.48-1992 (R1997) (Permanence of Paper).

LIBRARY OF CONGRESS CATALOGING-IN-PUBLICATION DATA
Graham, Richard, 1934–
Independence in Latin America : contrasts and comparisons / By Richard
Graham. — Third Edition
        p.   cm. — (Joe R. and Teresa Lozano Long series in Latin American
and Latino art and culture)
Includes bibliographical references and index.
ISBN 978-0-292-74451-6 (cloth : alk. paper) —
ISBN 978-0-292-74534-6 (pbk. : alk. paper)
1. Latin America—History—Wars of Independence, 1806–1830.   I. Title.
F1412.G64   2013
980'.02—dc23   2012040856

doi:10.7560/744516

For

MARSHALL

JUNE

ANNIE

MILES

COLE

THOMAS

MARINA

Contents

Illustrations

Acknowledgments

M ANY HAVE CONTRIBUTED TO THIS BOOK. I ESPE-
cially want to thank my undergraduate students, who heard
a good deal of its content in lectures and asked provocative questions, regularly forcing me to clarify my meaning or be more precise. Fellow scholars,
sometimes through casual conversations, sometimes more formally by commenting on academic papers, have added qualifications and nuance. For the
documents presented in this volume I am especially grateful to Peter Guardino
and Pamela Murray. Jim Dunlap and Barbara Sommer helped identify some
appropriate illustrations, and the staff at the Center for Southwest Research–
Zimmerman Library of the University of New Mexico made their reproduc-
tion possible. Richard and Shirley Cushing Flint advised on the translation
of Spanish-language documents. Deborah Read prepared the maps with care,
patience, and skill.

Sandra Lauderdale Graham took much time away from her own research
and writing to read and critique all these chapters, engaging with the argument,
sometimes to question my logic, always to suggest improvements.

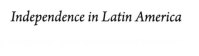

Independence in Latin America

Introduction

IN THE COURSE OF FIFTEEN MOMENTOUS YEARS, THE Spanish and Portuguese American empires that had endured without serious challenge for three centuries came to an end in the mid-1820s. The subsequent states now operated within a new paradigm, generally acknowledging the principle of constitutionalism and popular sovereignty, even if not always observing its rules. And within these states—and mainly as a result of the war itself and of the new governmental structures—national solidarity and national identity soon came to be taken for granted, as people identified themselves not only as inhabitants of America, but as Argentines, Venezuelans, or Mexicans. Moreover, the notion that society consisted of individuals and not of a body made up of castes, guilds, and other corporate orders had become commonplace. How all this came about is explored here.

Before turning to the events in question, it is worth noting that three factors delimited the course and ultimately shaped the meaning of these independence movements. First, colonial elites sought to maintain control over Indians, blacks, and the poor in general. Second, peasants, slaves, and workers sought—sometimes successfully, sometimes not—to assert themselves in the face of difficult economic conditions or altered political realities. And third, a world economy increasingly centered in northern (or northwestern) Europe now impinged directly on the life of Latin Americans, not only in terms of their livelihoods but also through a set of accompanying ideas that encompassed both a scientific approach to the natural and social world and an ideology of individualism and democratic government.

Already in the previous century the transformed economies of northern Europe had created a growing demand for raw materials and luxuries from New World colonies. Planters, ranchers, and miners jockeyed to supply these "colonial" goods directly to the consuming centers rather than through Spain or Portugal and to import manufactured goods on the same basis. But to produce those goods they often relied on unfree labor, and, in order to control the workers, they counted on the political stability and governmental authority that Spain and Portugal could supply. So many of them faced a conundrum: They desired independence in order to pursue perceived economic advantage but faced the danger of thereby losing control over coerced laborers. And then, although the social and political theories associated with growing economic connections to northern Europe were held only by a relatively small number in Portuguese and Spanish America, this group proved influential well beyond its size because it was socially connected to the economically dominant and — once independence was secured — to the politically powerful. These circumstances set the contours, directed the outcomes, and lent significance to the portentous events examined in this book.

To speak of independence requires an understanding of what it meant to be a colony. There have been many types of colonies in the history of the world. But in the Atlantic world of the seventeenth and eighteenth centuries, the predominant one existed for the economic benefit of the metropolis and depended on holding a monopoly over colonial trade. That is, merchants of the metropolis, or, rather, a subset of these, secured from their respective governments the exclusive right to trade with the colony. To secure this monopoly against competitors from other countries or from the colony itself meant that the metropolitan government had to maintain its political power and its authority over the colony. Navies had to protect the coast from smugglers; navigation acts had to be passed to limit shipping to one's flag, customs offices set up to inspect imported goods, governors appointed, and courts established. To pay for all this, governments levied taxes on the colonials. And if colonial products were to be shipped in sufficient quantities to make the trade worthwhile, workers who would otherwise prefer to produce their own food had to be persuaded or compelled to produce nonedibles such as tobacco, cotton, sugar, cacao, or coffee and to labor in mines to bring up gold, silver, or diamonds. Those areas of the New World where soils or climate led only to the production of crops such as wheat or barley that Europe supplied for itself — as was true in Pennsylvania, New York, and New England — can be considered a different type of colony. Also, cattle-raising regions managed to produce hides and other pastoral products for export in a system wherein total labor needs were low and coerced labor was inappropriate. But in the remaining areas a great number of unfree or, at any rate, involuntary laborers dominated by a strata of wealthy local proprietors proved the rule. Alongside these owners were the agents of privileged European merchant houses that monopolized overseas trade and an imposing list of bureaucrats directed by a metropolitan government. In Spanish and Portuguese America — collectively referred to here as Latin America — an elaborate Catholic Church hierarchy lent legitimacy to the entire system. Evidently implicit in this colonial structure were three sources of tension: that between workers and the propertied; that between the American producers of exports and consumers of European-made imports on the one hand and the European monopoly merchants who wished to control this trade on the other; and, finally, that between the merchant communities of the respective colonial powers in Europe, each of which would wish to maintain its own exclusive rights while raiding the colonies of others.

But the *timing* of the move toward political independence in Latin America resulted not from these multiple strains but from very specific events on the European continent. Whereas English North America had initiated its independence movement almost thirty-five years earlier and was often looked to as a model by the insurgents in Latin America, it was the 1789 French Revolution and especially the succeeding wars that led directly to the onset of the independence struggle I examine here. Whenever Spain allied itself with France against the British, it found itself cut off from its American colonies. Then when Napoleon in 1808 embarked on a determined effort to dominate the Iberian Peninsula, the Portuguese government itself moved to Brazil, making Brazil, in a sense, independent, although not totally free of Portuguese control until 1822. In Spain, Napoleon's invading army and puppet government encountered fierce opposition, leading patriots there to establish a constitutional regime in 1812, a move with far-reaching effects on Spanish America. The restoration of the former absolute monarchy in 1815 marked the end of the first phase in this story for Spanish America.

For events in Latin America can be broken chronologically into two distinct wars for independence, divided from each other around 1815 or 1816. This second war, recounted in chapter 5, resulted from the experiences of the first, unsuccessful one and from the behavior of the Spaniards after the revolutionaries' first defeat. The puzzle explored in chapters 2, 3, and 4 is how the widely divergent regional and group reactions to social divisions within each area, to the possibility of trade with England, and to the transformations promised by Enlightenment liberalism are all linked to the onset and course of the first war. The setting and background for all these events are explored in chapter 1; the resulting changes are assessed in chapter 6. I have deliberately refrained from commenting on the documents that conclude this book in order to allow readers to come to their own conclusions about them, although the text itself provides their context.

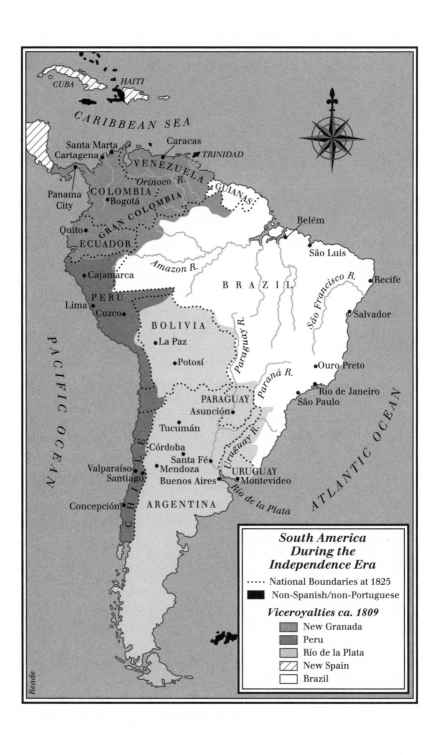

CUBA HAITI

CARIBBEAN SEA

Santa Marta   Caracas
Cartagena   *TRINIDAD*
        VENEZUELA
Panama   *Orinoco R.*
City   COLOMBIA   GUIANAS
        Bogotá
        GRAN COLOMBIA
Quito
    ECUADOR   Belém

                                São Luis
        Cajamarca
                Amazon R.   B R A Z I L   Recife
    PERU
Lima   São Francisco R.
    Cuzco   Salvador

        BOLIVIA
        La Paz   Paraguay R.
                                        Ouro Preto
            Potosí   Paraná R.
                                        Rio de Janeiro
        PARAGUAY   São Paulo
        Asunción

        Tucumán   Uruguay R.

    Córdoba
Valparaíso   Santa Fé   URUGUAY
Santiago   Mendoza   Montevideo
        Buenos Aires   Río de la Plata

Concepción   ARGENTINA

PACIFIC OCEAN

ATLANTIC OCEAN

Reade

South America
During the
Independence Era

···· National Boundaries at 1825
■ Non-Spanish/non-Portuguese

Viceroyalties ca. 1809

    New Granada
    Peru
    Río de la Plata
    New Spain
    Brazil

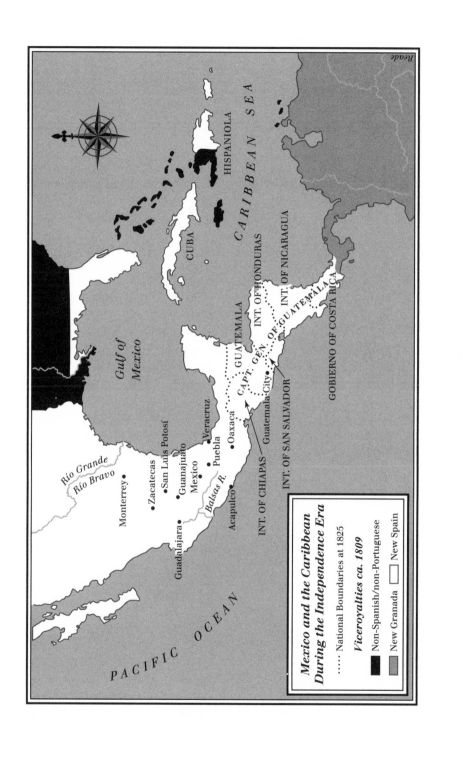

CARIBBEAN SEA

HISPANIOLA

CUBA

Gulf of
Mexico

INT. OF HONDURAS

INT. OF NICARAGUA

CAPT. GEN. OF GUATEMALA

GUATEMALA

Guatemala City

GOBIERNO OF COSTA RICA

Río Grande
Río Bravo

Monterrey

Zacatecas

San Luis Potosí

Guanajuato

Mexico

Veracruz

Puebla

Balsas R.

Oaxaca

Acapulco

INT. OF CHIAPAS

INT. OF SAN SALVADOR

Guadalajara

PACIFIC OCEAN

**Mexico and the Caribbean
During the Independence Era**

...... National Boundaries at 1825

Viceroyalties ca. 1809

▮ Non-Spanish/non-Portuguese

▮ New Granada   □ New Spain

CHAPTER ONE

Colonies in Flux

T HE EIGHTEENTH CENTURY SAW THE CROWNING OF A new dynasty in Spain and a reinvigorated government in Portugal. Administrative and policy changes altered the imperial structure of power and generally lessened — or tried to lessen — the control exercised by colonial elites over their own affairs. England as center of the new economic order increasingly threatened to endanger Spanish and Portuguese colonial trade monopolies. The power of the church to vouchsafe the authority of the state declined, while the competing ideas of the European Enlightenment grew. Tension and friction between various social strata in Spanish and Portuguese colonies became more intense. As Simón Bolívar later put it, "A great volcano lies at our feet. Who shall restrain the oppressed classes?" — a question made especially relevant by the Haitian Revolution.[1]

RULER AND RULED

So linked were societies on the two sides of the Atlantic that military, diplomatic, and political events in the Iberian Peninsula had major repercussions for the structures of government in Latin America and exacerbated tensions within the colonies. The War of the Spanish Succession broke out at the beginning of the eighteenth century when Louis XIV of France decided to enforce his family's claim to the throne of Spain and hoped eventually to unite the two kingdoms, a decision to which other powers objected. At the end of this war in 1713 France agreed that it and Spain would remain forever separate, but a major branch of the Bourbon line would replace the Hapsburg dynasty on the Spanish throne. The first three Bourbon kings, Philip V (reigned 1700–1746), Ferdinand VI (r. 1746–1759), and Charles III (r. 1759–1788), inspired by the example of their French cousins and at first surrounded by French advisers, set to work to transform Spain. In so doing they wrought major changes on Spanish America as well.

Perhaps the most important alterations made by the Bourbons were the result of their view of the relationship between king and subject. The Hapsburgs had thought of themselves as patriarchs who occupied their position not because of the divine right of kings but, so to speak, because of the divine right of fathers. According to the Hapsburg view, God had ordained the family the basic unit of society, and the family was hierarchically structured with the father at its head. The king was also the head of a similarly structured "family," with every member of society occupying a place within it fixed by God. This political philosophy, which permeated the entire social organism, fostered and depended on relationships of authority-dependence, benevolence-loyalty. No legislation could change the deeply meaningful link between king and subject, just as no law could alter the biological connection between father and child. Legal theorists in the sixteenth century had clearly laid out the king's responsibilities to protect his subjects. Viceroys were expected to avoid confrontations and work out compromises with the locals when needed. The Bourbons in the eighteenth century took a different tack. Although not entirely free of such a familial viewpoint, they were more apt to think of the king as a ruler than as a father and to judge him by his effectiveness rather than by his benevolence. Many Spanish Americans, however, clung to the image of the paternalistic state and resisted the Bourbons' new approach. The long process through which people came to direct their loyalty toward an abstract state rather than toward the person of a monarch had not yet really begun even in Spain and Portugal, much less in Spanish and Portuguese America. But the Bourbons did not understand this.

Furthermore, Spanish Americans considered themselves legally linked to Spain merely by their king. At the time of the discovery of America, Spain had consisted of two distinct kingdoms, albeit united by a common throne, and each kingdom had its own traditional institutions, courts, and councils to advise the king on local affairs. Subsequently there were also separate institutions for the kingdoms of Naples, the Netherlands, and (from 1580 to 1640 when the Spanish king claimed its throne) Portugal, despite the fact that they all shared the same ruler. The overseas territories were made up of kingdoms, and together they were represented in Spain by a separate council, known as the Council of the Indies, that advised the king on American matters. Under the Hapsburgs this council was the highest administrative, legislative, and judicial body that the Spanish Americans dealt with before appealing to the king. So Spanish Americans did not consider themselves colonials of Spain but subjects of the king. When superimposed on the patriarchal view of the state, this self-image eventually became more than a legalistic question, for these kingdoms were envisioned as distinct families with the same father. If the father were to be removed, nothing would make one family subordinate to the other. In contrast, the Bourbons conceived of all Spanish territory as a single state and believed that the purpose of the Spanish American colonies was to advance the interests of the metropolis. In this view they were supported by most political leaders in Spain.

The Bourbons put a high value on efficiency. Scientific administration was, in theory at least, the keystone of their approach. Direct lines of command, the ability to pinpoint responsibility, clear separation of jurisdictions, and specialized functions were the major goals of the reforms that the Bourbons imposed on Spain and Spanish America. Their first step was to create a cabinet that met to consider the affairs of the entire realm whether in Aragon or in Spanish America. Then, impelled by the same logic, they broke up the affairs of the empire into component parts: for instance, military affairs were handled by the minister of war while relations with other colonial powers were assigned to the minister of foreign affairs. The area-specific Council of the Indies dwindled in importance.

The Bourbon kings noted that if American affairs were to foster the welfare of Spain, the economic life of Spanish America would have to be revitalized, especially given the cost of Spain's frequent wars. One such change was the naming of intendants for Spanish America. Intendants, first used in France and then in Spain, were administrative officers whose principal objective was to increase royal revenue both by stimulating the local economy with such improvements as bettering roads and by firmly enforcing the collection of taxes. As idealized, the system of intendants was a perfect example of the Bourbons' belief in rational, centralized administration. Its application in almost all of Spanish America by 1786 meant the end of a complicated and extremely subdivided political system in which the viceroy had exerted his power through a large number of provincial officials of different ranks and titles. The old scheme was now replaced, at least in general, by a simplified structure of authority in which a relatively few intendants reported directly to the viceroy on some matters and directly to the king on finance.

The Bourbons actually took vast areas completely out of the control of the two viceroys who had until then ruled all Spanish America from their seats in Mexico City and Lima. In 1717 the crown set up a third viceroyalty, that of New Granada, with its capital in Bogotá. It encompassed the territory now included in Venezuela, Colombia, Panamá, and Ecuador (for the sake of simplicity all areas are henceforth referred to by their modern names). In 1776 the Bourbons established the Viceroyalty of Río de la Plata, stripping from the Viceroyalty of Peru most of the territory now encompassed by Argentina, Uruguay, Paraguay, and Bolivia (including the rich silver mines of Potosí). They also created two captaincies-general (virtually viceroyalties but without their prestige) for what are now Chile and Venezuela.

The viceroys, under both the Hapsburgs and the Bourbons, were advised by *audiencias*, a kind of miniature Council of the Indies that, like it, also acted as a court. Under the Bourbons the appointees to audiencias tended to be almost exclusively Spanish-born and not American-born, reversing the trend under the Hapsburgs. In this way they enhanced royal control and diminished the influence of the locally well-off.

People of entirely Spanish heritage but born in America ("Creoles") still exercised a vestige of governmental responsibility in the *cabildos* (sometimes called *ayuntamientos*), that is, in the councils charged with local government. Their jurisdiction included both rural and urban areas and sometimes extended for hundreds of miles, but their focus was always a central city. The cabildos had gradually lost much of their actual power, however, first because an increasing number of petty details were covered by laws issued from Madrid. Then, as the crown became more desperate for money it often sold, sometimes in perpetuity, the seats on the cabildo to the highest bidder. Few people looked to the cabildo as a source of vitality or new ideas. Its members, though, still enjoyed high social rank and accompanying prestige. As the only local government authority, the cabildo remained important as a symbol, as the place where residents found representation. Ironically, the intendants sent out by the Bourbon kings in the eighteenth century to supply a more immediate link between locals and the king often gave cabildos new life by their reforms. So in the end the cabildos remained a place of recourse for the people in time of trouble. Clashes between locally oriented cabildos and the Spanish-dominated audiencias became commonplace, especially as conflicts built.

In Brazil local government remained stronger than in Spanish America. From the beginning, it had received less attention from Lisbon than Spanish America from Madrid. The real empire of Portugal from the early sixteenth century had been India and the spice islands of Southeast Asia. Brazil, without known precious minerals until the end of the seventeenth century, had been only a second thought, and the Portuguese paid scant attention even to the sugar-rich coastal strip stretching from Recife to Salvador, unless it was threatened by other nations. So Portuguese Americans were practically left to govern themselves until the eighteenth century. The basic unit of government—beyond the sugar plantation or cattle ranch itself—was the *senado da câmara*, or *câmara* for short, an elective city/county council. The câmaras were usually dominated by planters, who, in contrast to their Spanish counterparts in the cabildo, wielded real power either because they were too far from Portugal to be effectively controlled or because they had been granted rights, privileges, and exemptions by successive Portuguese kings. Eventually the discovery of gold and then diamonds in Brazil's southeast, in the area near Ouro Preto, provoked major changes in Portuguese government policies under the leadership of the marquis of Pombal.

The Portuguese king's chief minister from 1750 to 1777, Sebastião José de Carvalho e Melo, Marquis of Pombal, echoed and often anticipated the reforming zeal of the Bourbons. He may be considered the "enlightened despot" of Portugal, akin to Charles III of Spain, Frederick the Great of Prussia, or Joseph II of Austria, eighteenth-century rulers who combined absolutism with forceful economic and religious reforms. Pombal could be frightfully cruel and imprisoned many who opposed him, but he also won a great deal of respect for his energy in reorganizing public services and streamlining colonial government. He consolidated in royal hands the last of the proprietary colonies created in sixteenth-century Brazil. He enhanced the authority of the viceroy over the governors and captains-general in all the provinces of Brazil, and, in 1763, he moved the seat of the viceroyalty from Salvador to the now prospering city of Rio de Janeiro through which Brazil exported its gold and diamonds. He worked to lessen the power of the câmaras. But unlike the Bourbons, Pombal recognized the value of incorporating Brazilian-born men into the imperial machine. As Brazil had no university, sons of ranchers or sugar planters received their higher education at the University of Coimbra in Portugal, so Pombal did not have far to go to find capable Brazilians trained in Roman law and the principle of centralized authority. These he placed in many administrative posts in India, Africa, and Brazil. Pombal's legacy was a strengthened empire.

Both Charles III and Pombal sought to raise revenues from the colonies by reforming taxation. The long-established sales tax in Spanish America was raised from 4 percent to 6 percent and its collection placed directly under royal appointees rather than farmed out to private bidders. The intendants were given particular responsibility for seeing that tax collection went well and reported on these matters directly to the king instead of the viceroy. Pombal established a new, centralized treasury department in Portugal under his personal direction and paid close attention to colonial revenues. The mining economy in the region surrounding Ouro Preto became notorious for its tax evasion schemes, so one of Pombal's successors, lacking his political skill, in 1788 decreed a per capita tax to make up for alleged arrears in public revenues. In both Portuguese and Spanish America (as in English America) protest and even rebellion resulted from these new tax policies. In Peru riots broke out in 1780, opening the way for an Indian uprising. In Colombia the next year an armed revolt of tradesmen and artisans was principally driven by resistance to the new imposts. And in Ouro Preto, Brazil, authorities uncovered a conspiracy in 1789, led by those who owed the most in back taxes, whose purpose was complete independence from Portugal for their region. Yet on the whole most people in Spanish and

Portuguese America accepted the rule of their respective monarchs as legitimate and continued to do so until 1808 and even well beyond. Their major objection centered on restrictions applied to colonial trade.

TRADE WITH WHOM?

In the long competitive struggle among the merchants of Spain, Portugal, France, Holland, and England, those of Spain and Portugal gradually lost ground. Over a period of some two hundred years, from approximately 1500, the entrepreneurial classes in England, both rural and urban, managed to accumulate more and more of the national wealth. In the seventeenth century they secured sufficient power to wrest a large measure of state control from the nobility. The government then became more than ever interested in protecting and expanding overseas opportunities for the commercial classes. Jamaica was seized from Spain in 1655, not only to place a sugar-producing island within British hands, but also to provide a base for an extensive smuggling commerce to the Spanish mainland. The British Parliament also passed navigation laws to ensure that Jamaican sugar and Virginian tobacco could be transported only on ships belonging to British businessmen. These and other enumerated articles could only be shipped to England and not to mainland Europe. And new laws forbade the colonists from importing manufactured goods from anywhere else. Meanwhile, wars against the Dutch helped secure even more trading opportunities. Treaties (called the "unequal treaties") were forcibly imposed on the Portuguese according to which British merchants in Portugal (from 1642) would be judged by English judges according to English commercial law and be allowed (from 1654) to trade directly to Brazil. Later a limited number of English businessmen even gained the treaty right to set up shop in Brazil itself. After the "Glorious Revolution" of 1688 in England, these steps on behalf of the commercial class proved irreversible. Finally, at the conclusion of the War of the Spanish Succession (1700–1713), Spain had to cede to British merchants the monopoly right to supply slaves to its empire as well as to send one ship a year to trade at an annual fair in Panamá. At every step state power was pointedly used to advance the commercial interests of British merchants overseas.

In the eighteenth century England entered what is usually referred to as the industrial revolution. Although its true flowering came in the nineteenth century, cotton mills already proliferated in the eighteenth, requiring a new raw material that must come from overseas and sharply increasing demand for dyes such as indigo and cochineal. This new wealth and urban growth also encouraged a taste for stimulants or desserts like tobacco, cacao, coffee, and sugar both in Britain and in northern Europe generally. Also, the expanding production of textiles and other manufactured goods impelled a search for ever more consumers for these products. The Spanish and Portuguese empires offered an obvious potential market, and British authorities officially ignored but unofficially encouraged smuggling and contraband trade into those colonies. Especially notorious was the subterfuge by which the right to send one five-hundred-ton ship to Panamá was abused: It unloaded goods during the daylight hours but was resupplied at night by other English ships from Jamaica, with the result that it stayed in port unloading for weeks and even months while local authorities looked the other way. By the end of the century a quarter of all British exports went to the West Indies, that is, principally to Spanish America.

The year 1776 brought permanent changes in colonial relationships within the Atlantic world. Before that date the British would hardly have openly advocated the end of colonial monopolies, for they themselves held a major colony and sought to maintain exclusive rights to trade there. But once the United States declared its independence and then succeeded in winning it, little could restrain the British. In fact, ten years earlier Britain had already declared Jamaica a free port, open to foreign ships, since British industrialists had become more interested in selling their products and buying raw materials than in protecting the trade of their erstwhile allies, the monopoly merchants. Meanwhile, British theoreticians had been rethinking economic policies, and in 1776 Adam Smith (1723–1790) published his *Inquiry into the Nature and Causes of the Wealth of Nations*, arguing (among other things) that the maintenance of colonies for the exclusive trade of monopoly merchants made no sense. The British were thus freed practically and intellectually from any restraint in attempting to end the colonial monopolies of Spain and Portugal.

Meanwhile Spain declined economically. Many of the great silver mines of Mexico and Peru began to exhaust the easily reached veins. With a lagging economy went sagging government revenues, making it all the more difficult for Spain to protect the far-flung empire it had established in the sixteenth century. So while British merchants sought new markets and new sources of supply for an expanding industrial complex, Spain was increasingly unable to withstand their onslaught.

In self-defense the Iberian powers became more self-consciously committed to maintaining the colonial monopoly of trade. These views found expression in many treatises but can be exemplified here by the words of two early-nineteenth-century administrators sent out to rule the colonies. The viceroy of Peru, responding in 1812 to local complaints about limits and restrictions on trade, noted that freedom of trade "would be tantamount to decreeing the separation of these Dominions from the Mother country since, once direct trade with foreigners [is] established[,] . . . the fate of European Spain would matter little to them."[2] A governor in Salvador, Brazil, responding to the town council's request for fewer controls on commerce, put it this way in 1807: "If I were to embrace slickly written arguments deduced from arbitrary principles, I would say—along with modern economists—that any brake or restriction is prejudicial to the freedom of commerce, even colonial commerce. But I cannot help believing the opposite, knowing that colonial establishments like this one have as their primary purpose (or truly their only one) the welfare and utility of the Metropolis, to which colonies should remain directly dependent, . . . trading with it exclusively."[3]

To preserve such a monopoly required changes in trade policies. Before the eighteenth century, all Spanish-controlled transatlantic trade was conducted through four ports: Cádiz in Spain and Cartagena, Panamá, and Veracruz in America. The result was, for example, that manufactured goods produced in England to be consumed in Buenos Aires went first to Spain and then to Panamá, taken across the isthmus, loaded again on ships sailing to Peru, and then transported overland across towering mountains and broad plains all the way to the coast of Argentina. In Spain only Cádiz was permitted to participate, for its merchant guild held great political power, and in each of the entrepôts through which their goods passed, other merchants, usually agents for the Cádiz monopolists and often their relatives, maintained tight hold on the profitable interchange. If Spain had produced the goods, it might have been able to uphold this commercial system indefinitely, but this was no longer the case. Even legally traded goods were imported to Spain from England or other European countries to be sent overseas. Sometimes through war and sometimes through subterfuge, the British managed to invade the American markets, exchanging cottons and knives for cacao, sugar, and hides, not to mention bullion. Non-Spanish masters had the daring; Spanish Americans, especially those outside the monopoly ports, had the desire for cheaper goods; and Spanish officials often connived locally to make this a widespread practice.

The Bourbons set to work to reform and modernize this commercial system. First, they liberalized the regulations, making it easier and cheaper to trade legally through Spain. Second, they created monopoly companies modeled on the Dutch or British East India Company, in which capitalists from other parts of Spain besides Cádiz could participate. These companies were assigned special areas in the Americas as their preserve to defend and develop. And third, a steadily increasing number of ports were allowed to trade with each other. The culmination of this policy was the so-called Decree of Free Trade (1778) that allowed twenty-four ports in America to trade with almost any port in Spain. Commerce was still limited to Spanish subjects and, in effect, still fell into the hands of the great Spanish merchants who had the necessary capital. Also, by curtailing smuggling, these measures further intensified the exclusive claim of Spanish merchants on the trade of the colony. Yet the decree was a great boon to ports like Buenos Aires that had previously suffered most from the old restrictions, and its transatlantic trade multiplied several times over in volume and value.

New economic activities encouraged a shift in the center of economic gravity in Spanish America away from the mining areas and toward new centers, previously on the frontiers. Lima in the South American west began to lose ground, while Caracas in the north and Buenos Aires in the southeast increased in importance. Mexico City managed to cash in on both the old and new regimes, but even in Mexico the coastal regions entered a period of unprecedented growth.

The Portuguese had never centralized trade in Lisbon. Even foreign ships were occasionally given legal permission to trade to Brazil, not to mention the selected British merchants whose rights had been secured through the "unequal treaties" mentioned above. Pombal did create monopoly companies to foster the development of the northernmost coastal regions of Brazil, and they had a limited but noticeable success, especially in fostering cotton cultivation. But the real stimulus to Brazilian commerce came from expanding consumption in northern Europe and, eventually, from economic disruptions in the colonies of France and Spain.

Changing trade patterns meant changed needs for labor. The center of Indian population had always been in the highland areas of Spanish America, and that was also where most mines were located. But tropical exports aimed at European markets were produced in more sparsely populated lowland regions. To cultivate them profitably either the Indians would have to be moved from the highlands or black slaves would have to be imported from Africa. Iberian peoples had been accustomed to African slave labor for centuries. They had used African slaves on the Atlantic islands (Madeira, the Canaries, and the Cape Verdes) even before the discovery of America and had introduced them into the New World in the sixteenth century. With the expanding needs of growing plantation economies, owners looked with heightened interest for labor in Africa. Slave traders, especially the British after the treaties of 1713, brought in an ever-increasing number of human cargoes to Spanish America.

Colonial Brazil also relied on slave labor but became more interested in mines just as Spanish America was turning toward plantations. Gold mines discovered near Ouro Preto at the end of the seventeenth century finally gave Brazil the wealth and importance it had previously lacked. Cities now flourished, and Brazilians had the leisure to engage in the arts for the first time. But the mines in Brazil (mostly placer mines) were worked by slave labor and not by salaried workers as in Mexico or draft labor from Indian villages as in Peru. And Brazilian sugar planters still dominated most urban centers and kept their eye firmly on European markets.

A CORPORATE SOCIETY

The Hapsburg political and economic system had been reinforced by a social structure in which everyone was assigned a fixed position within a multilayered set of social categories (to be sure, always more flexible in practice than in theory). Most people belonged to a self-governing body of some sort — a craft or merchant guild, a cathedral chapter, a religious order or a convent, a lay confraternity dedicated to a saint and committed to charitable work, a university, a professional organization, a military corps, a cabildo, or an Indian village community. In most of these corporations their officials — chosen by members, not appointed by higher officials — represented the groups before the government, making such bodies intermediate institutions of the state. By the same token, these representatives had responsibilities toward their constituents and had to listen to their grievances and heed their aspirations. To a large degree these social and political arrangements remained in place through the Bourbon period into the early nineteenth century, but because the wars of independence would bring drastic changes to them, that ordering of society deserves close attention here.

As it stood, each corporate body had its special rights and privileges. Guilds, for example, were organized as if they formed a family in which the apprentices and journeymen, as virtual children, were in a fixed relationship to the masters. Each guild — whether, say, of water carriers, carpenters, pottery makers, goldsmiths, shoemakers, masons, or cotton weavers — had its particular identifying clothes, its own patron saint, and — most important — its own court where masters passed judgment on cases involving conflicts between members of the guild and sometimes between themselves and members of less privileged corporations. There was not a single judicial system for everyone. In many places Indians were left to rule themselves in what were called "Indian Republics" where their leaders or village elders judged disputes and enforced sentences. Stockmen had their own guild and court where large landowners judged the fate of alleged cattle rustlers. Cases involving commercial law were decided by the state-sanctioned merchant guild dominated by the wealthy merchant-creditors who engaged in international trade. The right to special courts, special clothes, special places in parades, and other honors were called, collectively, *fueros.* We may call this a "corporatist" society and define its guiding principle as "corporatism."

This judicial system, divided up by occupation and corporation, reflected a more general view of society. Instead of being formed by individuals protected in their rights and mobile in relationship to one another, society was made up of multiple castes, ranks, and corporations, simultaneously layered one atop another or existing side by side. The individual had multiple identities and multiple loyalties without a truly all-encompassing one, except as a Christian (and, marginally, as a subject of a king). Insofar as they identified themselves in terms of place, they did so with regard to a city or a province, not as Argentinians, Brazilians, or Mexicans. There was no nation as we understand the term.

The family formed a kind of corporation too, with internal ranks and external connections. Its head, the father, had authority over its other members and represented them all before other families or the political authorities. Yet it is important to note that both Spain and Portugal were joint-property regimes, and women there had more legal rights than in most other contemporary societies. Partible inheritance laws meant that daughters inherited equally with sons. Women played a large and responsible role in organizing church festivities or preserving church property. In convents women ruled themselves in routine, day-to-day matters, and they played prominent roles in confraternities. In Spanish America many upper-class wives hosted gatherings where men and women together discussed new ideas and new books. And when foreigners visiting the area reported on the alleged seclusion of women—actually meaning upper-class women—they ignored the evidence all around them that women transported and marketed foodstuffs and crafts, ran taverns and inns, carried water from public fountains where they also did the laundry, and interacted with men throughout the day. Finally, insofar as men gained status by heading an orderly, law-abiding family, they had to heed the desires of other family members, as did the officers of other corporate units.

In much of the Spanish American highlands, Indian villages with inalienable common lands continued to be a typical arrangement. In a sense they too had their fueros. They were legally corporate bodies and not merely collections of individuals, and each had its own court system where village elders exercised justice and its own chosen headman whom the Spanish called "cacique," a word they had picked up from Caribbean Indians. Although they paid a tribute per head (collected by the cacique), they were legally exempt from some other taxes. Many of these villages successfully perpetuated their distinct cultures. The Bourbons took measures to alleviate the lot of Indian villages by forbidding the practice of forcing them to buy a certain amount of manufactured goods, a practice that had been effective in pushing Indians to seek employment for cash outside the village. Although not long enforced, this prohibition—along with many other royal decrees over the years—led many Indians to envision the king as their protector, sometimes even as a sort of deity who would eventually rescue them from oppression. Nevertheless, in Spanish America generally the lot of Indians noticeably worsened on the plantations, and the growth of commercial agriculture in the highlands to feed growing cities pushed many villagers off the land. The eighteenth century was a sad time for them.

Pombal in Portugal, more than the Bourbon kings, saw the Indians as potential subjects and desired their integration into Portuguese-speaking society as fast as possible. For one thing, he hoped to acquire internationally sanctioned legal claims to the Brazilian hinterland by designating as Portuguese the Indians who inhabited it. Although he forbade the enslavement of Indians, he forced religious orders to cease proffering them protection in an effort to encourage their assimilation into Portuguese society. Indians did not have corporate status in Brazil.

Well above the Indians in social position were the mestizos (persons of mixed Indian-Spanish descent). It is sometimes estimated that only six hundred thousand Spaniards ever migrated to America; but, through race mixture more than through force, they imposed Spanish culture over a vast empire. Although mestizos' social position lay between the Indians and the whites, they were accepted by neither. Many mestizos, restless and ambitious, were anxious to prove they were just as good as the whites. Whites often accused them of being unreasonably aggressive, and certainly many mestizos visibly did resent the prejudices and obstacles they confronted. Yet, although most mestizos remained in lowly positions, there were numerous examples of mestizos who, becoming wealthy, were able to buy their way into the white world for themselves or their descendants and be accepted in society as whites. For that matter, many of the so-called best families in the eighteenth century were descended from conquistadors who had married into the Indian nobility in the sixteenth. The mestizos' very ability to compete with the Creoles may have intensified prejudice against them, and racist feeling was perhaps on the increase in Spanish America at the end of the colonial period.

Blacks—slaves, freedmen, and freeborn—were a significant presence in Spanish America, even though they were far fewer than in Brazil. Slaves were especially numerous in the coastal areas of Venezuela, Mexico, and Argentina. In New Granada in 1800 there were 70,000 slaves and twice that many free blacks. They were concentrated in certain areas, such as the coastal regions facing the Pacific and the Caribbean, especially around Cartagena and at the gold mines just north of the border of present-day Ecuador, and in the sugar-producing Cauca River valley west and southwest of Bogotá. In Peru there were some 40,000 slaves and another 40,000 free or freed blacks by the beginning of the nineteenth century. Here too they were concentrated in the lowland area on the coast, especially near Lima.

Pardos, that is, free mulattos (persons of mixed African and European descent), were even more discriminated against than mestizos and bore a number of legal disabilities. They had to pay a head tax (unless they were in a militia unit), just as the Indians did, but, unlike them, were not exempt from certain other taxes. They were specifically prohibited from marrying whites, could not wear certain clothes or ride horses, and were restricted to certain neighborhoods. The Bourbons, in an effort to make productive workers out of everyone, revoked many of the laws that had earlier circumscribed their freedom and even allowed some of them to buy the legal status of whites in exchange for substantial sums (see Document 2). On the other hand, in the 1790s the Bourbons disbanded many of the preexisting militia units that had been specifically for pardos. This meant that these former militiamen lost their fueros and were reduced to paying the tribute.

Social conditions in Brazil differed from those in the highlands of Spanish America. The Indians living in Brazil at the time of first contact with Europeans had not been part of so-called high civilizations like the Aztecs or Incas but lived in semisedentary villages, moving from place to place every few years after harvesting the corn or manioc on which they depended. Or they roamed the wilds relying on hunting and gathering. Through enslavement, conquest, and disease, they were rapidly eliminated from most of the coastal region of Brazil and pushed into the interior. By the eighteenth century, instead of Indian laborers, African slaves worked the cane plantations and produced the sugar. Some 2.5 million enslaved blacks were imported across the Atlantic to Brazil from Africa before 1800. The majority of them, both men and women, worked under slave drivers on plantations or in mines to produce export crops, but cities also teemed with slaves, their work more often skilled, requiring independence and initiative. Urban owners commonly let these slaves hire themselves out, finding their own customers, bargaining over wages, returning to their masters a fixed amount per day or week, and even living independently. Many bought their freedom with the surplus that they kept and saved. The long-standing practice of manumitting slaves to reward faithful service, to celebrate special occasions, or in exchange for cash (either already accumulated by the slave or promised in the future) led over time to large numbers of free blacks and mulattos. In 1780 there were four hundred thousand free blacks and mulattos in Brazil, as compared to a million and a half slaves. In the coastal city of Salvador two separate militia regiments, one for free blacks and the other for pardos, served viceroy and king. These men prided themselves on their discipline and loyalty. But, if there seemed to be an easier acceptance of the free colored than was true in Spanish America, the Brazilian upper class still saw African Brazilians—be they free or slave—as a potential threat to the social order, and resisted any steps that would weaken their control over them.

At the other extreme of the social spectrum in Spanish America were the white Creoles, that is, those who considered themselves, in effect, Spaniards born in America. They occupied many rungs of society, but, along with those born in Spain (the "peninsulars"), Creoles monopolized the most prestigious social positions, shutting out Indians and mestizos, along with blacks and mulattos. The great landowners and miners formed an aristocracy that was acutely

FIGURE 1.1. *Brazilian Sugar Mill and Slaves*

class-conscious. Creoles lorded it over other groups, but peninsulars often looked down on them, despite the fact that many were only one generation removed from Spanish birth, thought of themselves as Spaniards, and found that their daughters were sought after as wives by new Spanish immigrants. The Spanish-born often maintained that Creoles were naturally inferior, that is, that the American climate, or perhaps the American longitude, was somehow enervating. They alleged that by nature people born and raised in America, regardless of their parentage, lacked intelligence, drive, and stamina. In general Creoles resented the fact that peninsulars who had occupied lowly positions in Spain and frequently began in America as peddlers, small shopkeepers, or artisans found their upward mobility helped along by the solidarity of others born in Spain. The Spanish-born seemed to find it easier to evade taxes, get around laws, receive government loans, and secure land titles, all because they enjoyed clientelistic ties to government officials who were also peninsulars. Even if Creoles could amass great fortunes, operate huge estates, and hold all other American groups in contempt, they could not run the government, for under the Bourbon kings the Spanish-born occupied all the chief positions of power and tended to scorn Creole pretensions. Spanish-born bureaucrats, naturally responsive to the wishes of the king, often tried to ameliorate the condition of the Indians over the opposition of Creoles.

One opportunity the Creoles did gain under the Bourbons was to hold commissions in the local militias. Faced with war on the European continent, the expanding imperial ambitions of other nations, and limited financial and human resources in Europe, the Bourbon regime set out to expand and revitalize these militias in America. Spanish officers were dispatched to train these part-time troops, and Creoles were then promoted to the rank of officers. Militia officers also gained for the first time the right to the military fuero, exempting them from the authority of other judicial bodies. In Brazil the locally well-connected Creoles* also held commissions in the militia. In times of threatened attack, as often happened in the late eighteenth century, they were mobilized and got to display their authority and add to their prestige while learning the rudiments of military organization. But whereas military units were regularly dispatched to the Americas from Spain, in eighteenth-century Brazil the regular army itself was largely officered by the Brazilian-born, and, among these, sons of the planter class were preferred in promotions. Only later were armies sent from Portugal.

To summarize, in both Brazil and Spanish America the colonial system engendered social tensions. In order for that system to work, some must be compelled to work to produce colonial products for colonial trade. Those who commanded others necessarily encountered resistance and felt the difficulty of getting others to do their will. At the same time, many in the colonial elite chafed at the restrictions placed on them from above by the monopoly merchant-usurers, by authorities from the Iberian Peninsula, and, especially, by the tax collector. In certain places they were all too eager to evade the rules and trade with the foreign interloper. Some even thought that, better yet, they could oversee their own affairs entirely. But could they win that privilege without endangering their own control over the laboring many?

RELIGION AND THE ENLIGHTENMENT

In solidifying the edifice of colonial rule, religion provided a firm cement. Before the eighteenth century, state and church had been so closely related in the Iberian world that they should be considered one. Even a conceptual distinction between them may be misleading unless it is understood as merely a heuristic device. The Portuguese and Spanish kings had long been granted patronage over the church. That is, in exchange for financing and fostering the preaching of the Gospel, the crown received the right to make all ap-

---

*For the sake of simplicity, I use the familiar term *Creole* to refer to any person of entirely Spanish or Portuguese descent born in America, despite the fact that in Brazil the term *crioulo* meant a person of entirely African descent born in America.

pointments of churchmen. In addition, the crown would collect the tithe, a tax for church purposes. Even papal bulls could be published only after they had been approved by the king, who also controlled and limited the number of religious orders that sent members overseas and restricted the travel of individual friars. Originally the Inquisition functioned primarily as an arm of the state designed to maintain ideological purity.

The ordinary expenses of the bishops, cathedrals, and parish priests were paid by the state from the revenue derived from the tithe. In Portuguese America the state merged this revenue with its general fund and paid out fixed salaries, whereas in Spanish America the bishop was the king's agent in supervising the collection of the tithe and dispensing the resulting funds. Consequently, in prosperous areas of Spanish America the bishop directly controlled extensive resources, whereas in Portuguese America churchmen depended much more on other government officials. Parish clergymen, in addition to their stipends, received fees for baptisms, marriages, and the performance of other religious offices. In addition, both the secular church and religious orders received numerous bequests, most often to pay for the saying of masses for the souls of the dead. These could represent a substantial portion of the deceased's estate. Once real property was given to such corporate bodies, it was rarely sold, either because it was inalienable by the terms of the bequest or because the church, unlike individuals, was never forced to divide its property among its heirs. Over time the church became enormously wealthy. In Mexico City in 1811 church properties or ones on which it held mortgages accounted for 47 percent of the total value of the city's real estate and up to half its physical extent. In Lima in 1791 some 29 percent of the city's buildings similarly belonged to church entities. Not surprisingly the church became the principal banker in Spanish America. Although it held foreclosable mortgages on a vast number of estates, usually borrowers paid only the interest and let the principal ride, even from generation to generation.

Much of this wealth was used to finance charitable institutions and mission work. Social services like hospitals and orphanages were carried on exclusively by lay organizations under the auspices of the church, while regular orders typically ran schools and colleges. The Jesuits in Spanish America alone oversaw some 120 secondary schools. Although some of these institutions fell into disrepair or became merely sinecures for churchmen primarily interested in luxurious living in the cities, others continued to be vigorous centers of social concern. Often the imperial task of extending the frontiers of Spanish culture and Spanish power into the jungles of South and Central America and into the high deserts of North America was carried out by courageous missionaries. The Christianization of Indians in the more settled areas seems to have been generally successful. In countless Indian villages social life revolved around their

FIGURE 1.2. *The Church of Guadalupe, near Mexico City*

churches, linking sacred belief to the polity. Church festivities, processions, and images animated village life, and its patron saint was used as the town's principal symbol. In effect, the space within which face-to-face relationships were possible for each village was defined by where one could hear the ringing of the church bells.

The Catholic Church was not immune from change in the eighteenth century. Although the Bourbon kings maintained the ancient union of church and state, they were much more conscious of the church as a separate entity than had been true in the Hapsburg period. Probably for this reason, increasing friction resulted between crown and church. The church fuero was successively restricted, and it may be for this reason that many clergymen later joined revolutionary movements. The Bourbons also systematically reduced the independent power of the Inquisition. Finally, in 1804, at a time of dire financial need, the crown not only selectively seized some church properties, but announced that it would issue public bonds to the church in exchange for taking over its endowments. Then, and this is the crux of the matter, it demanded that all borrowers amortize their loans over a relatively short time, paying back the principal and not just the interest on their loans. The measure created a financial panic as cash-strapped debtors were suddenly forced to find buyers for their encumbered properties. As the resulting moneys were shipped off to Spain to pay for its wars, borrowing funds in Mexico became extremely difficult for everyone, including miners, big landowners and small farmers, merchants and shopkeepers. Those who relied on credit to operate their business were particularly hard-hit, but the measure also affected government officials and humble widows, lawyers, and priests. For a long time the Spanish government seemed unaware of their plight, although the measure was eventually suspended in 1808. Since the Portuguese-Brazilian church hierarchy was relatively weak and poor, Pombal did not feel compelled to attack it the way the Bourbon kings did.

But both Pombal and Charles III harbored deep suspicions about the Jesuits, who were more loyal to the pope than to the king. Pombal charged them with plotting with the Spaniards to prevent the extension of Portuguese boundaries in South America in areas where the Jesuits maintained missions. Furthermore, the Jesuits in both Portuguese and Spanish America, besides operating the leading secondary schools, were efficient administrators of property and consequently came to own some of the best land and compete successfully with local merchants. Some people were jealous; others approved of their vigor and their drive. Indians felt protected by them. But Pombal and Charles III saw them only as threats to royal authority. Finally, in 1759, Pombal ordered their expulsion from all Portuguese territory. The Bourbons followed suit eight years later. The measure resulted in uprisings among some Indians and other groups whom the Jesuits had protected. Although many colonists welcomed the move, others condemned it as an example of royal anticlericalism.

These various measures, taken together, weakened the Catholic Church, one of the bulwarks of the Iberian empires. As the distance between church and state widened, these steps unwittingly undermined the belief that the state was God's surrogate on earth. The ideological foundation of the old order suffered some erosion, although most people continued genuinely to believe that a king was "the Lord's Anointed" and that to challenge his right to rule was to abjure one's faith in God.

These changes happened just as a new set of ideas gained a small but growing acceptance. These new ideas derived from the European intellectual movement historians have dubbed "the Enlightenment," which had a noticeable effect on colonial intellectuals and professionals. It is a myth that Latin America was kept in cloistered isolation from all new ideas by a veritable iron curtain imposed by retrograde governments. The truth is that precisely these governments, led by "enlightened despots," injected a modern and scientific worldview into overseas domains, along with new understandings of man and of the world that the Enlightenment embodied. Several noted European astronomers, botanists, and geographers were sent out at royal expense to conduct studies, collect specimens, observe the stars, and make meticulous drawings. The Portuguese government funded a major ten-year scientific expedition to the Amazon beginning in 1783.

A striking example of the new scientific spirit in America was José Celestino Mutis (1732–1808), a Spanish physician who had moved to Bogotá in the early 1760s. As trained personnel were scarce, he was asked to teach mathematics and astronomy at the university, where he subsequently built an observatory and taught the heliocentric Copernican system. With characteristic eighteenth-century curiosity, Mutis then began the study of botany and carried on an active correspondence with the Swedish scientist Carolus Linnaeus. The viceroy, with the encouragement of the Spanish government, provided Mutis with a subsidy to begin a vast botanical project to systematically collect specimens and drawings of South American flora. His botanical work was carried on by his American-born pupil Francisco José de Caldas (1770–1816), who kept up an active correspondence and intellectual interchange with Benjamin Franklin, one of the most important Enlightenment thinkers in the New World. Eventually Caldas turned his attention to institutional obstacles to change and to the goal of independence.

Viceroys and other bureaucrats themselves organized literary societies, held soirées, and prided themselves on being as up to date in their ideas as they were in their stylish French-inspired clothing. The upper and middle classes, both men and women, followed their example, seeing themselves as part of European civilization, whether it was through meeting at cafés, organizing balls, or gathering to talk about the most recent books arriving from overseas, creating a public space where new ideas circulated with some freedom.

The social and political ideas associated with the Enlightenment—the social contract between rulers and ruled, the political and economic freedom of the individual, the importance of reason over revelation in guiding social policy, the belief in social progress through education—also invaded Latin America, although without the same official protection enjoyed by scientific study and with even less widespread acceptance. Remember that John Locke's (1632–1704) view of human psychology—shaped, he believed, entirely by experience and not by one's noble or common birth—lay at the very heart of the new competitive British economy and that his political argument set out the principal tenets for parliamentary democracy. His emphasis on the individual would form the hallmark of the new economic and political system. In Spain the ideas of Voltaire and the other French philosophes had been popularized by Benito Feijóo (1676–1764), and although many of the original sources were banned by the Catholic *Index* of prohibited books, he and other writers spread Enlightenment concepts far and near. In any event, some well-educated Creoles knew those works, and attempts to suppress the circulation of the new views were always in vain. Libraries of famous and not-so-famous men in Brazil (e.g., those implicated in the conspiracy uncovered in 1789) included works by many European thinkers as well as the French *Encyclopédie*. On the other hand, no printing press was allowed in Brazil and no university was established there. A governor once declared that "advanced studies would only serve to nurture the self-pride of vigorous young inhabitants and destroy the political and civil ties of subordination that ought to bind the colony to the metropole."[4] Even among the Creoles of Spanish America the social and political implications of the Enlightenment became important only at the time of independence.

By that time their understanding of these ideas was deeply colored by the French Revolution. Many believed that expectations raised by intellectuals had fired the crowd that stormed the Bastille in 1789. The response to Enlightenment ideas now varied according to whether these events were seen favorably or not. The class basis of the French movement was understood clearly only by the more conservative Latin Americans, and they abhorred the result. The radical or reform-minded ones, despite their own aristocratic or semiaristocratic origins, greatly admired the Declaration of the Rights of Man enacted by the French Assembly in 1789 guaranteeing both the legal freedom of the individual and private property rights. Practically no one, however, failed to condemn the violence and bloodshed of the subsequent Reign of Terror directed by the French National Convention, the Committee of Public Safety, and the firebrand Maximilien de Robespierre. Most sighed in relief at the conservative reaction that culminated in the seizure of power by Napoleon Bonaparte in 1799. As he led French armies that then swept across Europe, many Latin Americans admired him for his daring and his personal verve, even if a few were troubled by the decline of individual freedom under his rule. But freedom was now associated with the Terror, and the ideology of liberty was seen as a two-edged sword to be drawn only at great risk. These conclusions were bolstered by events in Haiti.

HAITI

Two colonies in the Americas became independent before those of the Spanish and Portuguese, and their experiences had a marked impact on the movements examined here. The first was that of the United States. The course of its war for independence is too well known to be recited here, but one point did not escape the attention of Latin Americans: Slave owners such as George Washington and Thomas Jefferson were able to win their country's independence without ending slavery. Indeed, it has been argued by the historian Edmund S. Morgan that in the United States the slavery of blacks made possible the ideal of freedom for the whites.[5] In any case, those in Latin America who came to desire freedom from colonial rule for their countries without personal freedom for their workers were encouraged by the North American example. Haiti, though, filled them with dread.

Haiti, or Saint-Domingue as it was then known, was a prosperous French colony in the Caribbean producing coffee, indigo, cotton, and, especially, sugar on the western end of the island of Hispaniola. The shape of the country is that of a crescent with two peninsulas pointing to the west at the northern and southern edges of a huge bay. A haven for buccaneers in the seventeenth century, Haiti was formally annexed by France in 1697. By 1780 its ports teemed with French ships, and French monopoly merchants profited handsomely from its trade. The plantations were worked by half a million slaves, while only 30,000 whites and some 28,000 free mulattos made up the rest of the population. The richest plantations lay along the northern peninsula, so it was there that the largest number of slaves were concentrated.

Society was sharply divided into distinct groups. By the 1780s the wealthy planters, like many of those in Spanish and Portuguese America, were becoming dissatisfied with their lack of political power and with the restrictions on trade imposed with new vigor by monopolists. As events played out, they hoped for local rule under the old French monarchy and were generally unsympathetic to the French Revolution. Poorer whites—artisans, tradesmen, and the descendants of the original indentured servants—favored the Revolution and the end of the monarchy. Free mulattos, ambitious and hardworking, made up a third group. Several became planters, and many acquired smaller tracts of land in the less fertile and hillier southern peninsula or along the north-south axis linking the two peninsulas. They owned approximately a third of the colony's land by 1789 and a quarter of the slaves. While they resented the racial discrimination they suffered at the hands of whites, whether rich planters or, even worse, poor whites, they did not wish to end slavery. They chafed under a series of legal restrictions placed on them in the 1760s by whites, forbidding them to bear arms or wear certain kinds of clothes and making the penalties for violation of any law more severe for them than for whites. The French Declaration of the Rights of Man seemed to promise them equality at last. Finally, there were the slaves themselves. Given their high mortality, planters relied on regular new shipments of slaves from Africa. In 1780 probably two-thirds of the slaves in Haiti had been born in Africa. They were treated harshly, perhaps more harshly than anywhere else in the Americas. In addition to these four groups, of course, there were the Frenchmen who filled government positions and were charged with maintaining the commercial monopoly on behalf of merchants in France. Ironically, these merchants formed one of the groups in France that most enthusiastically backed the French Revolution. But they were not likely to support any alteration of the status quo in the colony.

When King Louis XVI of France was finally compelled to summon a meeting of the Estates General in 1788, the white planters of Saint-Domingue determined to send delegates and try to secure self-rule. Only six of the thirty-seven chosen delegates were actually seated, and that only after lengthy debate; but those six articulately called for the loosening of the trade monopoly and the appointment of a fellow planter as administrator in the colony. Unstated, but even more important to them, was their intention that there be no alteration in the colonial social order. In this last point they were opposed, on the one hand, by the emancipationist French Société des Amis de Noirs (Society of Friends of Blacks) and, on the other, by lobbyists financed by the rich mulatto planters of Saint-Domingue.

The far-reaching social transformations the Revolution wrought in France could not fail to have repercussions in the colony. When news regarding the storming of the Bastille in 1789 reached the town of Le Cap, the poorer whites rioted and demanded the dismissal of the royally appointed governor. Wealthy planters responded by creating their own colonial assembly (later replaced by one officially sanctioned by the French Assembly) from which both mulattos and poor whites were excluded. This assembly passed a number of regulations that, taken together, amounted to a virtual declaration of independence, although its members insisted on their continued loyalty to the king. When they refused to take orders from the French Assembly, the pro-Revolution governor and army garrison took their action as a challenge, eventually forcing the entire assembly to flee the island. Meanwhile, the mulattos, angered by their exclusion from the deliberations of the assembly, rebelled in protest. They were quickly defeated, their leaders imprisoned and cruelly tortured. From Paris contradictory instructions arrived, contributing to the general unease.

Such signs of disarray among the free may have been the spark that set off the slave revolt in August 1791 in the plantation region of the northern peninsula. Although it has been argued that French officials actually instigated it to bring whites and mulattos to heel, surely no great impetus was needed to encourage the slaves, who were well informed of events and often had a clear sense of their goals and opportunities, to take this moment to rebel. Their pent-up rage found expression in the destruction of some two hundred sugar mills and six hundred coffee estates during just the first eight days of their movement. Soon they were in control of the entire northern region outside the towns, although fighting continued for months.

Later in 1791 mulattos rebelled in other parts of the colony, and this time, as white planters had been dispossessed in the north, mulattos met with considerable success. They declared that their government would be open to all who possessed a given income except white planters. By these restrictions they excluded the poor generally, including former slaves, and rich whites, leaving wealthy mulattos in sole control of the center and the south.

Although the French Assembly attempted to regain authority over the rebellious colony by dispatching army after army, European political and diplomatic events soon impinged directly on the fate of Saint-Domingue. By the end of 1791 an alliance of several countries had formed in Europe to oppose the French

FIGURE 1.3. *Revolt of African Slaves in Haiti*

Revolution and reimpose absolute monarchy in France. Spain joined the effort and instructed its officials in the Spanish part of the island of Hispaniola to attack the French. Ironically, to back their anti-Revolutionary effort in Europe, the Spaniards offered to support the slaves in their continuing struggle for freedom in Saint-Domingue. The British also joined the anti-Revolutionary alliance in Europe and also decided to attack the French colony but, more logically, sided not with the slaves but with the planters, who declared themselves royalists. In August 1793 the French governor, in an attempt to regain the upper hand militarily against the British, declared the freedom of all slaves (a measure that was ratified by the French National Convention in February 1794 by a decree of emancipation). The governor's stratagem had its desired effect as most former slaves began to abandon the Spaniards and side with the French, gradually driving out the British. With their defeat in 1797, most white planters, whom the British had backed, fled the island.

At the head of the blacks was Pierre-Domingue Toussaint l'Ouverture (1743–1803). Born in Haiti as a slave, he had become a trusted coachman, learned to read French, and acquired an education on his own. He had joined the slave rebellion soon after its outbreak and gradually became its leader. He had engineered an alliance between the former slaves and the Spaniards, and he was among the first to agree to join forces with the French against the British after news of the decree of emancipation had arrived. He considered himself a Frenchman, trusted in the definitive abolition of slavery by the National Convention, and backed the principles of the French Revolution. The French made him a general, and he gradually took over the direction of the military effort, making even the French-born officers into his virtual subordinates. Once the British were gone, and aided by the African-born Jean-Jacques Dessalines (1758–1806), Touissant set to work against the mulatto faction. It was an ugly war in which some ten thousand mulattos were killed.

From 1797 to 1801 Toussaint's rule went unquestioned. He promulgated a constitution that maintained a nominal tie to France but granted the French government practically no authority regarding internal affairs. The ports of the "colony" were opened to the trade of any nation. Although Toussaint insisted on identifying himself with the French, Saint-Domingue was to all intents and purposes now a free country. Increasingly it was called Haiti, the name for the area used by pre-Columbian inhabitants. Securing for himself from the newly elected assembly the post of governor-general for life, Toussaint set about restoring law and order as well as economic prosperity. He fostered the renewed planting of sugar, rebuilt the irrigation system, and forced former slaves to work the plantations, now with the title "cultivators." Sugar production soared, and Toussaint was widely popular even among these coerced workers, although his immediate subordinates resented his authoritarianism.

Napoleon Bonaparte, however, had other plans for the island. Napoleon dreamed of building a French colonial empire that would stretch from Louisiana to the Amazon. Haiti was crucial to his plans. He had only contempt for a black man who claimed to be French. As soon as he had secured peace with the British at Amiens in 1802, he dispatched an army of twenty-five thousand troops commanded by his brother-in-law General Charles Victor Emmanuel Leclerc, and instructed him to reestablish French authority and restore the social order as it had once been. Toussaint resisted this army the best he could, but he was unable to convince all his followers that Leclerc was an enemy (Leclerc's instructions being secret). Toussaint suffered several defeats before being forced to surrender in 1802 and was sent in chains to France, where he died in prison the following year.

Once news arrived in Haiti that the French were reenslaving blacks in other French colonies, however, a new rebellion broke out, this time led by Dessalines and one Henri Christophe (1762–1820). They understood that either Haiti must be independent or blacks would lose their freedom. While they were still gathering their forces, a yellow fever epidemic struck the French army. In just weeks eight thousand men had died, including Leclerc himself, and fresh reinforcements from France suffered the same fate. Then war began again in Europe, dooming Napoleon's dream of an American empire. He sold Louisiana to the United States and recalled those troops that still survived in the Caribbean island. On January 1, 1804, Dessalines proclaimed the independence of Haiti.

The subsequent fate of the former French colony was not a happy one. Dessalines declared himself an emperor and ruled absolutely. He and his followers discriminated sharply against the remaining poor whites and the mulattos. In 1806 he was assassinated, leaving a power vacuum and provoking civil war and anarchy. At one point the country broke in two, a black republic in the northern peninsula and a mulatto one in the rest of the country. In the end the mulattos emerged as dominant throughout but never with absolute authority or legitimacy. And the years of war had left a devastated land. Other countries refused to recognize its independence, and some boycotted its exports. In any case, the former slaves often preferred to raise their food on small plots they themselves controlled rather than toil on plantations to produce an export crop while they went hungry.

Haiti's example struck fear into the hearts of the planter class in Spanish and Portuguese America. Creoles there, as had been true in Saint-Domingue, desired free trade and political autonomy. But they saw themselves surrounded not only by mestizos or mulattos who desired social recognition, but by slaves or oppressed Indians whose rage could easily be unleashed by any sign of division among the white ruling groups and most of all by the disruptions of a war. They understood that what had begun in Haiti as an effort to secure independence had ended in the destruction of those very elites. Francisco de Miranda (1750–1817), one of the precursors and early participants in the Latin American independence movement, said, "Much as I desire the independence and liberty of the New World, I fear anarchy and revolution even more. God forbid that other countries suffer the same fate as Saint-Domingue. . . . Better they should remain another century under the barbarous and senseless oppression of Spain."[6] Similarly in Brazil, a man who in 1791 had spoken out in favor of the "equality of men" the very next year confessed his fear that what had happened in Haiti would also occur in Brazil, "which God forbidding I shall never see."[7] He was right to fear such developments. In 1805 "black and half-breed" members of a Brazilian militia unit were found wearing on their chests "portraits of Dessalines, Emperor of the Blacks in S. Domingue."[8]

The increasing demand in northern Europe for colonial products was accompanied by the export of a new ideology, whether expressed in terms of laissez-faire economic theory or as a vision of the social contract in politics. The exclusive right of metropolitan merchants to control all trade to the colonies seemed less and less acceptable to those who produced cattle hides or sugar or cacao. Increasingly self-conscious Creole elites in Spanish America, pleased with their newly acquired military ranks in the militia, hungered for a still larger decision-making role. But the experience of Haiti made them sharply aware of the potential dangers for them of pushing too far too fast toward local autonomy in societies built on the labor of unwilling workers. They knew they would need to rely on these workers as soldiers if it came to armed conflict. Could the colonial upper classes free themselves from metropolitan control without endangering their own dominance over the workers on whom they depended? Still, it was now possible to think of such action because the ideological underpinnings of the two Iberian empires had been frayed. Even more immediately important in Spanish America were some of the unpopular changes wrought by the Bourbon dynasty. The divisions within Latin American societies implied different visions of the future. While for some "freedom" would mean the end of forced labor, for others it would mean an end to the colonial mercantile monopoly, and for still others it would signify individual political liberty. As the nineteenth century opened, no one expected the complete rupture of the Portuguese and Spanish empires, but many sensed that old certainties had collapsed. While some viewed the prospect with enthusiasm, others saw it with alarm.

CHAPTER TWO

Reactions to Change

*E*ACH AREA OF LATIN AMERICA REACTED IN ITS OWN way to eighteenth-century changes. The lure of closer trade with northern Europe and the usefulness of Enlightenment ideas depended on the particular configuration of elite interests. The degree of social tension varied from place to place. Subsequent independence movements in the nineteenth century varied also. This chapter examines the bases of these differences before independence and projects their effects into the ensuing struggles. The importance of trade monopolies figured centrally in Argentina but much less in Chile. In several places a push for regional autonomy, separate from the former capital cities, captured local imaginations more than independence from Spain did. In Venezuela, Mexico, Peru, and Brazil social conflict, or its all-too-visible possibility, distinctly shaped upper-class attitudes regarding Spanish or Portuguese rule. As well, the will to modify the ordering of society, opening it to individual mobility, varied greatly across the region.

ARGENTINA AND URUGUAY

The Viceroyalty of Río de la Plata, lacking geographic and historical unity, remained unwieldy as a governmental unit from the time of its establishment in 1776. Its multiple and distinct regions reached as far as the massive Andean ranges, then referred to as Alto Peru and since renamed Bolivia. The piedmont areas, now in Argentina, included the wine-producing zone of Mendoza, the sugar-rich areas around Tucuman, and the proud and ancient university city of Córdoba. The steaming lowlands that are today Paraguay also belonged to Río de la Plata. And at the center of the viceroyalty lay the vast pampas, or grassy plains, that stretched for nearly five hundred miles west of the city of Buenos Aires. Cattle roamed free and wild on these plains, multiplying rapidly during two hundred years of neglect. Almost as wild as the cattle were the gauchos, or plainsmen, who slaughtered the cattle principally for the hides. Scattered within this open range were small nuclei of agricultural settlement that became more numerous and uniform the closer they were to the city of Buenos Aires. Finally, the viceroyalty included the rolling grasslands that today are in Uruguay.

The defense of Uruguay against incursions from the Portuguese was the chief reason for the introduction by the Spanish government of viceregal prestige, pomp, and ceremony to the otherwise bedraggled Buenos Aires. The Portuguese had established a settlement directly across the estuary of the Río de la Plata in 1680 and from this base had carried on a successful smuggling operation into the Andean mining regions. Whenever war broke out in eighteenth-century Europe, Spain and Portugal positioned themselves on opposite sides, with immediate repercussions in this region. Although Spaniards repeatedly drove the Portuguese out of the eastern bank of the estuary and pushed them into what is today southern Brazil, at the ensuing peace conference the Portuguese would regain much of the lost territory and then surreptitiously extend their control still farther into this sparsely settled region. Finally, in 1776 King Charles III dispatched to the region ten thousand troops and a viceroy charged with putting a stop to Portuguese expansion. Although the king succeeded briefly in this goal, the region remained a pawn fought over by Portuguese- and Spanish-speaking peoples even after the viceroyalty was replaced by independent republics.

A great rivalry existed between the two cities in the region, Buenos Aires and Montevideo. The harbor was better at Montevideo than at Buenos Aires, the surrounding region was far richer in pastoral resources than the pampas right around Buenos Aires, and the first plant for preparing jerked beef had been erected there. Yet the Bourbons favored Buenos Aires. The appointment of a viceroy to Buenos Aires exacerbated these tensions, and hostility between the two cities deepened.

The Decree of Free Trade of 1778 had even more far-reaching results. It permitted Buenos Aires to trade directly with Spain instead of indirectly via Lima and the circuitous route that led along the Pacific coast through Panamá and across the Caribbean and Atlantic to Spain. The transformations were profound. No longer strangled by isolation from international markets and foreign sources of supply, no longer forced to survive only by virtue of its smugglers' ability, the region around Buenos Aires experienced rapid economic growth. Prices of imports declined, and a large legal export business developed, al-

FIGURE 2.1. *Buenos Aires from the Plaza de Toros*

though principally through the hands of Spanish-born monopoly merchants. The silver from the fabled mine at Potosí, earlier shipped through Lima, now flowed through Buenos Aires, where new wealth accumulated in the hands of these merchants. In addition, pastoral products were increasingly important exports by the early nineteenth century. Hides, horns, and tallow, derived from the wild cattle that roamed the pampas, were all useful to European industry. Buenos Aires, whose inhabitants were called *porteños*, became the port for a vast and prospering area, exporting not only to Spain but also to the Caribbean. The population of the city grew from twelve thousand in 1750 to forty thousand by 1800.

Satisfaction with trade reform was short-lived. By the end of the century, cattle herds had been decimated, and the years of unrestrained prosperity had only served to whet the appetite for a still more direct exchange of products between Buenos Aires and other European nations, in particular England. Furthermore, Spain lagged behind England in its ability to supply manufactured goods and continued to burden all exchange with onerous taxes designed to bolster its own faltering finances. Many porteños believed Spain stood in the way of continued economic expansion. Yet Spain would not open the port of Buenos Aires to trade with other European nations because this would have destroyed the business of the politically powerful monopoly merchants in Spain (see Document 1).

By 1810 those with money and power in Argentina had not reached a consensus as to the proper organization of society and its government. Their disagreement swirled around four issues. First in ultimate importance was the issue of how society should be ordered. Should the old corporate structure, hierarchic in conception and religious in basis, be continued, or should it be replaced by a society of free individuals, vertically mobile regardless of their original "condition"? Second, and most immediately in evidence before 1810, was the issue of trade. Should it be monopolized by Spain or opened to other nations? Third, and most apparent after 1810, were questions about the best type of government. Should Argentina be ruled by a king—any king—or should it be a republic? And fourth, there remained what would become the most enduring issue of all: the division deriving from the divergent regional interests of "federalists," who demanded provincial and local autonomy, and their opponents, who dreamed of a unified, single government centered in Buenos Aires. Although the issues are simply defined, they were not simply resolved, for individuals grouped and regrouped around each question without consistency. Even similar economic interests, social relationships, or educational levels did not ensure a common position on many of these questions.

Creole intellectuals were the most visible early group to express opinions. By "intellectuals," I refer, here and in the remainder of this book, to doctors, lawyers, judges, and priests, as well as professors, teachers, journalists, and other writers. These educated professionals did not draw their income directly from landholding, mining, or commerce. Ideas were a central part of their lives. They did not speak as a group and were often in disagreement, but they shared a belief that ideas and theories mattered. On the whole they came from the upper middle class. In Argentina they concentrated in Buenos Aires but were also scattered in small numbers in interior cities. These men adopted the ideals of the Enlightenment, the French and American Revolutions, and the desire to transform their country accordingly. Such men as Mariano Moreno (1778–1811), Manuel Belgrano (1770–1820), and Bernardino Rivadavia (1780–1845) were typical. They believed that the natural laws that ruled economic and social affairs required the end of commercial restrictions, freedom of speech and press, equal rights for all men, and the attraction of immigrants from the non-Spanish world. The ideas of such men as Adam Smith and Jean-Jacques Rousseau excited them. They divided, however, on the ideal form of government, with some wanting a monarchy on the British model; others, a republic. Some wanted a strong, centralized government that could impose change on the "backward" interior, whereas others thought that freedom could be preserved only through local self-government and a loose federation of sovereign states. They united in seeking Argentine autonomy, but not all wanted a complete break with Spain. When independence became a reality, the other divisions among these reformers loomed larger still.

Buenos Aires, more than any other Spanish viceregal capital, was a commercial city, an entrepôt above all else. Merchants held a prominent place in its affairs, while Creole landowners, who had just begun to carve estates out of the open range, remained dependent on them. Merchants divided into two groups. Spanish-born agents or intermediaries of monopoly merchants in Spain dominated the newly created merchant guild and preferred to maintain the old regime. A second group of moderately wealthy Creoles envied the former's position. These Creole merchants shared the intellectuals' belief in the need for economic liberalism and direct trade with northern Europe but were not as committed to transforming the social order. The more conservative merchants were sure that monarchy was the best form of government. All Buenos Aires merchants, however, wanted a centralized government, believing this would prevent internal tariff barriers from hobbling their businesses. After 1810, once the old monopoly trading system ceased to exist, they became more united.

The merchants in the western cities differed sharply from their counterparts in Buenos Aires. They looked back nostalgically to the days of their own importance, when trade had been oriented toward Lima. They opposed any further rupture in the trading system and objected strongly to the centralization of government in Buenos Aires. The craftsmen and agrarian interests of the interior, no longer the chief suppliers of the Potosí mines, not surprisingly took the same position.

Cattle ranchers in the huge province of Buenos Aires were anxious to establish direct commercial connections with the consuming centers of northern Europe and were willing to go along with the intellectuals' insistence that the social structure must be transformed. Upwardly mobile, lusting after wealth, they had little use for the ancient modalities of social hierarchy, for noble titles, privilege, and monopoly. After 1810 they gradually became more preoccupied with gaining power and protecting their interests. Not ideologically committed to central government, they managed outwardly to support federalists in the subsequent internecine fighting while instituting de facto strong centralized government whenever they occupied the seat of power.

Other groups proved less significant in determining the early course of political events surrounding the struggle for independence, although they played important roles in later stages of the movement. Poorer whites throughout the region, anxious to preserve their social superiority but threatened with downward mobility because of economic changes they did not fully understand, developed a strong antipathy toward those born in Spain. Blacks, mulattos, and mestizos — the latter originally from western regions of the country — provided labor on eastern wheat farms in exchange for paltry wages. Meanwhile, the mixed-race gauchos, who had once roamed unfettered across the grasslands, began to find themselves gradually reduced to hired hands on private lands belonging to others. This process had not gone far enough, however, to provoke organized or widespread social discontent, and those on top could safely ignore gaucho interests for the time being. In fact, they mobilized the gauchos into rival armies with the promise of personal gain. Cowboys proved to be excellent soldiers in the civil wars that accompanied independence.

In Uruguay by 1810 the open range had ceased to exist, as most good land had been divided into vast estates worked either by miserable Indians drawn southward from the area formerly controlled by Jesuit missionaries or by mestizos migrating from the northwestern highlands of Argentina. Much of the meat produced in this region ended up as jerky to be exported as slave food to Brazil and Cuba. There were also some smallholder farms raising grain for consumption in Montevideo. The merchants in this city were not only absentee owners of many ranches, but they also participated in the illegal trade to Brazil. Yet local autonomy appealed more to rural interests than to the commercial elite.

The variety of backgrounds and the distinct interests of groups and regions within the Viceroyalty of Río de la Plata ensured that both the independence movement and subsequent regimes would be characterized by divergence and conflict.

CHILE

Just as the creation of the Viceroyalty of Río de la Plata reduced the area under the jurisdiction of the viceroy in Lima, so too did the formation in 1778 of the Captaincy-General of Chile. Although this area along the southwest coast of South America continued nominally to be part of the Viceroyalty of Peru, from this time forward the effective king's agent was the captain-general, who ruled from Santiago itself.

Chile then contained only one important region: the central valley, running for six hundred miles north and south between the towering Andes on the east and the lower coastal range on the west. Cultivation of wheat and other cereals, some viniculture, and the production of fruits to be dried and exported formed the bulk of economic activity. Cattle hides, pack mules, and small amounts of copper were also exported. All these goods went primarily to supply the market at Lima or the mines of Bolivia, with the exception of copper, which mostly went to Spain. The principal city in Chile was Santiago, but Concepción at the southern extreme of the central valley proved increasingly important.

The central valley had been won from the fierce Araucanian Indians two

FIGURE 2.2. *Valparaíso Bay*

and a half centuries earlier, but in the heavily forested area south of the valley over a hundred thousand Indians still remained unconquered. Those who had earlier been defeated were then absorbed through racial mixture into the wider society, and mestizos constituted the majority of the population of the central valley. They were tenant farmers, farmhands, menial workers, domestic servants, and skilled artisans. Agricultural workers, held in virtual bondage to their landlords, the *hacendados* (owners of large rural estates), still considered themselves privileged in comparison with others who wandered from place to place in search of a plot of land to plant in exchange for service. None of them, however, posed an overt threat to those on top.

Some landowners, claiming descent from the original conquistadors, hid their small admixture of Indian blood. In the eighteenth century this class was invigorated by intermarriage with the sons and daughters of Basque immigrants, whose commercial energy enabled them rapidly to accumulate considerable wealth. Old and new landowners cherished the right to entail their properties—a privilege granted by the king so that all landed inheritance went to the oldest son—and tried to purchase titles of nobility. They lived in relative splendor in the cities, with only occasional visits to their estates, sometimes to command the militia that they officered. They frequently felt themselves victimized, however, by Peruvian merchants who manipulated the price of wheat, or by Peruvian counting houses that financed their opulent lifestyle and then dunned them mercilessly. In addition, Peruvians controlled the carrying trade at the Chilean port of Valparaíso. By refusing to supply shipping at certain moments, they could force down the price of Chile's exportable grain. For these reasons the landowners welcomed Bourbon trade reform, which allowed them to sell their grain all along the Pacific coast and expand their shipments to Argentina. The construction of a road for wheeled vehicles from the central valley to the port city of Valparaíso had stimulated the economy, as had the opening of a route across the Andes to the Argentine city of Mendoza, with links to Buenos Aires. They did not seriously contemplate the possibility of exporting their goods to Europe and so did not demand even freer trade.

The merchants of Santiago and the port city of Valparaíso were mostly Spanish-born subagents of Lima houses or agents of Spanish firms, but there were a few Creoles among them. The latter participated actively in contraband trade, but the influx of goods legally imported from Europe had by the 1800s already saturated the meager Chilean market and exhausted all available currency. As a result, many merchants in both legitimate and illegal trade went bankrupt. Moreover, the long struggle between merchants in Santiago and Lima culminated in Santiago merchants successfully gaining the right to establish their own merchant guild, and a mint was established in Santiago. Along with the Bourbon policy of allowing trade to other Spanish American ports, these measures quelled most of their complaints.

In Santiago, Valparaíso, and Concepción, a small group of intellectuals was active in the last years of the eighteenth century. Swept on especially by the reforms being carried out in Spain and the ideas being propagated there but also by the ideas of Adam Smith and the French philosophes, these men were able to move in at crucial moments to influence the course of events. Since they could not make a strong case for the right to export products directly to Europe, they found other issues. They played on the dissatisfaction of both merchants and landowners over taxes imposed by Spain—especially those collected at the end of the century to finance Spain's wars against the English and sometimes against the French—and on the resentment of Creoles over their diminishing political power. These intellectuals maintained that prosperity would come only when Chile was controlled by Chileans, by which, of course, they meant the small crust of Creole aristocracy. The diversification of agriculture, the establishment of industries, and the introduction of modern technology were all dependent, they said, on a philosophy of government that had as its central aim local development rather than the immediate supply of revenues to the mother country. Once those revenues remained in Chile, they said, progressive measures could be taken to facilitate rather than hinder the economy. Playing on these ideas, educated professionals managed to widen the circle of their listeners, but they would never have been able to do much if it were not for later events in Europe.

COMPARISONS

Intellectuals — broadly defined — in both Chile and Argentina offered a rationale for breaking the imperial lines of authority, although they chose to emphasize different issues. A determination to make decisions for themselves characterized leadership cadres in both places. In Chile's central valley and in the region around Buenos Aires, landowners felt no threat from the changing patterns of trade, unlike the landowners of western Argentina, who faced ruin. But, as heirs to ancient families, the landowners of Chile held more conservative views than did the arriviste cattle ranchers of eastern Argentina.

Four other differences are striking. First, the possibility of direct exports of local products to northern Europe was of overriding importance in Argentina but hardly considered in Chile. Second, the promise of cheaper imports was much more attractive to Argentina than to Chile. Third, Chile was more concerned with the preeminence of Lima than with throwing off the yoke of Spanish power. As was true for Uruguayans, the rivalry between colonial centers often loomed larger than the conflict between Creoles and Spaniards. Finally — and as a logical consequence — the hostility directed at monopoly merchants was much more intense in Buenos Aires than in Santiago.

VENEZUELA

The Viceroyalty of New Granada included, as its eastern portion, the area that is today Venezuela. Named a captaincy-general in 1777, it was practically removed from the jurisdiction of the viceroy in Bogotá. Along its northern coast the hot, humid climate proved ideal for the production of tobacco, indigo, and especially cacao. At the higher elevations of the piedmont running east and west parallel to the coast, coffee bushes flourished. Large plantations worked principally by African slaves supplied exports for overseas trade. Their owners lived in cities on the higher ground, including the Andean spur reaching deep into the region from the southwest. South of the coastal range and east of the Andes are the treeless plains, or llanos, swampy in the rainy season, scorched in the dry. South of the plains run the muddy waters of the Orinoco River, beyond which the forbidding jungle stretched to the Amazon River.

Pushed by their ambition to ship ever larger quantities of plantation products, landowners bought ever greater numbers of black slaves. By 1800 there were some 87,000 slaves in Venezuela, not counting the thousands who had run away. It did not take much perspicacity for slave owners to sense the simmering discontent of their workers. Alexander von Humboldt, the German scientist who visited Venezuela in 1799, noted that this reality dampened any enthusiasm for independence, for slave owners "believed that in revolutions they would run the risk of losing their slaves."[1] Their fears became greater after some three hundred slaves revolted in 1795, sacking plantations, killing the planters, and proclaiming their desire to follow the Haitian example and adopt "the law of the French, the republic, the freedom of slaves."[2] Four years later another unsuccessful revolt — this one by free pardos in the militia — actually received help from Haiti. Slaves and free pardos together outnumbered whites two to one.

Pardos met and mingled with everyone but found acceptance by only a few. They rubbed shoulders with new immigrants from Spain and the Canaries as tradesmen and artisans and intermarried with them. Other free pardos sought to escape the master-and-man relationship characteristic of the plantations and the discriminatory treatment they encountered in the cities by fleeing to the llanos. Mixing with the Indians and mestizos of this region, the pardos joined them in cattle raising. Taking their name from the llanos, the *llaneros* roamed relatively free, described by contemporaries as living to drink, gamble, and sometimes kill. They were fiercely devoted to leaders who commanded their loyalty as much because of their machismo and charisma as their prowess with the lasso and machete. The llaneros despised the sedentary way of life of Creole planters and deeply distrusted their ambitions.

Creole landowners were often at odds with the merchants, despite their common social preeminence. The merchants who were most disliked were the commercial representatives of the Caracas Company, a monopoly enterprise organized in Spain under royal auspices in 1728 and opened to the investment and direction of enterprising Basques. Its creation had been prompted by the boom in contraband trade to Venezuela. The company policed the coast and drove away smugglers, stimulated cacao production, introduced new crops to diversify production, and returned profits to Spanish investors reaching 20 percent a year. But the landowners were less than satisfied with company practices and results and believed the Caracas Company manipulated prices. When the company finally dissolved in the 1780s, it left behind a heritage of rancor against Spanish merchants.

The landowning aristocracy — few in number but rich in fortune — carefully maintained their distance from "inferiors." Insisting on the purity of their own racial heritage, they were alarmed at any "uppity" behavior by pardos. Toward the end of the eighteenth century racial feeling in the cities became particularly intense precisely because an increasing number of pardos with industry and drive had achieved moderate wealth. Sometimes they became the landowners' creditors, causing further alienation. Racial tensions were further exacerbated by the newly arrived Spaniards, who thought such attitudes irrational and would as soon proffer business opportunities and government posts to pardos as to Creoles. Upper-class whites were especially offended by the royal decision to allow a few pardos to legally change their status (see Document 2).

Grievances were often vented in the cabildos. These bodies enjoyed more prestige and exercised more power than other cabildos in Spanish America because the Spanish government had long neglected the area. This neglect encouraged cabildo members to think they were the arbiters of their own affairs. The existence of several cities of more or less equal wealth and the absence of a viceroy, leaving only a captain-general to rule in Caracas, probably contributed to their sense of independence.

When near the end of the century the Bourbons ended this era of neglect and began to tighten their command, Venezuelans deeply resented it. The European wars at the turn of the century resulted in increased taxes and further irritation. French and English ships, according to Spain's shifting alliances, alternately raided the port towns, and workers had to leave the plantations to defend the coast. On the eve of independence Venezuela seethed with discontent.

In contrast, the topography of neighboring Colombia had always hindered the effort of any government there to exert control over its far-flung regions, tucked into mountain valleys or spreading across lowland plains. In most towns Indians were in the minority, and their lands had long passed to outsiders. Gold mines produced wealth for a fortunate few and penury for workers. Plantations in the lowland areas, worked by black slaves, provided some export products, but the economy of Colombia was mainly oriented to internal consumption in regionally self-sufficient areas. Independence, therefore, would be a series of highly localized movements, lacking coordination and sometimes even resisting it.

MEXICO

The Viceroyalty of New Spain, stretching from California to Central America, shone as the brightest star in the Spanish imperial firmament. New Spain had a population of 6.5 million, more than any other viceroyalty, and it was also the most prosperous. Principally because of its silver mines, New Spain supplied two-thirds of all the revenues Spain derived from its empire, in addition to subsidizing imperial administrations in other colonies.

At the center of the country, both topographically and politically, lay Mexico City, in a delightful valley at an altitude of almost eight thousand feet. In 1800 it held about 140,000 people, making it one of the largest cities in the world. Its needs stimulated agricultural development in its hinterland. Northward from Mexico City stretch two mountain ranges in a somewhat lopsided "V."

FIGURE 2.3. *Mexico City and the Mountains Beyond*

The western range reaches as far as the Rocky Mountains; the eastern range is shorter and ends around Monterrey. Northwest of Mexico City lies the city of Guanajuato, the center of one of the most prosperous areas in Mexico at that time. Fabulously productive silver mines dotted the hills about the city, and a rich agricultural and pastoral region supplied it and the mines with food and woolens. To the west, the burgeoning administrative and commercial center of Guadalajara was the center of another thriving agricultural region. Farther north, in more arid sections, cattle raising predominated, and more mines were located at San Luis Potosí and Zacatecas. Southeast of Mexico City, in another fertile valley, lay the city of Puebla, a textile center. Toward the south the knotty mountains dissolve into strands that separate tropical valleys from cool highland ones. The city of Oaxaca (then called Antequara), in one of these high valleys, was the center of a large, self-sufficient region of Indian villages that also produced indigo dye. Along the Balsas River, draining into the Pacific, and in the hot, humid plains that stretch to the Gulf of Mexico sugar, cacao, and tobacco plantations added to Mexico's export wealth and helped diversify its economy. Imports flowed in legally from Spain through Veracruz and illegally from other countries through every cove and sleepy harbor on the Caribbean coast. These goods—especially cloth—then competed with those produced by craftsmen in highland cities such as Oaxaca and Puebla. On the Pacific coast Acapulco was the terminal point of a prosperous trade with the Philippines, to which Mexicans shipped silver coins in exchange for silks and other products of the Orient. Transport between and among these different regions was almost entirely by mule train.

Mexico's increasing prosperity produced marked social tensions, for some groups and individuals were on the rise, while others were in decline. At the beginning of the nineteenth century there were approximately fifteen thousand Spaniards in Mexico, alongside a million Creoles. Spaniards stood at the top of the social pyramid, as elsewhere in Spanish America. They represented the interests of monopoly merchants and administered the bureaucracy that channeled revenues to Spain. The Bourbon reforms had depressed Creole hopes of participating in this uppermost strata, although these reforms also opened up more trading opportunities for everyone, benefitting a number of Creoles.

Immediately below this administrative and commercial elite were two other groups. One may be thought of as the nouveaux riches. They had recently accumulated staggering fortunes, having invested mercantile capital—their own or borrowed—in plantations and especially in mines, some of which proved to be bonanzas. Either Spanish immigrants or the sons of immigrants, they had succeeded through energy, ambition, good contacts, and luck. They sometimes blamed Spain for any obstacles they encountered in their attempt to rise even further or faster, but their loyalties were divided. While their economic interests tied them to Mexico, their social roots made them sympathetic to Spain.

Another group, often in decline, were the Creole descendants of the original conquistadors or old-time settlers. These Creoles had rested too long on the glories of their antecedents and had paid too little attention to cultivating their inheritance. They clung desperately to the vestiges of their former position, one of these often being a proprietary seat on a cabildo. They inclined to the professions, especially law, for through its practice, without dirtying their hands, they could maintain appearances. Some entered the clergy or became teachers. They resented the lack of more positions for themselves in government, the church, and overseas commerce. They often provided the intellectual justification for rebellion against Spain.

The next group—either Creole or mestizo in the broadest sense—was made up of an upwardly mobile lower middle class. Storekeepers, small landowners, administrators for absentee landlords, independent muleteers, owners of textile mills and their skilled operators, parish priests in the more impoverished areas, self-employed artisans who owned the tools with which they worked, and occupants of lowly government positions such as postal clerks and night watchmen—they had enough wealth and education to imagine a better deal but not enough influence to secure it.

A final, mixed group formed in the cities and included the workers themselves, employees of the large government-owned cigar and cigarette factory, journeymen employed by artisans, street vendors, servants, and the permanently or temporarily unemployed. Especially in Mexico City, many were Indian or mestizo migrants from the countryside who, no matter how bad the living conditions they encountered, knew they were better off than those they had left behind in rural areas facing a short supply of land and a rising population.

Indians in the central valley of Mexico and even more so those in the highlands south of Mexico City—that is, the areas of the pre-Columbian "high" civilizations—had succeeded in continuing village life much as it had been at the time of their conquest. They had successfully resisted any massive encroachment on their common lands, although many Creole-owned haciendas (landed estates) had been established in their midst. They were compelled to pay the tribute levied on each village collectively according to the number of males in a specified age bracket but were exempt from most other taxes. Centuries of attrition had, of course, changed many ancient villages. Chieftains, or caciques, had become the creatures of the Spaniards, and visits by the parish priest had cast a new layer of ritual and meaning over the old religious practices. Yet these Indians still dressed in traditional clothes, spoke their ancient languages, preserved the bedrock of their spiritual life, and did not think of themselves as "Indians" but as Mixtecs or Zapotecs, that is, speakers of a common language, or as belonging to particular village communities.

In the areas around Guanajuato and Guadalajara the situation was different. The country around Guanajuato had never really been Aztec territory, and the Spanish presence had more easily disrupted village life. The wealth of the mines and the heightened demand for food in the cities had also eroded the ancient relationships of people to land and of people to each other. In the half century before 1810 the expansion of Creole- and mestizo-owned small farms had further encroached on the best Indian lands, just as the Indian population was increasing. As a result more and more Indians sought employment on farms as day laborers, sharecroppers, or debt peons. Debt peons, having received goods on credit at the hacienda store, found themselves unable to pay off their debts from their meager earnings and were legally compelled to do so before being allowed to move elsewhere or find other employment. The result of this general shift from village to farm was to depress wages. The Indians here, who typically understood Spanish or even spoke it and participated actively in a money economy, knew they did not benefit from the prosperity of the region. A drought in 1808–1810 exacerbated their plight while increasing the profits of those landowners who hoarded grain awaiting still higher prices. Meanwhile Indians felt beset by cultural invasions that challenged their autonomy, their way of life, their cosmology, and even their identity. Their discontent was palpable. In the neighboring region of Guadalajara similar pressures were felt. The villages there were stronger, but in the face of increasing population, more and more Indians found themselves with no choice but to leave communal lands and seek employment on nearby estates. These estates then competed with the villages even for the use of marginal lands, because the burgeoning demand for foodstuffs in the rapidly growing city of Guadalajara meant that land had become an increasingly scarce commodity. Social and ethnic tensions were rife in these regions on the eve of independence.

In the northern ranch country the life of the Indians had been even more affected by the Spaniards, but the change had happened long before. They were now cowhands or peasants, kept in a lowly position and mixing with poor mestizos. Beyond them, in the hills of the northwest and the plains of the far north, warlike Indian tribes, almost entirely untouched by the Spanish presence except for the use of horses, pushed steadily southward.

In Mexico not only were there the two broad categories of the ambitious and the satisfied, but the ambitious saw their future in diverse ways. The nouveaux riches hoped for increased wealth under a system they monopolized. The mestizos wanted to participate more fully in wealth-producing enterprises, and the Indians could hope for little but revenge. With so many conflicting interests present, a unified program of change along several fronts is difficult to imagine. As it was, it fell to the crown to act as a mediator among hostile groups.

CENTRAL AMERICA

The Captaincy-General of Guatemala included a great variety of regions, encompassing what are today the countries of Costa Rica, Nicaragua, Honduras, El Salvador, Guatemala, and Belize, as well as the Mexican state of Chiapas and some parts of Yucatán. In the sixteenth century native inhabitants in what eventually became Costa Rica had been relatively few, and European settlers, without their labor, had to settle for small plots of land. By the nineteenth century Costa Rica was predominantly European in ethnic background, with little race mixture. At the other extreme, in Chiapas and Guatemala, a large population of communally organized village Indians, most of whom spoke no Spanish, contrasted with the narrow segment of white or mestizo city residents. El Salvador, Honduras, and Nicaragua fell somewhere in between, with a predominantly mestizo population. Along the low-lying Caribbean coast English loggers and settlers often allied themselves with the Miskito Indians and descendants of runaway black slaves from Caribbean islands to harass the Spaniards or to smuggle goods to the highlands.

Economic activities also differed sharply from place to place. The Creole hacendados in highland Guatemala produced mainly foodstuffs for the cities, relying both on draft labor from Indian villages and, increasingly, on debt peonage. The major exports to Europe were the dyes so important to the flourishing English textile industry. Dyewoods from the eastern tropical lowlands were taken directly by the British loggers on the coast. Indigo, the deep blue dye produced in a labor-intensive process from leaves of *Indigofera* bushes, formed a growing part of the region's exports in the late eighteenth century, especially from the Pacific coast lowlands of El Salvador and Guatemala. By the end of the colonial period, however, indigo faced growing competition from producers in South Carolina, Venezuela, and the East Indies. Cochineal, the orange-scarlet dye extracted from an insect, took its place. These products were generally produced by mestizo smallholders who fiercely exploited the Indians they brought down from the highlands as draft laborers during the harvest season. Merchandising was handled almost entirely by merchants in Guatemala City, who in 1790 succeeded in establishing their own guild. The Bourbon-declared freedom to export directly to Spain instead of via Veracruz greatly benefited the dyestuffs trade. Older merchant houses increasingly faced challenges for their control of the colony from a number of energetic immigrants from Spain and their children, who joined the Creole hacendados to form a local aristocracy, dominating the cabildo of Guatemala City.

COMPARISONS

The diversified economy of Mexico meant that all regions would profit from any move that increased contact with the industrial centers of Europe. Coastal planters already welcomed smugglers. Mine owners would be glad to get more in exchange for their silver. The urban middle classes, feeling that the future belonged to them, believed that closer contact with northern Europe could only be good. In this, Mexico resembled Venezuela, which had become prominent in the first place only as the expansion of the European economy stimulated plantation agriculture and where the lure of commercial freedom attracted many. This was also the case in lowland Central America. On the other hand, and not surprisingly, Spanish monopoly merchants in Mexico, Venezuela, and Guatemala frowned on such a prospect.

Venezuela and Mexico most resembled each other in the intensity of class feeling. Although the social structure of Venezuela was perhaps less complicated than that of Mexico, a similar friction between Creoles and less favored groups characterized it. The pardos of Venezuela and the mestizos of Mexico understood that a more open society would make social mobility easier. Venezuelan slaves and Mexican Indians were seen to threaten social stability, although Indians in traditional villages in the south of Mexico and the north of Central America may have wished mainly to be left alone. Class friction would play equally large parts in struggles for independence in Mexico and Venezuela but in almost opposite ways. Wealthy Mexicans, fearing Indian power, gradually retreated to the safety of colonial rule, whereas those in Venezuela were surprised to find slaves eventually joining the Spanish forces against them.

PERU

While the coastal area of Peru is arid, the snow-fed rivers that flow to the Pacific watered plantations, worked by African slaves and some acculturated Indian laborers lured down from the highlands. The chief crops produced on these estates were grains, cotton, and sugar. Producers did not look to Europe for markets but instead supplied local cities and highland mines. Indians of ancient civilization and lowly status populated the mountain valleys, many working for minimum pay as draft laborers in the silver mines.

The wealthy lived in the coastal city of Lima, where sixteenth-century Spaniards had established their capital, shunning the preconquest center of Indian power in Cuzco. Lima was an aristocratic, Spanish-oriented, commercial town with no roots in Indian tradition. The silver from the mines was exported through the adjoining port of Callao, and, before the trade reform of 1778, all legally imported manufactured goods from Europe destined for southern Colombia, Ecuador, interior Peru, Bolivia, Argentina, and Chile passed through this port and the warehouses of Lima's merchant guild members. As the vice-regal seat, Lima housed a large Spanish bureaucracy, and many of its residents were Spaniards. Most of the city's elite, whether born in Spain or America, were royal employees. A significant number of Creoles and a few Spanish bureaucrats resided in Cuzco, the area's second largest city, but it was a city most *limeños* (residents of Lima) had never visited.

That Lima—which would be practically the last center of Spanish power in America—was one of the centers of Enlightenment thought in the last decades of the eighteenth century is one more proof that ideas alone did not make the revolutions of Spanish America. A whole generation of articulate liberals studied at the Real Convictorio de San Carlos, a college-seminary established after the expulsion of the Jesuits in 1767. But these intellectuals aimed at reform, not revolution.

This limited program may be a tribute to their realism, for no prominent group stood to benefit from independence. The legal restrictions on commerce favored the colony's most wealthy and powerful, and independence could only diminish the orbit of their economic power. Creole aristocrats enjoyed the glow of viceregal splendor and the ancient tradition of a colonial preeminence. By the early nineteenth century the predominant groups had two complaints. First, the Bourbons had taken Alto Peru, present-day Bolivia, out of

FIGURE 2.4. *Lima with Bridge over the Rimac River*

their jurisdiction and placed it, with its rich silver mines, in the new Viceroyalty of Río de la Plata (albeit still leaving some newer and exceedingly productive mines in Lima's orbit). They further resented the fact that the Bourbons had allowed Buenos Aires and other ports to trade directly with Spain and no longer only through Lima. Supplies for the miners in the highland now came through Argentina, even undercutting the hitherto busy textile shops of Cuzco. Certainly they would also have preferred lower taxes, more local control, and more freedom to exploit the Indians, that is, the revocation of most Bourbon reforms, but they did not think of independence. They desired to return to a better past, not to move on to a vaguely envisioned future. The big fear among upper-class whites, whether Creole or Spanish-born, was that the Indians of the highlands would revolt. Indians made up 60 percent of the population of Peru; "pure" whites accounted for only 13 percent. Even in Lima whites were outnumbered by Indians, mestizos, free pardos, and slaves by a ratio of two to one.

Sometimes Indians did revolt, most notably in the rebellion led by "Tupac Amaru II" in 1780. José Gabriel Condorcanqui Noguera (1738–1781), despite his mestizo origin and prosperous business as a muleteer, claimed descent from an Inca (i.e., king). He had acquired an education and became incensed at the plight of the Indian masses. He understood the Bourbon reforms as having abrogated the Hapsburg deal whereby descendants of the ancient Indian rulers were to be treated as a separate corporate group. Assuming the name of the last known Inca, Tupac Amaru, he called for a general rebellion in the highlands. He demanded the end of forced labor, the suspension of the most oppressive taxes, which had greatly increased under Bourbon rule, and the freedom of slaves. He drew his lieutenants from the colonial middle class, including a number of Creoles, many mestizos and Indians, and a few blacks—farmers, artisans, and muleteers like himself. His wife, Micaela Bastidas Puyucahua, handled the campaign's logistics and may have played a major advisory role. Tupac Amaru's program was not anti-white, but anti-European. Yet bloody massacres resulted in which his Indian followers vented on their white oppressors the rage they had contained for centuries. Because of this, he hesitated to attack the ancient city of Cuzco, an essential target, and the Spanish authorities, recovering from their initial surprise, put down the Indian uprising within six months. Some one hundred thousand persons lost their lives, and punishment was wreaked on the leaders with unrestrained violence. The arms and legs of Tupac Amaru were tied to four horses to tear him apart.

This rebellion had several far-reaching effects. The legitimacy of Spanish rule over the Indians was now definitively questioned throughout the Andean highlands. Other, even more radical rebellions erupted later in Bolivia that, although also defeated, signaled a changed order. Although the Indian tribute was now collected with even greater efficiency, the perception was that the former status quo had been permanently broken and could not be restored. But, most immediately important, Tupac Amaru's rebellion frightened propertied Creoles away from any revolutionary inclinations they might have otherwise developed, for they witnessed the Indian majority's seething discontent.

Regardless of the ideas of a few intellectuals, the basic position of Creoles both in Lima and in the highland city of Cuzco was one of satisfaction with colonial status. Neither closer economic ties with northern Europe nor a changed society attracted them. There were sources of dissatisfaction but not necessarily with colonial status. They would have preferred to return to the way things were before the Bourbon reforms. Only military force brought in from outside would bring about independence for Peru.

BRAZIL

Although Brazil is not divided by towering mountain ranges, its vast size has exerted almost as divisive a force as the more spectacular topography of Spanish America, creating enduringly diverse regions. The oldest area of Portuguese settlement was a narrow strip of land running from the tip of the northeastern bulge around Recife southward beyond Salvador and ranging in width from fifty to one hundred miles. This area is characterized by a generally rolling terrain, a humid climate, and rich soil. The land was early divided into sugar plantations, where thousands of African slaves labored in the fields and in the mills. Unlike the situation in Lima, the masters did not typically resort

FIGURE 2.5. *Brazilian Plantation House*

to sumptuous living in the cities. Deeply involved in the daily affairs of their plantations, these entrepreneurs managed a large number of slaves with whom they were in relatively close contact. Some relied on brute force to compel their workers, but others found it useful to negotiate with them, granting some the right to plant food crops on less fertile tracts of land or playing other paternalistic roles. In either case it was clear to all that planters held overwhelming power over the slaves, their families, and other dependents. But planters often found themselves in debt to Portuguese merchants in the cities to whom they sold their crops and from whom they bought supplies. From 1550 to 1650 this northeastern region was the biggest supplier of sugar to the world, and it continued to be a major actor in that market. Because of the revolution-caused disruption of the Haitian economy at the end of the eighteenth century Brazilian sugar sales again soared. The hinterland of this coastal strip was a sparsely inhabited, semiarid region devoted primarily to cattle raising.

The São Francisco River connected the coastal region to the area of "General Mines," or Minas Gerais. At the end of the seventeenth century vast reserves of gold and then diamonds were discovered in this area, rapidly upsetting the regional, economic, and social balance of the entire colony. Many sugar planters with their slaves abandoned everything to join the gold rush. Others came in such numbers from overseas that the Portuguese government, fearing depopulation, prohibited emigration. Around the placer mines, large towns like Ouro Preto grew up seemingly overnight, overshadowing some older cities. The turbulent, socially mobile lives of these newcomers contrasted with the fixed relationships noted in Recife and Salvador. After the middle of the eighteenth century the mines began to play out, and the economy slowed, cushioned, however, by a secondary agricultural economy needed to feed the growing city of Rio de Janeiro. New taxes imposed by Portugal bred restlessness and discontent. An abortive conspiracy was organized in Ouro Preto in 1789 to declare independence and establish a local republic, and, although supported only by a handful of conspirators, their move was symptomatic of local sentiment.

The mines had been originally discovered by mestizo explorers based in São Paulo. These restless, ambitious, footloose men had in the seventeenth century extended Portuguese control over the bulk of the area that is now Brazil, despite the legal rights of Spain. At the end of the colonial period the inhabitants of São Paulo were still proud of their role in handing over to the king such vast areas and great treasures and resented the scant appreciation they received in return. The regions they had opened up had been cut away from their jurisdiction, the wealth they had discovered had fallen into the hands of new arrivals from other parts of the country or from Portugal, and the code by which they lived on the rivers and in the forests had been circumscribed by the imposition of formal institutions directed by colonial administrators.

The discovery of the mines had drawn the political center of gravity southward, and in the 1760s Pombal relocated the capital of the entire colony from Salvador to Rio de Janeiro. By the beginning of the nineteenth century Rio de Janeiro, long an important port, profited as chief entrepôt for the legal and illegal commerce of the region. Despite its beautiful setting among green hills and sandy coves, the town of Rio de Janeiro itself was a backward provincial capital, beset by disease and characterized by muddy, filthy streets. Even the elevation of the colonial governor to the titular position of viceroy had not done much to give Rio de Janeiro the luster of the much larger Mexico City or even of the smaller Lima.

Among Brazil's various regions, no single one achieved complete preeminence. Its configuration has been described as that of an archipelago. Although this meant that few people thought of themselves as "Brazilian" and more likely identified themselves with their local capitals, it also meant that Brazil before 1808 did not experience the same tension, competition, and rivalry as existed between Montevideo and Buenos Aires or Santiago and Lima, that is, between lesser provinces and a single predominant center. These would develop in Brazil only later.

Creole sugar planters in Brazil—both in the northeast and around Rio de Janeiro—were generally satisfied with their colonial status, for the Portuguese, being relatively lax in administration, allowed the colonial upper echelon a

FIGURE 2.6. *Rio de Janeiro as Seen from the South*

great deal of local political power to add to their wealth. In addition to presiding over their vast slave-worked properties, they dominated the câmaras, or municipal county councils. The centralizing effort to create an efficient Portuguese empire, ably directed by the marquis of Pombal, did begin to trim the wings of these local bodies, but the new program was not enforced overnight, and Creole irritation remained minimal. Furthermore, not only did the Portuguese not restrict commerce as severely as did the Spaniards, but because England protected Jamaican sugar by placing a high tariff on the Brazilian product, the major market for Brazil was the European continent itself, for which Portugal was a natural entrepôt. Obviously it would have been even better for them if they could import machinery and cheap textiles (to clothe their slaves) directly from northern Europe, but it was not their highest priority. Nor did sugar planters, unlike a few leaders in the mining regions, care that there were prohibitions on manufacturing.

Planters and miners alike, however, did resent the wealth and prominence of Portuguese merchants in the coastal towns. They believed the merchants overcharged for the imported goods they sold, paid too little for the sugar they bought, and lent money at too high an interest rate, often foreclosing on indebted planters. Predictably these Portuguese-born merchants wanted Portugal to intensify the restrictions imposed on trade with foreigners and to combat

FIGURE 2.7. *Rio de Janeiro as Seen from the North*

smuggling. They clung to their monopoly of contracts to supply equipment to the navy or furnish stores to any government establishment, and greatly valued the colonial relationship that protected them.

By the end of the eighteenth century an energetic lower middle class had formed in Recife, Salvador, and Rio de Janeiro that included Brazilian-born whites, mulattos, and free blacks. They were easily stirred up against Portuguese storekeepers, who seemed to make money at consumers' expense. Caught between the upper grindstone of Portuguese predominance and the nether one of cheap slave labor, this class became irritable, tense, and eventually volatile. In 1798 mulatto tailors and common soldiers plotted revolt in Salvador. One participant, a free mulatto, declared that he sought "a government in which whites, pardos, and blacks would enter equally, without distinction by color [but] only by [their] capacity to command and govern."[3] Their mixed race and less than elite social position led to much harsher punishments of these would-be revolutionaries than those meted out to the wealthy leaders of the 1789 tax revolt in Ouro Preto. By this time the experience of Haiti had further heightened fears of a race war among both urban whites and sugar planters.

Intellectuals, inspired by the ideals of the Enlightenment and devoted to the inclusion of their country in the main currents of the Western world, encouraged urban discontent. But there were not only few issues to play on but also few intellectuals. There was no university or institution of higher education in all of Brazil, and not everyone could afford to study in Portugal. Furthermore, the fact that no printing press existed in Brazil before 1808 greatly limited the possibilities for intellectuals to spread their ideas. If it had not been for events outside Brazil, decades would probably have passed before they could have mobilized enough favorable opinion to create an independent country.

COMPARISONS

At first sight it may seem odd to compare Peru with Brazil. The towering Andes have no counterpart in the geologic formation of Brazil. Spaniards had found the Indians in the Andes to be highly sophisticated creators of complex and densely populated civilizations, while in contrast the Portuguese had encountered relatively few and mainly seminomadic Indians in Brazil. The Portuguese had thus turned to African slaves to supply the labor of the colony, in numbers far exceeding those in Peru.

There is, however, one marked similarity between these two areas: those excited by the Enlightenment found few cracks of dissatisfaction among the powerful into which to wedge new ideas. Wealthy Creoles had few reasons to complain in either place. Unlike the situation in Argentina, Venezuela, or Mexico, the trading monopoly did not grate for most leaders in either Brazil or Peru. And, as was also true to some extent in Mexico and Venezuela, social tensions worked to dampen Creole interest in altering the existing colonial order. Aside from plots or abortive revolts in Bolivia, Ouro Preto, and Salvador, independence came to both Brazil and the central Andes from outside and was formalized only in the 1820s, a full decade after independence movements began elsewhere. The need of the well-off to maintain control over their workers far exceeded their desire for change.

CHAPTER THREE

Toward War

T HE INDEPENDENCE OF LATIN AMERICA WOULD NOT
have occurred when it did had it not been for major changes
taking place in Spain and Portugal, and it would not have occurred after that
had it not been for the demands of some Latin Americans for change. Because
of European events, Spanish Americans found themselves without a king while
Portuguese Americans received a king in their very midst. In Spanish America
groups that stood to gain from local autonomy were able to take some steps
toward independence. Because of its other preoccupations, Spain was unable
to muster enough force early enough to snuff out these initiatives but was able
to do enough to alienate still more Spanish Americans. Meanwhile intellectuals provided a unifying rationale for drastic change. I begin by considering who
wanted change, before examining the precipitating events in Europe and the
early responses they elicited.

WHO WANTED CHANGE?

Interest Groups

In view of the eventual importance of Creole militias in initiating
moves leading to independence in Spanish America, one has to ask, what was
the outlook of the upper and middle classes from which their officers were
drawn? Although it is safe to say that in every area there were some more or
less well-off Creoles who were willing to support independence (or, at least,
local autonomy), the strength of their commitment varied greatly from place
to place. This diversity of views exemplifies the complexity of examining the
"why" of the movement.

In some regions the landowners' interest in independence was clearly based on economic issues. The planters of Venezuela, coastal Mexico, and Colombia and the ranchers around Buenos Aires knew that their products were consumed in northern Europe and that they would get better prices through direct sales. But in other regions the economic factor was relatively unimportant. The hacendados of Chile sent their grain mostly to Peru and by 1810 were free to send it to other ports along the Pacific coast. Those of the Colombian highlands distributed their products locally because the difficult terrain prevented them from supplying the coast in any significant quantity. None of these landowners, or those in the highlands of Mexico, was interested in direct exports to overseas markets in northern Europe. It is not surprising, then, that landowners in different regions took opposite positions regarding independence.

Nor was the advantage of the lower cost of imported manufactured goods of equal interest to all consumers, although the landed class always supported steps that facilitated this importation unless it crossed their other interests. In Chile, for instance, landowners received silver from Peru in exchange for their wheat, and this silver went further when the prices of manufactured imports were lower. Similarly, the gold exported from Colombia paid for more manufactured goods if sent directly to England. The haciendas of highland Mexico supplied foodstuffs to the mining towns, and the mineral wealth received in return paid for sumptuous town houses that in turn called for imported European furnishings. Even the hacienda itself required tools and other iron products best supplied from abroad. On the other hand, if the imported products competed in price with local ones, then the feeling was reversed. Weavers in highland Peru and in Puebla, Mexico, for instance, looked with disfavor on measures that opened the region to foreign competition.

Where landowners remained loyal to Spain, their loyalty resulted from other, countervailing and mostly noneconomic considerations. Most noticeable is the case of Mexico, where, in the event, the landed interest perceived much more advantage in maintaining Spanish power than surrendering to what they believed to be a maddened horde of Indians. In Peru the fear was so direct that virtually no one moved to break the tie with Spain. In Venezuela men of property did join the struggle for independence, but conflict between them and the lower classes soon caused them to have second thoughts. In Cuba slave-owning planters understandably shied away from talk of rebellion, all the more so as they had long enjoyed an exceptionally freer commerce with northern Europe and the United States than did other Spanish colonies and received more governmental funds in forts and other public works than they paid in taxes. Even where social tensions do not seem to have been present, it was only when the demand for higher prices on exports and lower ones on imports combined with other interests, such as a push for lower taxes generally or greater power locally, that the landowners were stirred up to fight for independence.

Among merchants there was the obvious distinction between those who profited from the existing monopoly trading system and those who did not. The former were mostly Spanish-born agents of large merchant firms in Cádiz. Even after the trade reforms of the 1770s, large-scale legal commerce remained in their hands. In outlying areas like Santiago, Montevideo, or Guatemala City, setting up officially sanctioned merchant guilds to limit competition met their maximum aims. Although the old, established merchants of Lima or Veracruz resented the increased trading freedom encouraged by the Bourbon kings and imposed by the turn-of-the-century wars, they correctly surmised that independence would not improve their situation. The most that can be said is that perhaps some of these businessmen only lackadaisically defended a system that seemed to them already moribund.

Those who bought from the monopoly merchants, on the other hand, were often Creole middlemen. The owners of these small businesses were ambitious, unreconciled to remaining forever in the shadow of the larger merchant houses and susceptible to the wiles of the contrabandist. When the leaders of independence movements moved to loosen the restrictions on foreign trade and end many of the earlier smaller monopolies, these merchants benefited and eagerly gave the new governments their support. This was true in Buenos Aires and Caracas and would have been true in the minor cities of Mexico, such as Veracruz, had not some independence leaders threatened the safety of all trade by undertaking much more radical change. The position of Creole merchants in Lima and western Argentina—who almost unanimously looked back nostalgically to better days, opposed any measure that would transform Buenos Aires into an even larger entrepôt, and saw independence as a step in the same direction as the "disastrous" Bourbon reforms—contrasted sharply with those in Mexico City, who, because of their more vigorous trade and the profits some had derived from the Bourbon measures, disagreed among themselves as to whether independence would be good or bad.

The position of craftsmen before the threat or promise of independence has not yet been adequately studied. A fear of competing foreign imports would surely have strengthened their loyalty to Spain, but many of them derived more protection from the difficulties of internal transport than from legal rigidities. The textile shops in Puebla (Mexico), Quito (Ecuador), and Cuzco (Peru) felt threatened by foreign competition, but their counterparts in Socorro (Colombia) did not apparently share their viewpoint. In some areas, for example, southern Colombia, we can ask whether it was direct economic interest or a highly traditional social order that contributed to the strength of loyalist sentiment among this class.

Closely related to the issue of trade, but in a sense overriding it, was the question of power. There is little doubt that the Creole aristocracy and professional middle class wanted more power and wished to wrest it from the supercilious Spanish bureaucrats. This ambition was linked to the issue of free commerce, because with control in their hands they could foster their own economic interests, whatever they were. Gaining power would also — and importantly — give them the right to tax and disburse funds in their own behalf. They may also have believed that mestizos and mulattos could more easily be kept in "their" place and Indians further exploited, if they, the Creoles, wrested authority away from the peninsular Spaniards, whether through complete independence or regional autonomy within a tolerant European-based monarchy. People had multiple reasons to complain about the existing system, but whether they saw national independence as a way of righting their situation depended on the particularities of their case.

Ideas

The role of Creole intellectuals assumes real importance once we understand that society was fragmented, with some groups desiring change and others abhorring it. Intellectuals, that is, the entire class of those preoccupied with debating ideas about society, the polity, and the economy, pushed in two major directions. The first played on the financial or other interests of others. For instance, in Argentina, Chile, Venezuela, and parts of Colombia they successfully expounded a well-elaborated ideology, convincing a significant portion of their region's Creole leadership of the advantages of a break with Spain. They argued that in order to significantly alter economic conditions and transform Spanish America into a scientifically oriented and entrepreneurially active society, basic changes were needed. For these intellectuals it was not possible to speak of economic progress without casting a new look at tax structures, commercial restrictions, and monopoly agents, as well as at the corporate society itself and the potential economic and political role of the free individual.

Another current of thought looked to the past. The idea that sovereignty returns to the people in the absence of the king was hardly at the forefront of anyone's mind before there seemed to be no king. When called upon, however, some intellectuals were able to dredge up learned references to the arguments of sixteenth-century and earlier scholastic thinkers, about natural law and divine purpose. According to their arguments, in the absence of a legitimate ruler, sovereignty devolved onto the people. There was no talk among this group of ending the corporate society to free the individual, or even any consideration of economic reform. The most prominent proponents of this point of view emerged in Mexico, Peru, and Ecuador, although they were present in several other places.

These two intellectual currents—the economic one and the philosophical one—often merged, twisting and turning about each other throughout the course of the war, and were sometimes even found in one individual. But everywhere these ideas left an almost visible mark on political culture. As always, different emphases were applied at different times and places, and people stressed those ideas that fit their particular needs or what they perceived to be their needs.

Spanish government officials had long considered the new Enlightenment-inspired political and social doctrines sweeping Europe in the eighteenth century dangerous and subversive to the establishment, but their effort to prevent the penetration of such notions proved in vain, for ideas have a life of their own. Once any Latin American had had contact with the new critical approach, nothing could prevent him or her from thinking "subversive" thoughts and even "infecting" others. The fate of Antonio Nariño (1769–1822), a somewhat quixotic Colombian intellectual, demonstrates the dangers of openly espousing such ideas. In 1794 he translated and published the French revolutionaries' *Declaration of the Rights of Man*, apparently unaware of the effect this would have on a government fast becoming jittery over the regicidal behavior of French revolutionaries. Nariño had the curious idea that he could make money from this editorial venture, despite the fact that he had to print it in the secrecy of his home. Spanish authorities seized him and shipped him off to Spain in chains. Once aboard, the chains were released, and in the port of Cádiz he escaped as his ship was docking and proceeded disguised through Spain to France and then to England. Nariño then trustingly returned to his native land, where he was promptly clapped in jail, to be released only in 1803 for medical reasons. He was even then required to remain on his estate under virtual house arrest. But preventing the distribution of a translated *Declaration of the Rights of Man* was one thing; stopping the spread of its basic ideas was quite another.

In 1808 or so most Spanish American intellectuals, even those solely impelled by the ideas of the Enlightenment, would have been satisfied with reform. If Spain had granted more local autonomy early on, perhaps they would not have pushed for independence. But Spain did not, and independence became their goal. Although their notions fell far short of a genuine revolution, they eventually succeeded in profoundly altering the patterns of society and politics. These patterns would be far different in 1825 than they had been in 1808. Intellectuals, however, would have had little influence at all and independence would have been long delayed were it not for political upheavals in Europe that created an entirely new situation for Americans.

EUROPEAN EVENTS

Spain and France, 1788–1805

The "enlightened despot" Charles III of Spain died just a year before the French Revolution broke out. His successor, Charles IV (r. 1788–1808), was well meaning but stupid and did whatever his wife wished. At middle age, according to salacious rumors, her fancy turned to romance with a handsome if overweight twenty-five-year-old officer in the palace guard. Manuel Godoy (1767–1851) was of middle-class, not noble, background and thought of himself as a liberal, but, seen from the outside, he was primarily an opportunist. As the queen's favorite, Godoy was rapidly promoted not only into her bedchamber but also to the post of chief minister of the realm. Charles IV gave him full powers over domestic and foreign policies, and Godoy became a mean and petty dictator. The old aristocrats were outraged at this climber's success, and the reformers were appalled to see such a charlatan pretending to their principles.

Spain's alliances in Europe shaped its relationships with the colonies. The Revolution in France frightened Spanish leaders, to the extent that Spain abandoned its historic enmity toward England and in 1791 temporarily joined it in a coalition against France. By late 1793, however, this coalition began to fall apart. Meanwhile, the end of the Terror in France and the assumption of power there by the more conservative Directorate assuaged Spanish fears. France and Spain signed a new treaty of friendship in 1796, making Spain Britain's enemy. In the on-and-off wars of the next decade, Britain, whose navy controlled the seas, systematically cut Spain off from its American colonies. Even when sometimes the Spanish government, facing other crises, officially allowed colonial trade with friendly neutrals, envisioning that this trade would be with the United States, it was the British who in fact reaped the greatest advantage. On one such occasion the British trade with Veracruz tripled in the course of one year. In any case, whether legally or not, British vessels continued to ply the Spanish coast in the Caribbean, in the Río de la Plata region, and even on the west coast of South America. According to the terms of the Treaty of Amiens between France and England, signed in 1802, England was permanently allowed to keep Trinidad, which it had captured from the Spaniards in 1797. It then consistently used this island as a base for clandestine trade with Spanish America. In these ways the economic independence of the colonies was being forged long before political independence became a live issue.

The alliance between France and Spain continued after Napoleon's rise to power in 1799. French armies joined Spanish ones in attacking England's ally Portugal, not only seizing part of Portugal's territory, but successfully demanding that the boundaries of French Guyana be legally extended southward to the mouth of the Amazon River. France now held territories in both Louisiana and Brazil, controlling access to two continental river systems, and was well situated in relation to the Caribbean. So Napoleon's grand dream of a new French empire seemed a real possibility. But neither Napoleon nor the British fully implemented the Treaty of Amiens, and Britain declared war once again in 1803, taking Napoleon by surprise. He now had to concentrate on Europe. He hastily sold Louisiana to the United States, recalled troops from Haiti, and persuaded Spain to join him against Britain once again. Napoleon, having decided to invade England, needed additional Spanish ships to transport men and equipment across the channel. But the French and Spanish fleets were hounded into port at Cádiz. When they attempted to break out, Lord Nelson decisively defeated them off Cape Trafalgar in 1805.

England, Spain, and Spanish America, 1797–1807

If Napoleon could readily discard or postpone his overseas ambitions, British policy makers faced more difficult choices during these years. Should they concentrate on separating the American colonies from Spain, leaving the continental war to their allies? Or should they focus on defeating the French in Europe, in view of their allies' defeats or inactivity? Instead of making a firm decision, the British pursued an ambivalent policy that did much to feed independence sentiment in Spanish America but not enough to accomplish it.

The difficulty of resolving this dilemma was not only strategic but also political and economic. The British business community was in desperate straits because the newly mechanized factories were producing more products than the markets could absorb. The years of war with France had broken old commercial ties with the continent, and the Treaty of Amiens had failed to restore them while simultaneously curtailing trade in Spanish America. If the Spanish colonies could be captured, the business community would have a sure market and the government would have a secure source of bullion to finance Britain's allies. But England lacked the resources for a massive colonial war, and the only alternative was to encourage revolution secretly. For the English had not forgotten their experience in North America. Nor had Francisco de Miranda.

Miranda, born in Venezuela, went to Spain as a young man to join the army. He fought against the British in the American Revolution, which the Spaniards and the French supported. Although he did not think much of the United States, Miranda somewhere absorbed liberal ideas and a belief in colonial freedom. He eventually abandoned the Spanish army and roamed Europe seeking support for his schemes to free Spanish America. He found that the London business community and also the naval captain Sir Home Popham were interested in his plans. Popham introduced Miranda to his influential political friends in Britain, a step that ultimately led to Miranda's semiofficial conversations with William Pitt, the prime minister. These consultations resulted in a plan to invade Venezuela with a few thousand troops. But the plan was abruptly halted when Pitt was persuaded that Spain could still be won away from France and included in a Third Coalition but obviously not if England aided a movement aimed at provoking independence in Spain's colonies. Miranda departed England in disgust in 1805 and headed for the United States, and Popham was dispatched to capture the Cape of Good Hope from the Dutch before Napoleon could extend his power there too. Neither Popham nor Miranda forgot the possibility of liberating Spanish America, however.

Miranda, doggedly determined to carry on even without British support, recruited two hundred men and sailed out of New York for Venezuela in January 1806. He was so completely out of touch with affairs in his home country that he thought his mere appearance off the coast of Venezuela would result in an uprising. Instead, when he landed the local inhabitants stared at him uncomprehendingly, and Spanish forces quickly routed him. Miranda fled to the West Indies, where he secured the promise of support from British Admiral Thomas Cochrane. Encouraged, Miranda tried again, again without success. The British cabinet received the news of his attempts at the same time that they were trying to arrange peace with France. An attack on Spanish colonies seemed particularly ill timed, but the cabinet nevertheless instructed Cochrane to send "full details of the situation in which the Continent of South America now stands."[1]

Meanwhile, Popham became bored with patrolling the Atlantic around the Cape of Good Hope. He heard that Napoleon had smashed the Third Coalition at Austerlitz in December 1805. Since this assured Spain's loyalty to France, Popham assumed that Pitt would approve if Popham took measures against the Spaniards like those that he and Miranda had once imagined. In April 1806 Popham set off for the Río de la Plata region with an army contingent commanded by William Carr Beresford to capture either Montevideo or Buenos Aires. News that Buenos Aires had just received a shipment of silver from the interior tipped him toward it. The city was captured almost without effort in June 1806. But victory proved short-lived, as a rapidly organized Creole militia drove the British from the city in August.

Beresford in the meantime had sent home not only news of the initial success but also over one million dollars in booty, paraded through the commercial section of London in September. The business community in London was electrified. In the previous year British exports to Spanish and Portuguese America had already mushroomed from earlier levels, and they felt that if this trade could be relieved of the frightening fluctuations that accompanied its illegality there was no telling how high the figure would reach. The merchants rushed to send out goods on consignment to Buenos Aires and pressured the British government to support their enterprise with guns.

Some members of the British cabinet had advocated a more forceful Latin American policy all along. Now, as had not been the case with Miranda's adventure, a British force had been successful, even if unauthorized, and must be supported. Napoleon's victories and his decrees closing Europe to British trade made the decision an easy one. The government ordered the preparation of a military force, the dispatch of which became even more urgent when news arrived that Beresford's troops had been forced out of Buenos Aires.

Yet even with the modest aim of recapturing Buenos Aires, the British were unsuccessful. Although an army of over ten thousand men landed in Buenos Aires in June 1807, it was met with fierce house-to-house combat and confronted marksmen crouched on every rooftop and in every church tower. The invaders, after suffering a thousand casualties and losing two thousand prisoners, struck a truce. By September the defeated British were on their way home. The Argentine militia, officered by upper- and middle-class Creoles and manned by whites, mestizos, and blacks of all classes, even slaves, had won again. On the one hand, the British defeat clearly indicated that Spanish Americans were not ready to be "liberated" from Spain's control, but on the other, it signaled that they not only had what it took to defeat a trained European army on their own, but could be mobilized for a "national" cause that united all races and classes. It also proved an object lesson in that the British goods brought in during these months caused prices of such imports to fall precipitously, completely undermining the position of monopoly merchants.

Portugal, 1807–1808

News of this debacle reached London only a few months before the announcement of a pact between Napoleon and the Russian czar. Napoleon now dominated practically all of Europe, and he intended to control the remainder. To weaken Britain he forbade any area in his control to trade with it, but, partly because British merchants had long been prominent in Portugal, it continued to keep its ports open to British traders. Napoleon was furious, even though, ironically, he knew that his armies were often dependent on British goods brought in through those very ports. In mid-August 1807 Napoleon demanded that Portugal declare war on Britain and join his "Continental System," embargoing ships sailing to or from it.

Portugal considered three alternatives. One was to yield to Napoleon's demands. But if Portugal declared war on Britain, that would be the end of her dominion in Brazil because Britain controlled the sea. A second course of action would be to openly ally with Britain. Britain, however, demanded that Portugal permanently remove its restrictions on British penetration of the Brazilian market—Britain's economic plight was intensified by Napoleon's closing of European ports—and that the Portuguese court be moved to Brazil for safety. Or third, Portugal could delicately play France against England, desperately trying to save through sophisticated diplomacy and delay what Portugal's limited military capability could not hope to safeguard. Negotiations were spun out and out so that Napoleon's ultimatum requiring compliance by September 1, 1807, was not carried to its conclusion until late November. Portugal made it seem that it was preparing to cooperate with Napoleon but kept England fully informed of every step, secretly preparing to ally with Britain should it be necessary—but with a twist. Not only would the court move to Brazil, but so would the entire machinery of government in all its complexity. Every detail was foreseen. Bureaucrats secretly surveyed and charted all the ships to measure available space. They established a line of command, selected papers, and put treasury accounts in order. They took no overt action because any sign that the government indeed planned to flee would have provoked an immediate French invasion. One vexing problem could not be overcome, though. Portugal's small size meant that an invasion could be known in Lisbon only four days before French armies would arrive at the city. The Portuguese gambled that this would be enough time to carry out the massive task of removing not just the sovereign but the entire government as well. They won that gamble. When Napoleon's officers reached the Lisbon quay at the end of November 1807, they saw only the distant sails of the departing ships.

The careful planning that enabled the Portuguese government to escape French domination is all the more impressive because the court in Brazil was to be the center of an entire empire. On the forty or so ships that sailed from Lisbon traveled the prince regent (later King João VI); his mother, the queen, who was mentally incapacitated; and his wife, Carlota, who was the sister of Ferdinand VII of Spain and would soon dream of replacing him as sovereign in Spanish America, together with her young sons, Pedro and Miguel, and other members of the royal family. The entire cabinet, several layers of the bureaucracy, a large number of judges, and most of the upper clergy—joined at the last minute by their friends and the friends of their friends—also went aboard. Along with them went box after box of government files and portions of the royal library, in addition to the crown jewels.

On arrival in Brazil, the Portuguese government's first action was to throw open the ports of Brazil to the trade of all friendly nations. British merchants now had at their disposal a market of two million to be clothed with cottons made in British mills. Napoleon had done more for British businessmen than either Popham or Miranda. And with Rio de Janeiro now the capital of the entire Portuguese empire, Brazilians had effortlessly secured a kind of independence.

Spain, 1808–1814

Thus encouraged, British leaders looked once again at their prospects in Spanish America. In early 1808 General Arthur Wellesley was charged with studying the military aspects of a campaign to liberate Venezuela. Wellesley concluded that conquest was out of the question but that, if the Venezuelans wished it, liberation was within the realm of possibility. The British recalled Miranda from his virtual exile in the West Indies and assured him that at last his hopes were to be realized. Britain would free Spanish America from Spanish "oppression."

But Miranda's hopes were soon dashed once again. For at this point Napoleon decided to take direct control of Spain. He had already cajoled Godoy into allowing French troops to cross Spain to reach Portugal and had then established a corridor across Spain between France and Portugal. The old aristocrats continued to chafe at Godoy's crass behavior and looked to Prince Ferdinand, who was by then old enough to think for himself (which does not mean he did so) for salvation. They hoped he would lead a revolt against his father and Godoy. When Napoleon demanded and secured the right to occupy northern Spain, officers in the army, supported by a skillfully manipulated mob in the streets, successfully demanded the abdication of Charles IV in March 1808, putting Ferdinand on the throne. But then in May Napoleon lured both Charles and Ferdinand to southern France under the pretext of offering mediation. Instead, he demanded that they both abdicate and thus make Napoleon's brother Joseph Bonaparte king. Offered the choice between a risky attempt at escape, perhaps to America, and the gift of a comfortable estate in France, Ferdinand chose the latter.

The Spanish War of Independence resulted. No sooner did news spread that Ferdinand had been kidnapped than the people of Madrid erupted in protest. French soldiers put down their revolt overnight, executing hundreds in the streets on May 3, 1808. But then revolts broke out all over Spain, and eventually a mob succeeded in temporarily driving Joseph Bonaparte himself from Madrid. But like the wars that subsequently swept Spanish America, this was also a civil war. Many Spaniards had always looked to France for their inspiration and felt that a new king could perhaps revitalize Spain as the Bourbons had done a century before. The Spaniards who thus collaborated with the foreigner were mostly moderate liberals, and this collaboration with the foreigner helped discredit liberalism in Spain throughout the nineteenth century. The opponents

FIGURE 3.1. *The Spanish War of Independence*

of the French were either conservatives or ultraliberal nationalists who readily fell to quarreling with each other.

The French found it hard going, nevertheless. The patriots organized councils (*juntas*) to direct defense efforts in each Spanish province and city. These councils quickly decided on guerrilla warfare as the most effective way to resist the enemy. The word *guerrilla* originated at this time and place. It is a kind of warfare that places a premium on individual action, courage, mobility, and the commitment of the general population. It puts an army to its hardest test because, in its desperation, the regulars take actions that alienate the civilian population, whose disaffection provides the basis for guerrilla success. Napoleon soon complained that Spain was like a running sore. He had to pour in thousands of French troops to hold territory, for as soon as a French unit moved on to another target after apparently subduing one locality, Spaniards rose up again, attacking from the rear. Still, Napoleon did manage to restore Joseph Bonaparte to Madrid and little by little expand the area under his control.

The first British reaction to Napoleon's move on Spain was to think of Spanish America and to hasten the plan to have Wellesley's army invade it. But when delegates from several rebel councils in Spain arrived in England and told of the fierce struggle that the French still faced, it seemed to the British that the better policy was to help them. So Wellesley left for Spain instead, using Portugal as his base. In such a situation it was impossible openly to encourage revolution

FIGURE 3.2. *Arthur Wellesley, later Duke of Wellington*

in Spanish America; yet it was equally foolish to discourage it in case the peninsular campaign failed—and failure was a distinct possibility.

In late 1808 the various local Spanish councils sent representatives to a coordinating body, out of which developed the Central Junta. This group was forced to flee southward, eventually to Cádiz, where it could be protected by the British navy. At the end of January 1810, in desperation, it dissolved itself to be replaced by a five-man Regency ruling on behalf of the king. For many Spanish Americans the end of the Central Junta indicated the end of the regime. Their king was gone.

In its quest for legitimacy (for Napoleon pointed to Ferdinand's signed abdication and a liberal constitution promulgated by Joseph Bonaparte as the basis for his), the Regency summoned a Cortes, or parliament, to meet in Cádiz in September 1810. Most members of the Cortes were young radicals. The moderate liberals were collaborating with the French, and the conservatives were too attached to their properties or their responsibilities to run from the French. Although delegates were to be elected in every region, the areas under French control were represented by anyone in Cádiz from that place. In their deliberations members of the Cortes sought to outbid Napoleon in their adherence to Enlightenment ideas on politics and society.

The result was the liberal Constitution of 1812 that established a constitutional monarchy, so restraining the power of the king that the country became virtually a republic. Power would reside in a parliament (Cortes) chosen, albeit indirectly, by the people. By abolishing many of the institutions of the old regime — press censorship, the Inquisition, privileges of the nobility, feudal dues, the fueros, Indian tribute, draft labor — these constitution makers uttered a cry of ultraliberalism that reverberated throughout Spanish America for more than a decade. Viceroyalties were abolished. Many more cabildos would be formed in America, even in small towns, and all of them would be fully elective bodies with no hereditary members. On the other hand, it would be the members of these cabildos who would choose the delegates to the Cortes, not individuals voting directly, for cabildos were still understood to represent their communities, assuring the partial continuation of society's corporatist nature. Suffrage for the first-round voting (for cabildo members) was exceptionally broad for the time, including most males over a certain age, without any literacy or property qualification. Indians would be allowed to vote but not to be elected. And, with rare and specified exceptions, no African or descendant of an African would be allowed to vote. "Provincial deputations" would be elected as local administrative bodies. Audiencias would now serve only as courts of law. Such measures were implemented only fitfully in the colonies, but such elections as were held gave Spanish Americans a taste for nationwide representative government.

Yet the Cortes had major reservations about changing the basic tenets of colonial rule. In determining how many delegates from the colonies would be sent to the Cortes, the Regency had made sure that these delegates, even in the unlikely event they all came and arrived in time for the deliberations, would be outvoted by Spaniards three to one. In the absence of the colonial delegates, Americans resident in Cádiz filled the American seats. They joined those who little by little did arrive from America to ask for greater colonial autonomy and the end of the monopoly trading system. On both counts they were ignored. The Cortes majority, for all their liberal credentials, thought it generous enough to accept residents of the colonies as part of the "Spanish nation," whereas what those colonials wanted was to be separate nations, albeit within a kind of Spanish commonwealth. On this crucial issue the Cortes refused to accept change: The colonies were to remain colonies. In Cádiz, the very center of the monopoly trade that characterized colonial relations, the monopoly merchants who financed the anti-French effort were highly influential. Even though virtually no Spanish ships could actually sail to America, when the British demanded that the ports of America be legally opened, Spanish leaders replied that their efforts in fighting the French were a sufficient sacrifice for the cause.

Meanwhile, the military struggle in Spain began to turn against the French. Wellesley's army and its Spanish units slowly consolidated their hold and steadily occupied more territory. At the end of 1812 French armies were also forced to retreat from Russia, and the next year they were driven out of Spain. In spring 1814 allied armies converged on Paris.

Napoleon released Ferdinand VII on the startling condition that he retain the old Spanish-French alliance, but by the time Ferdinand occupied his throne in March 1814 there really was no Napoleonic government left. In May Ferdinand tore up the Constitution of 1812, undid most of the Cortes's reforms, and proceeded to persecute both those who had collaborated with the French and the radicals who had dominated the Cortes. As was once said of his cousins the French Bourbons, he had forgotten nothing and learned nothing.

SPANISH AMERICAN RESPONSES

The Constitutional Crisis

The ideas of the intellectuals in Spanish America would have been in vain—or at least long delayed in their effect—if it had not been for these unsettling events in Europe. When Napoleon usurped the Spanish throne, his act created a crisis regarding the preexisting (unwritten) constitution of Spanish American government. Conceivably, Spanish Americans could have continued to obey viceroys, audiencias, and intendants. And they could have received instructions from the Spaniards in Cádiz who were fighting against Napoleon. But although this policy was adopted in some places, it was rejected in most because Spanish Americans did not think of themselves as colonials. Napoleon had removed their own king, usurped his throne, and left them entirely without a government. It was up to them to organize their government. Without a king, where did loyalty lie? The ties that bound people to their own home place were the only other reliable emotional commitment to territory. With the king gone, only the immediate locality remained. In this way the regionalism that has so often been decried as the tragedy of the Spanish American wars of independence was, in fact, their very root.

When the Spanish Central Junta and succeeding Regency failed to recognize the validity of this regionalist sentiment and autonomist impulse in the colonies, attempting instead to enforce their rule even without the king, they met with resistance. The old animosities between those born in Spain and those born in America came to the surface. The intellectuals provided justifications and suggested alternative forms of government that could be useful, and the Creole militias provided the necessary armed force to initiate the war. Except in Venezuela (and to some extent in Mexico), the first movements did not aim at outright independence. Such a considered program and definite goal was hewed out only during the course of warfare against "illegitimate" Spanish pretenders and after years of self-governing experience. Although pressures toward independence would surely have surfaced eventually, the timing resulted from European events.

Military Force

European events also shaped the military struggle. If Spain in 1810 and the years immediately thereafter had been able to marshal its full military might against the revolutionaries in Spanish America instead of occasionally dispatching small reinforcements, the course of events there might have been very different. In most places in America the war for independence was really a civil war. Evidently, a relatively minor increase in Spanish power or an equally small decrease in insurgent strength might have eliminated all foci of revolutionary action in America and prevented the drawn-out struggle that hardened attitudes and divided Americans from Spaniards. Such an outcome might well have maintained the Spanish Empire intact for perhaps another fifty years. In 1812 a single Spanish unit, moving out of Puerto Rico, successfully drew on the enthusiastic support of Creole royalists in Venezuela to sweep away its first independent government. In some areas, such as Peru, Spanish power during this initial period was never even challenged. Spanish armies marching from Peru expelled liberating Argentine soldiers from Bolivia in 1813 and crushed the revolutionary movement in Chile the following year. But the anti-insurgent operation could not be sustained with the limited number of troops arriving from Spain. Instead, Spanish forces based in Venezuela remained unable to subdue Colombia until Spain finally sent reinforcements in 1814. The armies from Peru did not have sufficient strength to move on Buenos Aires and turn back the effort there. In Mexico large-scale war raged continuously from 1810 to 1815 with Creoles on both sides, and only slowly were the Spaniards able to marshal sufficient forces to regain control, and even then only seemingly.

The chief military opposition to the Spanish forces in 1810 came from the Creole militia. In Buenos Aires, where memories were still fresh of their success against a large European army, Creole officers pressured the cabildo and the viceroy to create a local council to rule on behalf of Ferdinand VII, in effect ignoring the Central Junta in Spain. In Chile the story was much the same. In Bogotá, Colombia, militia officers fraternized with the very mobs that the viceroy had ordered them to disperse. The importance of the Creole officers may be judged by the contrasting situation in Mexico. Instead of siding with the revolutionaries, many Mexican militia officers were the first to take the leadership in crushing them. The explanation is that Indians in Mexico revolted in what may be seen as a separate war of their own. With all property and established social relations in jeopardy, most of the wealthier Mexican Creoles sided with Spain. If the Creole officers had similarly put down the revolutionaries in other parts of Spanish America, no real steps toward independence would even have been taken.

The ascendancy of Creole militia officers throughout Spanish America was short-lived, however. In Venezuela they failed to maintain the loyalty of their newly recruited troops, made up of freed slaves and pardos. In Chile and Colombia they fought among themselves, opening the way for Spanish reconquest. In Argentina they were eventually superseded by a regular army. But the point is that the Creole militia officers successfully initiated the independence movement by using the force they commanded, successfully held their own against the Spaniards for several years in much of Spanish America, and kept Argentina completely free of Spanish domination from 1810.

In most of the empire Spain was victorious by 1816, but it had taken too long and success had been incomplete. These factors were crucial in provoking a second, successful war for independence. Meanwhile, new groups that had never been heard from before emerged to prominence and had to be taken into account. The old system could certainly not be reimposed on them. The causes of the second War of Independence (after 1815) are to be found in the first one. It must be examined in more detail.

CHAPTER FOUR

The First War of Independence, 1810–1816

THE FIRST WAR OF INDEPENDENCE WAS DIRECTLY PRO-
voked by the constitutional crisis in Spain. Creole intellectuals
committed to social and political change, economic elites interested in forging
closer commercial relationships with northern Europe, or both, seized the moment to gain control of the councils that had been set up in a number of Spanish
American centers to deal with events in Spain. These leaders enjoyed momen-
tary success, but internal divisions led to their defeat. By 1816 or so peninsulars once again ostensibly controlled all of Latin America except Argentina and
Paraguay. Yet despite the setbacks for Americans that marked the conclusion of
this first War of Independence, it remains the more important one for it clearly
established the issues and created the sentiments that would prove decisive in
the second war. It also exposed the sharp internal divisions that cut across much
of Latin America. At the same time political and military events led to major
transformations in how people perceived themselves and others, pointing to
the emergence of self-conscious nationalisms.

ARGENTINA

The British invasions of Buenos Aires in 1806 and 1807 encouraged a
closer tie between the Río de la Plata region and northern Europe. Ranchers,
small merchants, and professionals welcomed the possibilities opened up by direct commercial connections. The alleviation of customs dues under the British
further emphasized the burdensome nature of Spanish rule. Creoles drew encouragement from the militia's victory over a well-trained and experienced
European army and by their heady experience in choosing their own viceroy,

when the Spanish appointee ignominiously fled Buenos Aires on the arrival of the British. These invasions are justifiably looked back on as a turning point on the road toward independence, even though it was the British who were sent packing. The government in Spain, racked by crises at home, did not send a replacement viceroy until the middle of 1809. The one who arrived was named not by the king but by the Central Junta of Seville. His claim to rule was based on the theory that these American provinces were part of Spain, not merely joint kingdoms under a common crown, and that the Central Junta was the king's only legitimate representative. He was uneasily accepted at first. His most immediate task as viceroy was to solve economic problems; with Spain largely occupied by foreign troops and the normal channels of trade closed, Creole ranchers and urban businessmen loudly demanded that in the present crisis they be allowed to trade freely with any country. The intellectuals, most notably Mariano Moreno, readily provided for their use reasoned arguments based on Enlightenment thought (see Document 1). The viceroy yielded, opening the port to non-Spanish shipping, ignoring the protests of monopoly merchants.

In May 1810 news reached Buenos Aires of the complete collapse of the Central Junta and most of the legitimist forces in Spain. Pressured by the local militia, the cabildo (following an ancient formula for times of crisis) summoned a general meeting of leading city figures called a *cabildo abierto*, or open cabildo. While a crowd, incited by political activists, vociferously demonstrated outside the hall, the cabildo abierto decided to depose the viceroy, now without claim to a mandate, and to organize their own ruling council as had been done earlier in Spain to govern on behalf of the captured Ferdinand VII. One of the council's first acts was formally to authorize trade with any country. It also exiled those Spaniards who opposed its policies and executed the Spanish leader of an attempted counterrevolution—all in the name of Ferdinand VII, the "rightful" king of Spain.

Although ready to unite behind the issue of trade, council leaders deeply divided on most other questions, differences that began to emerge at once. The leader of the council was Cornelio Saavedra, a conservative militiaman who opposed any effort to transform the ideological and social foundations of the established order. But he was outnumbered by Mariano Moreno (who as editor of the official newspaper published a translation of Rousseau's *Social Contract*), Manuel Belgrano, and Bernardino Rivadavia, all of them liberals who wished not only to break ties with the makeshift Spanish Regency but also to institute reforms such as weakening the relationship between church and state, establishing secular schools and a free press, and ending economic monopolies. Opposed to such steps, Saavedra resorted to the expedient of seating on the council delegates from interior cities, most of whom were as conservative as he. The enlarged council forced the resignation of Moreno after seven months in office—he died shortly thereafter—and conveniently dispatched Belgrano to enforce the hegemony of Buenos Aires over Paraguay, a task for which he was unsuited by both temperament and training. Another liberal member of the council undertook to extend its power over Bolivia and its silver mines, but loyalist forces based in highland Peru repulsed him.

The new and enlarged council, rid of most of its more liberal members, lost much of its political support within Buenos Aires, and its size made it too cumbersome for effective action. In September 1811 it named an executive triumvirate to rule with a rotating membership, but the resulting policies, not surprisingly, tended to be inconsistent. In the meantime the triumvirate's permanent secretary, the liberal Rivadavia, accrued increasing influence. Under his direction steps were taken to put a final end to the slave trade, to encourage European immigration, and to end all fueros, aiming toward the equality of all citizens in a society made up of individuals, not corporations. Rivadavia also sought to link the region ever more closely to the world economy centered in England.

The triumvirate was overthrown in late 1812 by a disparate group, some of whom felt Rivadavia had gone too far and others who thought he had stopped too soon. The succeeding triumvirate principally concentrated its attention on dealing with the centrifugal forces set loose by the break with Spain, for some people outside Buenos Aires province said that if the Spanish Regency had no authority over the Río de la Plata, why should Buenos Aires rule over the rest? A general congress convened in early 1813 and immediately split into two groups, one made up of centralists, who were predominantly reformers, and the other consisting of provincial representatives, many of whom were more conservative. The congress never wrote a constitution but did issue several laws. By using legal technicalities, liberals prevented some representatives from being seated, thus managing to form a majority that quickly proceeded to abolish the Inquisition, terminate titles of nobility, end Indian tribute, and declare that all children born henceforth of slave mothers were free. At the beginning of 1815 the congress appointed a young liberal, Carlos de Alvear, "supreme director." However, they still avoided a declaration of independence, precisely to skirt the divisive issue of centralism versus federalism and sidestep any decision on whether Argentina should be a monarchy or a republic.

The erratic and arbitrary actions of the self-seeking Alvear coupled with his liberalism-cum-centralism eventually led to his overthrow by discontents who relied on the power of the Uruguayan leader, José Gervasio Artigas (1764–1850), for support. By this time Artigas, fiercely committed to autonomy for his region and the end of direct control by either Spain or Buenos Aires, headed a loose confederation of five hostile provinces to the north of Buenos Aires. These provinces wanted the same direct access to foreign trade that Buenos

Aires enjoyed. Meanwhile the western and northwestern provinces suffered an economic decline because their wine, their sugar, and their textiles had to compete with imports from Europe or Brazil. Two of them, Córdoba and Santa Fé, went so far as to declare their outright independence from Buenos Aires, leaving unresolved the question of their independence from Spain. They then set up their own customhouses and began to tax imports from Buenos Aires. As well, these provinces were alarmed at the far-reaching liberal measures decreed in Buenos Aires. Such moves toward provincial autonomy could well have led to the creation of several independent states—as in Uruguay and Paraguay—especially for those along major navigable rivers that gave them outlets to the sea. In the event, however, conservative groups in Buenos Aires successfully appealed to these interior provinces for political support against the liberals and summoned still another constituent congress to meet not in Buenos Aires but in the interior city of Tucumán in May 1816. By that date, aside from some isolated pockets, only Argentina and Paraguay in all of Latin America were free of peninsular control.

URUGUAY

When news arrived in Montevideo of Napoleon's usurpation of the Spanish throne in 1808, the leaders of Montevideo immediately began to quarrel with those of Buenos Aires. They accused the viceroy chosen by the leaders of Buenos Aires of being pro-French, a traitor to the Spanish crown, and unworthy of their loyalty. They formed their own council with the Spanish governor in Montevideo at its head. These actions were not entirely surprising since Montevideo had been up to this point primarily a fortified city with a large Spanish garrison. The council voluntarily disbanded itself when Spain sent a new viceroy to Buenos Aires. But in 1810, when the council of Buenos Aires, claiming to govern on behalf of Ferdinand VII, replaced that viceroy and asked for the adherence of Montevideo, the latter refused, declaring its loyalty to the Spanish Regency, which, after all, also ruled in the name of the king. The Spanish Regency then named another viceroy for the region and made Montevideo the viceregal capital instead of Buenos Aires. In the end, for Uruguayans independence from Buenos Aires overshadowed independence from Spain.

But when Spanish officials used Montevideo as a base for operations against the new government in Buenos Aires, many Creoles in Montevideo became noticeably uneasy. Further, Artigas, leader of the Uruguayan gauchos and smallholders, defected to the side of Buenos Aires and began a lightning campaign against the Spaniards in Montevideo, reducing the area under Spanish control to the limits of the city itself. The Spanish viceroy appealed for help to the Portuguese monarch in Rio de Janeiro, whose wife, the sister of Ferdinand VII, claimed to be the rightful ruler of Spain in his absence. The Portuguese complied and sent in an army. Faced with the Spanish forces in Montevideo and the slowly advancing Portuguese in the interior of Uruguay, the Buenos Aires government signed a truce in late 1811 agreeing to let the Spanish viceroy control all of Uruguay. The Portuguese army, under British pressure, returned to Brazil. Inconsolable and fearing reprisal, Artigas retreated to the Argentine province of Entre Ríos, taking with him about four-fifths of the Uruguayan hinterland's population. There they remained for more than a year while regrouping and preparing to return and continue the fight against the Spaniards.

At the same time, Artigas's relations with Buenos Aires deteriorated. He sent delegates to the congress called by the liberals in 1813 to demand a federative government with local autonomy for the provinces. Since this congress failed to grant him what he wanted—failed even to seat his delegates—he turned against it, fighting both the Spaniards and the Buenos Aires government simultaneously.

When in 1814 the restoration of Ferdinand VII appeared imminent, the government in Buenos Aires became desperate to rid the Río de la Plata region of Spanish rule, for Montevideo served as a lodestone for Spanish forces invading from Bolivia and could also be used as a beachhead for armies dispatched by sea from Spain. Buenos Aires enlisted the support of William Brown, an Irishman, who, commanding a makeshift fleet, blockaded Montevideo from the sea. The wealthier residents of Montevideo, including the owners of meat-salting plants, actively aided the Spaniards in their efforts to resist the porteños. Nevertheless, in June 1814 Montevideo surrendered, and Buenos Aires again took control, doubtless hoping to prevent it from ever again competing for the commerce of the Río de la Plata. But when Buenos Aires once more attempted to extend its power into Uruguay's interior, Artigas resisted, recapturing Montevideo itself in early 1815.

Artigas instituted as enlightened a government as could be expected in such years of crisis while simultaneously expanding his power in northeastern Argentina. Among other things he declared that the lands and cattle confiscated from wealthy European Spaniards or disloyal Americans would be distributed in small homesteads to the "most unfortunate, . . . [to] free blacks, . . . Indians, . . . poor Creoles, [and] poor widows with children."[1] The recipients of these lands would be required to build two corrals and a shed within three months, on penalty of having their land given to another. The existing livestock on those confiscated lands would be distributed to the new landowners under the supervision of a judge. These land grants, had Artigas stayed in power long enough to make them, would have been declared inalienable to prevent the greedy from buying them up and reconstituting large estates. He also decreed the freedom of all slaves. These measures, not surprisingly, alarmed his fellow ranchers and property owners (see Document 3). Indeed, one reason the leaders in Buenos Aires resisted his demand for Uruguayan autonomy may have been a fear that his social reform policies might be applied as well in Argentina.

PARAGUAY

Buenos Aires had even less success reimposing hegemony over Paraguay than over Uruguay. A relatively poor area where settlers faced the persistent danger of Indian attacks and from which the principal exports were *yerba mate* (a leaf used in making tea throughout southern South America) and some tobacco, Paraguay had remained relatively isolated throughout the colonial period. Its hacendados oversaw a dependent workforce of mestizos and settled Guarani Indians. In the capital city of Asunción men born in Spain controlled commerce and even dominated the cabildo, not to mention the post of intendant. By the early nineteenth century Creoles and those mestizos rich enough to pass as Creoles resented not only the Spanish predominance in Asunción but also the fact that Paraguay's exports had to pass through fiscal bottlenecks in Buenos Aires to reach their markets.

When news arrived of the events in Buenos Aires in May 1810, a cabildo abierto in Asunción quickly repudiated the claims to authority put forward by porteños and promised its allegiance to the Regency in Spain. When faced with a military incursion of seven hundred men from Buenos Aires led by Belgrano, the Paraguayans quickly mobilized five thousand militiamen and easily crushed the invaders.

The hacendados, who controlled the Paraguayan countryside, now found an unlikely ally in Gaspar Rodríguez de Francia (1766–1840), a Creole lawyer who sat on the Asunción cabildo. Trained in theology at the University of Córdoba, he had an authoritarian streak and a taciturn and secretive personality. In May 1811 the Creoles deposed the Spanish intendant and formally (and definitively) declared their independence from Spain, stating that they would cooperate with Buenos Aires only as equals. Francia sat on the council set up at that time, but he frequently absented himself to travel in the interior, soliciting support from small landowners and Guarani-speaking peasants. When an elected congress convened in 1813, he had little difficulty persuading it to name him one of its two "consuls," and when still another congress gathered the next year they gave him the title "Supreme Dictator." Counting always on the support of both the poor and the propertied, he ruled the country until 1840.

The big issue remained free navigation of the Paraná River. If Buenos Aires failed to impose its will on this inland country, it could at least control its access to the sea. Based on its claims to sovereignty over Paraguay, Buenos Aires sometimes blocked all shipping in or out and always taxed it. It imposed an embargo on exports of Paraguayan tobacco and began buying its maté from Brazil. Meanwhile, the caudillos who arose on either side of the river in Argentina seized arms destined for Paraguay and raided river traffic without fear of punishment. Eventually Francia determined to go it alone, turning the economy and the culture inward, insisting on self-sufficiency, and rebuffing all foreigners. Public lands were turned into state enterprises for the production of livestock and foodstuffs, and small manufacturing enterprises made substitutes for the formerly imported goods. Aside from some trade with Brazil, Paraguay opted out of the international economy.

CHILE

At the time of Napoleon's usurpation of the Spanish throne in 1810, an interim governor ruled Chile. Events in Europe encouraged Chilean Creole intellectuals who desired independence to speak out against his ineptitude, bringing down on themselves his unrestrained and intemperate wrath. The governor's overreaction only widened the intellectuals' circle of adherents among the Creole aristocracy, men who doubted local Spaniards' true loyalty to the deposed king rather than to the French. Spaniards in turn suspected the Creole aristocracy of lacking loyalty to Spain and accused them of wishing to rule themselves in the guise of loyalty to Ferdinand VII. When the governor heard that the Central Junta in Seville had collapsed and a ruling council had been formed in Buenos Aires, he moved with special severity against three leading Creoles of Santiago, banishing them to Peru. This action resulted in open protests, for he had overreached himself. The audiencia itself forced his resignation in July 1810.

The next man in line for the governorship was in his dotage, but the audiencia supported him, hoping that his Chilean birth would satisfy the Creoles and that his age would make him easy to manipulate. The Creoles, however, were more adept at using him than were the Spaniards, and he agreed to summon a cabildo abierto. The Spaniards did not appear, either because they were not allowed by the Creole militia to enter the hall or, more likely, because they did not wish to undergo the humiliation of being outvoted. The cabildo abierto accepted the resignation of the new governor and named a council to rule in his stead, still on behalf of the absent Spanish king.

This council sought to win political favor by opening trade to all nations, dissolving the audiencia, and convoking a national assembly. Moderate and conservative Creoles controlled this assembly when it convened in July 1811, and

FIGURE 4.1. *Bernardo O'Higgins*

they wished to limit their actions to a few further reforms, to send delegates to the Spanish Cortes, and to stop short of any radical alterations in the status quo. But another group in the assembly, smaller but more liberal, wanted to declare independence and establish a republic.

One of these liberal leaders in the assembly was Bernardo O'Higgins (1778–1842), the illegitimate son of an Irish-born intendant in Concepción who had later become viceroy of Peru. O'Higgins, partially educated in England, had met Francisco de Miranda there and acquired many liberal ideas. When his father died he inherited considerable properties in southern Chile and returned there in 1802, a man of substance but with seditious views.

Alongside O'Higgins in spirit, although not a member of the national assembly, was the lawyer Juan Martínez de Rozas (1759–1813). He had once been legal adviser to O'Higgins's father and had subsequently held various positions of authority, but his Creole origins frustrated his desire for preferment beyond a certain level. A third liberal leader, a member of the national assembly, was the political economist Manuel de Salas (1755–1841), who was more interested in increased autonomy than in outright independence. His opinions carried much weight.

When the national assembly named an executive committee to rule while a constitution was being drawn up, without including a single liberal, the liberals resigned from the assembly in protest. Their resignation stirred to action the three Carrera brothers, Luis, Juan, and José, sons of one of Chile's wealthiest and most influential Creole families. Luis, Juan, and their father had already actively protested against the governor. José, in Spain at the time as an officer in the Spanish army, now returned to Chile and became fully committed to independence. He was dismayed by the moderate tenor of the national assembly and by the predominance there of a rival wealthy Creole family. When the liberal members resigned he determined on more forceful action. Winning over members of the Creole militia, he led a coup d'état that purged the national assembly of the more conservative leaders and introduced a majority of liberals.

The new national assembly immediately proceeded to transform the old institutions. It abolished the Inquisition, ended corporate fueros by creating a single national court system, set up a new educational network, and declared free the children born of slaves. By interfering in the system of parochial fees, putting parish priests on a fixed salary, and creating secular cemeteries, this assembly plunged the country into a long struggle between church and state that characterized the next century of Chilean history. This national assembly was short-lived, and many of its reforms were quickly undone, but it accomplished the task of spelling out in practical measures the implications of the Enlightenment.

José Carrera soon decided that if one coup d'état had worked so well, two would be better. He dissolved the assembly and created a triumvirate with himself at the head and O'Higgins as another member. Tiring of this arrangement, he led still a third coup d'état and placed himself in sole command. He introduced a series of reforms, among them setting up Chile's first printing press, decreeing the establishment of primary schools in every town, and combining three church seminaries of Santiago into the secular National Institute.

Other liberals were offended by Carrera's arbitrary methods and by the aspects of a family feud that he had introduced into the struggle. Civil war broke out between the forces he led and those commanded by O'Higgins and Martínez de Rozas. Both these men were from the southern province of Concepción and opposed Carrera's effort to rule the entire country solely from Santiago.

These quarrels laid the groundwork for a larger crisis. The viceroy in Peru dispatched a Spanish force by sea to southern Chile, and, marching northward from there, they met Carrera's men at Concepción, which fell in March 1813. Carrera's alleged mismanagement of the campaign brought about his deposition and temporary replacement by O'Higgins. O'Higgins moved to strike a truce with the Spaniards, for he preferred a pro forma declaration of loyalty to Spain and the election of representatives to the Spanish Cortes over continued bloody military encounters. Carrera, however, was outraged and led his fourth successful coup d'état. Although their quarrel was momentarily patched up, Carrera's rancor led him at a crucial moment to refuse reinforcements to O'Higgins, who with his army was forced to flee over the Andes to Argentina. The Spanish army proceeded to win battles and by October 1814 was in control of Santiago. A brutal repression followed, and Spanish merchants found their monopoly privileges restored. A new cabildo was formed, made up almost entirely of guild merchants.

VENEZUELA

Venezuela was the first Spanish colony to receive news of the usurpation of the Spanish throne in 1808. The French sent an agent to Caracas to ensure the allegiance of the colony, but he met with a cold reception from the captain-general and, once his mission became known, confronted a hostile mob commanded by Creole militia officers. When these officers requested permission from the captain-general to form a local council as in Spain, however, he temporarily threw them into jail for their audacity. Later, when news arrived of the final collapse of the Central Junta of Seville, the officers acted without the cooperation of the captain-general (whom they deposed in April 1810) and formed a ruling council. This council deported the captain-general and members of the audiencia, successfully solicited the support of most of the other cities in the region, opened the ports to world trade, lowered taxes on food, granted preferential tariffs to the British, and dispatched diplomatic missions to London and Washington to seek at least tacit support. Simón Bolívar (1783–1830) was one of those sent on this diplomatic mission to London, and there he recruited on his own initiative the support of Francisco de Miranda, who returned to Caracas with him. Bolívar and Miranda then elaborated a program and successfully pressed the congress that the council convened in March 1811 to declare independence. The American Confederation of Venezuela was created on July 7, 1811, and a constitution promulgated.

The act of declaring independence proved unfortunate. Bolívar and his friends, scions of rich landowners and educated in a European intellectual

FIGURE 4.2. *Miranda and Bolívar Signing Venezuela's Declaration of Independence*

milieu, did not realize how far they had outdistanced the majority of the population, even many in their own class. Many Venezuelans who would have been placated by a declaration of loyalty to the absent king considered a declaration of independence equivalent to cursing God. This act was suicidal. Those who would have supported the idea of a council modeled on the one in Seville were puzzled or dismayed. The pardos were distressed, for the Creoles, who had oppressed them the most, were now in control, and a high property qualification for voting, as specified in the new constitution, made it clear that this movement was not theirs. Spanish officials and clergy, who had often been solicitous of pardo welfare and who had sometimes ignored the prejudices of the Creoles, were out of power. Slavery continued, provoking a series of slave revolts. In all this uncertainty Spaniards readily enlisted the support of the pardos, while desertions plagued the revolutionary army, largely made up of pardo draftees and slaves marshaled by slave owners. Finally, many poorer whites had no sympathy for any cause espoused by upper-class Creoles. The revolutionaries had also forgotten how near Venezuela was to Spanish strongholds in the Caribbean.

Spanish troops from Puerto Rico landed in the loyal northwestern part of Venezuela in 1812 and had little trouble gathering local support in their rapid march toward Caracas. Despite the hurried elevation of Miranda to virtual dictator, nothing could stem the advancing Spanish tide. Miranda capitulated and tried to escape with the treasury, presumably to fight again as he had done before, but Bolívar, who had once idolized Miranda, put another interpretation on this act and turned him over to the victorious Spaniards in exchange for a safe conduct for himself to the West Indies. From there he went to Colombia,* where he pondered his past experiences and planned for the future.

Bolívar

Simón Bolívar emerged as the great hero of Spanish American independence. He was a native of Caracas, the son of a wealthy Creole who owned two cacao plantations, three cattle ranches, a very large number of slaves, and thirteen houses. He received his earliest education from a well-read tutor who was so thoroughly impregnated with the ideas of Rousseau that he made *Émile* his guide for the boy's instruction. Bolívar became an admirer of Enlightenment thinkers even before he went to Spain in 1799 to complete his education. In Europe Bolívar traveled widely and lived in Paris for a time when Napoleon was in his glory. He moved freely within high society, enjoyed Parisian pleasures, and studied Napoleon's military tactics, which he later copied in his own campaigns. Bolívar returned to Caracas and joined those Creole militia officers who in 1810 had voiced their political discontent.

When Bolívar arrived in Colombia two years later he found it in turmoil. He tried to persuade the members of the new insurgent government that they would not be safe from Spanish authority until Venezuela had been freed. When they refused to heed his warning he disobeyed their orders and, proceeding eastward, led a successful campaign against Spaniards in western Venezuela. When he returned bearing treasure, he was not court-martialed but promoted to general.

Bolívar dreamed of returning to Caracas in glory. After much pleading, the insurgent government in Colombia gave him a relatively small corps of five hundred men to undertake an expedition in 1813. With these troops he moved eastward with lightning speed, repeatedly engaging the Spaniards before they realized he was near, and occupied Caracas within three months. His campaign was a procession of triumphs against great odds, unparalleled since the days of the conquistadors. It was also instructive for him. During this campaign he perfected his ability to command and experimented with propaganda. He mastered the public manifesto and staged triumphal entries to win over the masses.

---

*The name "Colombia" was first coined by Bolívar for a country he later created out of the Viceroyalty of New Granada. This new country included approximately what is today Venezuela, Ecuador, Colombia, and Panama. By 1830 it had dissolved into its constituent segments more or less as we know them today (except for Panama), although Colombia itself was known as New Granada until 1863. I use the name "Colombia" in its present sense and refer, as do other historians, to Bolívar's creation as "Gran Colombia."

FIGURE 4.3. *Simón Bolívar*

When his great carriage was drawn through flower-strewn streets by dozens of pretty young women, the crowds went wild with adulation.

The campaign also revealed a destructive and even petty vengefulness to Bolívar's nature. During his absence the Spanish commander in Caracas had been unrestrained in persecuting revolutionaries, venting his anger even on Creoles who had not been involved in any republican effort. When Bolívar learned of these atrocities he declared that henceforth he would wage a "war to the death" on the Spanish-born. If they did not rally to his cause, they would automatically be considered the enemy, whether or not they were combatants. Those born in America would, on the contrary, be forgiven even if they had actively opposed him earlier. This war to the death cast a dark shadow over his career and pushed the seeds of hatred deeper into Venezuelan soil.

In any case, Bolívar's campaign had by no means completely crushed the Spaniards in Venezuela. They clearly perceived the divisions in Venezuelan society and now managed to enlist the full support of the llaneros, who were ready to fight against the hated city types and the haughty Creoles. To mobilize the llaneros the Spaniards turned to José Tomás Boves (1782–1814). Boves was a sadistic Spanish adventurer whom the Creole government had once arrested for smuggling. The Spaniards released him when they took over in 1812, and he immediately offered his services to them in exchange for booty. Boves had long been familiar with the ways of the llaneros and, by being as hard as they, had won their respect. Eventually ten thousand llaneros, almost all on horseback, were at his command. Incensed by earlier republican measures that threatened to end the open range to the benefit of would-be ranchers, mostly Creoles, these men also fought for the war booty that Boves distributed among them. In addition, Boves obtained the special loyalty of blacks and pardos by promoting them over the lighter-skinned officers in his command.

Bolívar was no sooner in possession of Caracas in 1813 than Boves loosed his hordes against him. Striking even more swiftly than Bolívar and outdoing him in forcefulness, Boves was soon successful. Bolívar's troops began to melt away. By mid-1814 Bolívar was once more in flight. The class divisions of Venezuela had defeated him.

COLOMBIA

There was relatively little reaction in Colombia to Napoleon's 1808 takeover of the Spanish throne. The legitimacy of the viceroy in Bogotá was not in question for he had been appointed by the king. He accepted the authority of the Central Junta of Seville and had relatively little difficulty quelling an abortive revolt in Quito the following year. When news arrived of the complete collapse of the Central Junta, however, the viceroy's power began to wane. Reformist landowners, merchants, lawyers, and priests in the coastal city of Cartagena mobilized the middle and lower classes, especially free blacks and pardos, in support of their effort to secure home rule. They petitioned and won from the local governor the right to participate in his decisions and to open the port to the trade of all nations. Meanwhile, the leading citizens of Bogotá demanded that the viceroy summon a cabildo abierto. He was forced to comply when the Creole militia defected from his camp. Inspired by the lawyer Camilo Torres (1766–1816), the cabildo abierto organized a governing council in July 1810. Although this council declared loyalty to Ferdinand VII, it refused to surrender its right to govern unless the king came to rule in person. Meanwhile, the council summoned a constitutional convention with representatives from all provinces and instructed it to create a charter to include a federal system in which provincial autonomy would be protected.

Despite this concession to local sentiment, jealousies immediately arose between Bogotá and the other Colombian cities, with Cartagena spearheading the opposition. Eventually the council in Bogotá, admitting reality, summoned a local congress to draft a constitution just for the surrounding province of Cundinamarca. The council then invited representatives from the other provinces to draft a pact among the acknowledged sovereign provinces. The representatives met, formed a congress, and in November 1811 established a loose confederation, the United Provinces of New Granada, with its capital in Tunja, well north of Bogotá. The congress made no formal declaration of independence. The province of Cartagena went its own way, declaring its independence both from Spain and from Bogotá, while other provinces in the Cauca River valley formed their own confederation.

Some in Bogotá, however, refused to accept these concessions to regionalist feeling. Among them was Antonio Nariño, who had emerged from house arrest in 1810. He insisted that unity was essential if Colombia was to withstand the onslaught of Spanish power, and he demanded that Colombia form a strong central government. When his preachments about unity fell on deaf ears he decided on more forceful action. Leading a coup d'état in Bogotá, he tore up the provincial constitution and proceeded to conquer neighboring provinces. Many of his officers resigned in protest and joined the beleaguered victims. Nariño also pushed for social change, for instance, the freeing of any slave who joined the cause, thus alienating mine owners and coastal planters. As he assumed increasingly dictatorial powers in the province of Cundinamarca, he seems to have become steadily more unbalanced. Under his frantic leadership Cundinamarca seceded from the United Provinces of New Granada in the name of centralism!

The Spaniards took advantage of this internal political turmoil and mounted an offensive against the insurgents. Only then did Nariño and the United Provinces finally agree to cooperate with each other militarily, but it was too late, and the war began to go badly. Nariño was captured in 1814, the local royalists in the northern city of Santa Marta revolted and reestablished Spanish control there, and the other provinces began to fight among themselves once again. Then the congress of the United Provinces decided that Nariño's province of Cundinamarca must be forced to join their union. At this moment Bolívar, having returned from Venezuela after his second defeat, was given this task. His troops occupied Bogotá at the end of 1814. He next turned his attention to driving the Spaniards out of the north, only to discover that Cartagena would not cooperate, partly for fear of losing its hoard of military supplies and partly because of personal jealousies. Disgusted, Bolívar left Colombia and retired to Jamaica. In May 1816 Bogotá fell to Spanish forces, and by August all of Colombia was back in their hands.

The leaders of the independence movement had invariably been drawn from the upper classes of Colombia. Fortunately for them, social tensions had not yet surfaced. Those with wealth, power, and name, consumed by their regional rivalries, managed to undo their revolution all by themselves, and the Spanish forces had an easy time of it.

PERU AND BOLIVIA

During the first War of Independence, as Spain was successively ruled by a Central Junta, a Regency, and the Cortes, many if not most regions of Spanish America went their own way, setting up their own interim — or permanent — governments. Not so in Peru, which remained loyal to Spain's successive regimes (as did Cuba, Ecuador, and Central America). In fact, when delegates selected by Peruvian cabildos in 1810 arrived at the Spanish Cortes in Cádiz, they argued against establishing a broad suffrage, even though this would have increased the weight of American delegations to future Cortes. Their reason? It would have enfranchised Indians and mestizos, whose political weight they feared. Creoles in Lima welcomed the 1812 constitution because it promised them power without requiring independence. For them it was an acceptable compromise. In Lima the viceroy began implementing the constitution almost on its arrival, although he did not disguise his personal distaste for it. Elections for Lima's cabildo were held in December 1812, Creoles winning twelve of the sixteen seats.

In Cuzco, the center of Indian Peru, Creoles welcomed the new Spanish constitution with fireworks and bullfights, for it erased the distinction between them and peninsulars. Elections for the cabildo were held in February 1813, and Creoles predominated among those elected. Members of the audiencia, however, almost all of whom were Spaniards, eventually blocked implementation of several constitutional provisions, even ordering the arrest of some cabildo members for alleged subversive plotting. In early August 1814 members of the Creole and mestizo middle class launched a rebellion with the announced aim of protecting the constitutional monarchy, headed by the Spanish Cortes, to which they had sent delegates. Their initial manifesto focused only on the complaints of Creoles, omitting any mention of Indians and their oppression. But their first ruling triumvirate chosen in Cuzco, seeking to appeal to the Indians, who, after all, made up the vast majority of the people in the region, invited into their governing group Mateo García Pumacahua (1740–1815), a descendant of an Inca ruler. They may have thought him a safe bet because he had opposed Tupac Amaru thirty years earlier. But they misunderstood his point of view. Pamacahua, who willingly joined their group because they declared their loyalty to the monarchy, had always believed that Spanish kings were the Indians' protectors. That is why he had opposed Tupac Amaru's rebellion against the king. And now the 1812 constitution promised equality not only for Creoles but for Indians as well. Pamacahua was ready to fight, but his notion of what the revolution was about differed from that of the Creoles, some of whom actually envisioned an eventual independent and republican country with Cuzco as its capital.

Pamacahua proceeded actively and effectively to recruit and organize large numbers of Indians into the revolutionary ranks, adopting the Inca headdress as the symbol of the movement. The revolutionary impulse spread from village to village in highland Peru, and at one point half the viceroyalty's territory was in revolt. As it spread, the movement became steadily more and more Indian. Indians joined the effort in the hope of regaining their land and redressing their many grievances but also to reassert their cultural traditions and religious identity. This emphasis on Indianness, however, alienated many non-Indians, who began to drift over to the pro-Spanish side. Meanwhile, many people in coastal Lima saw the entire highland movement as further evidence of the extreme danger of supporting any revolutionary activity, and militias enthusiastically joined expeditions marching against revolutionaries in both Chile and Cuzco. Some Indians in the highlands also joined their ranks, for not all of them found Pamacahua appealing. Six months of bloody fighting ensued, with revolutionaries fighting with the weapons they had—bows and arrows, slings, clubs, and lances—while the lowland militias arrived with guns and cannons. The royalists defeated Pamacahua's troops in several battles and unleashed horrible punishments on those they captured, slaughtering thousands. Pamacahua himself was hanged in a public execution, witnessed by a large number of Indians rounded up for the occasion. The news that Ferdinand VII had been restored to the throne in Spain and had rejected the 1812 constitution put a final end to the revolution in upper Peru.

Meanwhile and at several times, invading revolutionary armies from Argentina, most notably one led by Belgrano, had taken over parts of southern Bolivia, initial victories that proved deceptive. Troops recruited from the pampas were unprepared for the elevation in the highlands. Although Belgrano did succeed in attracting many Indian fighters, some of whom had participated in earlier Indian rebellions, they were focused on local issues and ill prepared to confront an organized army. What Indians principally wanted, the revolutionaries could promise but not give them: time to tend their own crops on village lands and freedom from labor obligations in the mines. On the whole, Belgrano had to rely on the relatively few local Creoles and mestizos. One of Belgrano's lieutenants was Juana Azurduy (ca. 1781–1862), a mestiza from the highland city of Chuquisaca (present-day Sucre). She had been educated in a convent but left it in 1805 to marry a man who was also a Belgrano follower. She eventually rode into battle leading her own band of male soldiers, although her personal guard consisted of twenty-five women warriors. She fought in some sixteen battles, even after Spaniards captured her husband.

In the end, though, the plainsmen from Argentina were driven off. Most people who lived in Bolivia had little interest in Enlightenment ideas and stood to gain nothing from closer contacts with northern Europe. On the whole, social tensions led the Creoles in Bolivia, as in Peru, to side with the Spaniards.

MEXICO

Events in Mexico eventually led to the same result. When the momentous news arrived there in July 1808 that both Charles IV and Ferdinand VII had abdicated, that French troops had occupied Madrid, and that the corrupt Spanish minister Godoy was now in prison, José de Iturrigaray, the viceroy appointed by Godoy, feared that he would be stripped of his lucrative position. He knew the Spanish community in Mexico City not only despised him as an unworthy representative of the mother country but also suspected him of siding with the French, believing that Godoy was a French lackey, a traitor to Spain. In the hope of saving his post, Iturrigaray summoned a joint meeting of the audiencia and the cabildo. No consensus emerged, though, for cabildo members argued that according to sixteenth-century authorities sovereignty reverted to the people in the absence of the king and that the cabildos represented the people, whereas the erudite judges of the audiencia would hear none of it. Iturrigaray finally sided with the cabildo, agreed with it to form a local council with members chosen by established corporations, and "consented" to head it, apparently believing that this would make him personally more secure. Satisfied with this, he proceeded to rule as if nothing had changed. The Creoles were momentarily satisfied, but Spanish merchants feared that a more representative body would be summoned to replace the council and that the lower classes would be mobilized to support such an effort. So in September they successfully carried out a midnight plot to seize Iturrigaray. The audiencia, privy to the plot from the beginning, met at two o'clock in the morning and named a new viceroy. Spaniards assumed control again. Revolution from above had ended ignominiously, but by overthrowing the viceroy the conservatives had done much to undermine the very legitimacy of the Spanish rule they intended to uphold, a legitimacy many understood as rooted in the notion that rulers were chosen by God, not by men.

Despite the insurrectionary ferment spreading among the well-entrenched Creoles, little else happened in almost two years to suggest the momentous events that were next to sweep over Mexico. In 1810 a new and able viceroy arrived: Francisco Xavier Venegas, a man closely associated with the monopoly-holding merchants of Spain. But as developments in Spain moved toward the defeat of the patriot forces there, secret societies and clandestine meetings of dissident Creoles became increasingly frequent in Mexico. Many believed Spain would become part of "godless" France. One group of conspirators, meeting in the town of Querétaro, planned a coup d'état for December 1810 in which the Creole militia would play a central role. But in their efforts to secure support, they approached some who betrayed the plot to the Spanish authorities. The plotters, warned in mid-September of their imminent arrest, scattered and hid, with one exception: Miguel Hidalgo.

Hidalgo

Miguel Hidalgo y Costilla (1753–1811) was a parish priest. Not particularly devout, he had had a good education, kept up with the ideas of the Enlightenment, and was deeply concerned with the plight of his parishioners, the Indians around the village of Dolores. Hidalgo had been banished there by the Inquisition because of his many peccadilloes and dangerous ideas. Most of his parishioners lived in grinding poverty made worse by bad harvests that had pushed up the price of corn to the breaking point. Although the cultivation of grapes and mulberry trees for silkworms had been forbidden in America because such competition would undercut merchants in Spain, Hidalgo encouraged the Indians in these ventures and also helped them establish a brickyard, a pottery, and a tannery. The companionship of unlettered Indians, however, was not enough to satisfy the roving curiosity of a well-read man who also enjoyed good living. He sought out like-minded fellows in nearby Querétaro, and it was these men who brought him into the conspiracy. Evidently he was not the driving force behind the plot, but when the others fled he decided on a plan of his own.

At dawn on Sunday, September 16, 1810, Hidalgo summoned his parishioners to the church. Addressing them in their native tongue, he pointed out their miserable condition and blamed the Spaniards for it. He simultaneously declared his loyalty to and perhaps his sympathy for the captured Ferdinand VII, whom the Indians had been taught to venerate as an almost messianic figure. He accused the king's subordinates of being untrue to their king. "Down with the Spaniards! Down with bad government!" The Indians scurried to assemble bows and arrows, machetes, pikes, clubs, and axes and followed Hidalgo to the next village, where a similar scene took place. "Long live the Blessed Virgin of Guadalupe!" became their cry as they appealed to the Madonna, who had long been the patron saint of Mexico City and now became a national symbol. Then to still another village marched the throng. Within a few days Hidalgo led a crowd of several thousand, including some mestizos and a few Creole plot-

FIGURE 4.4. *Miguel Hidalgo*

ters who hastened out of hiding. An attempt to transform this inchoate mass into a disciplined force failed. Supplies being scarce, they ransacked haciendas, consumed crops and cattle, and drew away agricultural workers as new recruits. Then the crowd flooded into towns, plundering shops, stripping houses, and smashing machinery in mines and craft shops. When they invaded Guanajuato, a major mining town already racked by discord between mine workers and mine owners, the bloodshed was unrestrained and the destruction of property devastating. It had become a war of revenge against centuries of oppression.

Although a few Creole intellectuals in Mexico City continued to defend Hidalgo, most people of substance and education considered him a madman. Hidalgo did little to stop the mostly Indian mob that threatened all whites, for he understood their frustration and sympathized with their outburst. When, however, he came to see how the campaign was understood by others, he began to have doubts himself, and his Creole companions were appalled. They had hoped for a rebellion, not a social revolution.

Hidalgo next moved toward Mexico City, leading some eighty thousand men. After a bloody daylong battle, in which the Indians suffered enormous losses, they nevertheless succeeded in driving back the Spanish military contingent of twenty-five hundred soldiers sent out to defend the mountain passes surrounding the city. Then, poised on the brim of the valley, Hidalgo hesitated, changed his mind, and directed his followers to turn away from Mexico City.

The reasons for Hidalgo's decision are still disputed. Some historians claim that his sensitive soul recoiled at the thought of witnessing another scene of pillage and bloodshed. Others have suggested more practical reasons. The plan for an immediate rising of Creoles, stimulated by the initial victories won by the underdogs, might have worked if Hidalgo had been able to launch an effective propaganda campaign making clear his goals and appealing for Creole support before the gory details about Guanajuato had reached them. But he lacked a printing press, and the royalists had several. They distributed thousands of handbills throughout the major cities describing the bloody ravages of Hidalgo's horde, accounts that were spread farther through sermons and word of mouth. Neither people of property nor their urban employees could identify with such a movement, and Hidalgo now understood this. Even more significantly, the village Indians of the valley of Mexico, who were to have been additional recruits for Hidalgo, turned against him. Finally, Hidalgo knew that a large Spanish army was descending on the city from the north. If he occupied the city his followers would likely turn to looting and drinking and be easy prey for the advancing army.

This loyalist army had been drawn from two sources: the regular Spanish army, originally posted in the north and on the coast to withstand threats from French or English invaders (and into which so many locals had been forcibly drafted that they formed the vast majority of the soldiers), and the Creole militias. The militias, despite some early exceptions, as in Guanajuato itself, gradually turned against Hidalgo and ended up siding with the Spaniards. Hastily brought together by the Spanish general Félix María Calleja (1753–1828), a peninsular military commander who had lived for many years in Mexico and was well connected to upper-class Creoles, this new army proved increasingly a well-disciplined and effective fighting force, all the more important since no reinforcements would come from Spain for another two years. Ironically, Calleja constructed a Mexican army, filled with Mexican troops and mostly commanded by Mexican officers. Should they ever turn on Spain, they would be a formidable enemy. But for now they opposed the revolution.

FIGURE 4.5. *Hidalgo and Morelos as Portrayed by a Modern Artist*

As Hidalgo turned back from Mexico City, his movement lost momentum. He fought one last major battle in early November 1810, in which hard-pressed Indians tried to stop the Spanish cannons with what they had left, even their sombreros. The battle was lost when a magazine exploded and the resulting grass fire spread panic among Hidalgo's ranks, allowing the royalist soldiers to move in ruthlessly, killing indiscriminately.

The first phase of the Mexican war for independence had ended. Hidalgo fled north and was betrayed, tried, and executed in July 1811. His head, mounted on a stake in Guanajuato, remained for ten years a grisly reminder of the fate awaiting rebels. Hidalgo had settled nothing, but he is remembered as the first hero of Mexican independence for he opened space for the oppressed, the non-elite, to participate in the national project.

The effort so far was more akin to the 1780 rebellion of Tupac Amaru in Peru than to the other struggles for independence in Spanish America. The long-pent-up hatreds of the Indians gave impetus to both movements, even though Hidalgo's followers were not, like those in Peru, village Indians with an ancient sedentary lineage. Well-educated leaders intent on reform rather than revolution and inspired at least partially by the new thought of the Enlightenment lit both sparks. Both leaders hesitated to invade major cities, the capture of which could have paved the way to final success. And in both cases the Indians had ages-long reasons for their outburst, motives that were all too clear to outside observers who, for this very reason, responded out of dread. The propertied shied away from any thought of revolutionary solutions to their problems. But timing often gives a meaning to historical events that is not built into their logic. It was the idea of independence — or at least autonomy — that sparked the initial activity of Hidalgo, a purpose read into his movement by both friendly and hostile observers. This meaning was picked up and borne further by his immediate successors. The social significance of the movement, as opposed to its political message, only affected the effort adversely and was not hailed for at least another generation.

With Hidalgo gone, and even as he lived, other leaders appeared in various parts of Mexico, many of them originally commissioned by Hidalgo to spread the revolution into their districts. The Spanish general Calleja noted that "the insurrection . . . returns like the hydra, in proportion to the number of times its head is cut off."[2] Often parish priests or other members of the middle class such as muleteers or shopkeepers took up the cause. Some chiefs were no more than brigands; others specifically sought the redress of their fellows' local grievances.

South of Guadalajara, for example, two Indians — Encarnación Rosas and José de Santa Anna — found widespread support among villagers who had been harshly treated by vengeful Spaniards in the wake of Hidalgo's defeat. Their redoubt was an island in Lake Chapala where a prison had once stood. Still fortified, it proved almost impregnable. Some thousand men armed with fourteen cannons and three hundred muskets held off the Spanish enemy. In mid-1813 pro-Spanish forces attacked with nine boats carrying six hundred men and four twenty-four-pound mortars. And still the Indians repulsed them. Attempts to lay siege to the island proved equally unsuccessful despite the assignment of eight thousand soldiers to the effort, because the villagers surrounding the lake managed to keep the insurgent garrison secretly supplied over three long years. During that time the insurgents regularly stole ashore to engage Spaniards in guerrilla war, often in concert with other insurgent groups, who communicated with them by using smoke signals. Finally the Spanish commander offered a truce, including a general amnesty for all participants and promises to rebuild the villages, restock their herds, supply seeds for the next planting season, and make Santa Anna the legitimate "governor" of the island fortress. Only then did peace return to the region. Meanwhile, to the south, a much more important offshoot of Hidalgo's revolt had seriously threatened to end Spanish rule in Mexico altogether.

Morelos

José María Morelos (1765–1815) was one of Hidalgo's lieutenants who continued to fight. The son of a Creole woman and a mestizo father, he had quit his transport business as a muleteer with a large troop on the Mexico City-

FIGURE 4.6. *José María Morelos*

Acapulco route to enter a seminary and study for the priesthood. The rector of the seminary at that time was Hidalgo. On completing his studies, Morelos was named priest of a parish in the less prestigious, hot and humid valley of the Balsas River to the south. When he heard about Hidalgo's mad rampage, he rushed to join his former teacher, who told him to return to the Balsas River valley and foster revolution there.

In this task Morelos proved more successful than his mentor, being both a skillful organizer and a man of perseverance. Depending on peasants who could be fierce fighters one moment and peaceful tillers of the soil the next, he proceeded to conduct a large-scale guerrilla war that intimidated the Creole landowners and shattered Spanish control in large segments of southern Mexico. He also welded disparate interests into one cause. He recruited farmers and ranchers, priests, students, muleteers, day laborers, and unemployed miners. Morelos attracted financial and moral support from those, including local bigwigs, who hoped to land on the winning side. With Creoles he pushed national pride and doctrines of popular sovereignty. Yet he also advocated complete racial equality and the abolition of the fueros so as to end the corporatist society and create in its stead a nation of individuals with a single judicial system. Even more extreme, he seized the property of those who opposed him, canceled all debts owed to them, abolished the tribute, and adopted other radical reforms designed to bind the loyalty of the masses. At a time when the conservatives claimed that rebellion against the king was tantamount to being against God, Morelos—like many other revolutionary leaders—insisted that he was the defender of the true faith against the Spaniards, who were only interested in aggrandizing their power for personal gain. He stressed that Catholicism was the only true faith. And he struggled successfully to keep his followers from engaging in a race war; this would be a nationalist effort (or at least a protonationalist one) above all else.

Morelos gathered a large and disciplined army. It probably included more mestizos than Indians, but Indians from communal villages that Hidalgo had failed to mobilize often joined Morelos's ranks. Yet he found it difficult to attract hacienda peons if their masters had played their paternalistic roles and supplied them with rations, housing, and security. In many cases, of course, those who joined Morelos's cause did so to settle local grievances, not to carry forward a national project. He armed his troops with captured Spanish weapons, and they rode on stolen horses. He took the rich city of Oaxaca in November 1812 and soon controlled all of Mexico south of Mexico City and Puebla, except Acapulco. With an army of some nine thousand men he was able at times to cut the capital city off completely from its food-supplying regions. Although he did not control Veracruz itself, its surrounding villages were on his side and often blocked communication between it and Mexico City for weeks on end.

Morelos used his power and influence to convene a congress of eight members elected indirectly from various provinces to draft a constitution (see Document 4). Meeting in the southern town of Chilpancingo, these delegates declared Mexico completely independent in November 1813. They then concentrated their attention on legal questions that perhaps should have been postponed. Bickering inevitably resulted. But the constitution they drafted remained as a kind of manifesto for the cause. It established the equality of all citizens without regard to their corporate status, made popular sovereignty a reality, and abolished slavery altogether. This constitution was known and quoted throughout much of Mexico, even as the Spanish Constitution of 1812 was being implemented in the Spanish-controlled areas at that very time. The juxtaposition of the two constitutions drew attention to how the Spanish docu-

d the localistic loyalties
se among many of their
ened the country's ports
during for Brazil through
led for years to achieve.
ence of Brazil was soon
hen the British insisted
rcent for all goods from
em for military support
: but to agree.

ons, encouraged indus-
 judicial system (a step
Rio de Janeiro a sophis-
e pomp and ceremony
ig of medical schools, a
garden. The royal press
in 1811 published a Por-
s, which so thoroughly

ment centralized power in Spain, in contrast to N
rightly declaring Mexico's independence.

By the beginning of 1813, at the height of his po
with an active fifth column in Mexico City. A conte
tuously described it as being made up of "shopkee
is to say, of low and common folk,"[3] but many lawy
and other professionals also joined up. Having deci
Morelos's commitment to independence than to l
nized an effective intelligence organization. The vic
that they informed Morelos's revolutionaries on "
nitions, and supplies, all of which [information] is
government—accounts of the resources of the g
its difficulties."[4]

Morelos also drew strong support from a well-c
Mexico City. María Leona Vicario was the daughte
who had educated her well. Her fiancé was one o
in charge of propaganda. She acted as one of the m
for information by using a secret code. In addition
female friends actively recruited fighters and arme
made it their habit to go by carriage out of the cit
their country houses on Sunday afternoons, carryir
den in their picnic baskets. On one occasion three
parts for an entire printing press. In the end seve
executed by firing squad, but Vicario only had he
imprisoned in a convent. She then managed to esc
Morelos's men. Once married and in Morelos's ca
cared for the injured, and kept Morelos's financi
her first child on the campaign trail (see Documen
were also active on the other side in this war; sor
longed to the Patriotas Marianas, a royalist organi

With hindsight we may conclude that Morelos
did not move on the capital when he could have de
Mexico City partisans, Morelos spent the entire
fortress city of Acapulco—apparently in a quixot
instructions received from Hidalgo three years ear
gathered strength and eventually smashed the stru
him isolated. That was not how the Spanish gener
things at the time, however (see Document 6).
did, it is true, eventually mount a vigorous and s
program in the south. General Calleja provided
arms on the gamble that most would not be used

FIGURE 4.7. *João VI*

a seat of imperial rule. This step inadvertently eroc
within each province, creating for the first time a se
Brazilianness. The new administration immediately c
to the trade of friendly nations—namely, England—
a king's signature what the rest of Latin America stru
This measure legally marking the economic indeper
followed, however, by another kind of colonialism
that the import duty of 24 percent be lowered to 15 j
England. Dependent as Prince Regent João was on
to drive the French out of Portugal, he had no recou

The new government fostered agricultural innova
tries, established a national bank, and instituted a ne
toward a single court system). Prince Regent João ga
tication that it had not known, bringing with him
of a genuine European court. He directed the found
national museum, a national library, and a botanica
became Brazil's first legal printing establishment an
tuguese translation of Adam Smith's *Wealth of Nati*

ranchers, priests, students, muleteers, day laborers, and unemployed miners. Morelos attracted financial and moral support from those, including local bigwigs, who hoped to land on the winning side. With Creoles he pushed national pride and doctrines of popular sovereignty. Yet he also advocated complete racial equality and the abolition of the fueros so as to end the corporatist society and create in its stead a nation of individuals with a single judicial system. Even more extreme, he seized the property of those who opposed him, canceled all debts owed to them, abolished the tribute, and adopted other radical reforms designed to bind the loyalty of the masses. At a time when the conservatives claimed that rebellion against the king was tantamount to being against God, Morelos—like many other revolutionary leaders—insisted that he was the defender of the true faith against the Spaniards, who were only interested in aggrandizing their power for personal gain. He stressed that Catholicism was the only true faith. And he struggled successfully to keep his followers from engaging in a race war; this would be a nationalist effort (or at least a protonationalist one) above all else.

Morelos gathered a large and disciplined army. It probably included more mestizos than Indians, but Indians from communal villages that Hidalgo had failed to mobilize often joined Morelos's ranks. Yet he found it difficult to attract hacienda peons if their masters had played their paternalistic roles and supplied them with rations, housing, and security. In many cases, of course, those who joined Morelos's cause did so to settle local grievances, not to carry forward a national project. He armed his troops with captured Spanish weapons, and they rode on stolen horses. He took the rich city of Oaxaca in November 1812 and soon controlled all of Mexico south of Mexico City and Puebla, except Acapulco. With an army of some nine thousand men he was able at times to cut the capital city off completely from its food-supplying regions. Although he did not control Veracruz itself, its surrounding villages were on his side and often blocked communication between it and Mexico City for weeks on end.

Morelos used his power and influence to convene a congress of eight members elected indirectly from various provinces to draft a constitution (see Document 4). Meeting in the southern town of Chilpancingo, these delegates declared Mexico completely independent in November 1813. They then concentrated their attention on legal questions that perhaps should have been postponed. Bickering inevitably resulted. But the constitution they drafted remained as a kind of manifesto for the cause. It established the equality of all citizens without regard to their corporate status, made popular sovereignty a reality, and abolished slavery altogether. This constitution was known and quoted throughout much of Mexico, even as the Spanish Constitution of 1812 was being implemented in the Spanish-controlled areas at that very time. The juxtaposition of the two constitutions drew attention to how the Spanish document centralized power in Spain, in contrast to Morelos's constitution forth-rightly declaring Mexico's independence.

By the beginning of 1813, at the height of his power, Morelos was in contact with an active fifth column in Mexico City. A contemporary Spaniard contemptuously described it as being made up of "shopkeepers, barbers, tailors, . . . that is to say, of low and common folk,"[3] but many lawyers, government employees, and other professionals also joined up. Having decided to pay more attention to Morelos's commitment to independence than to his social reforms, they organized an effective intelligence organization. The viceroy reported in desperation that they informed Morelos's revolutionaries on "the status of the forces, munitions, and supplies, all of which [information] is taken from the offices of the government—accounts of the resources of the government, its scarcities and its difficulties."[4]

Morelos also drew strong support from a well-organized group of women in Mexico City. María Leona Vicario was the daughter of a rich Spanish merchant who had educated her well. Her fiancé was one of Morelos's chief lieutenants in charge of propaganda. She acted as one of the movement's principal conduits for information by using a secret code. In addition to raising funds, she and her female friends actively recruited fighters and armed them at their expense. They made it their habit to go by carriage out of the city allegedly to visit friends at their country houses on Sunday afternoons, carrying weapons from the city hidden in their picnic baskets. On one occasion three women smuggled out all the parts for an entire printing press. In the end several women were caught and executed by firing squad, but Vicario only had her goods confiscated and was imprisoned in a convent. She then managed to escape with the help of some of Morelos's men. Once married and in Morelos's camp, she helped plan strategy, cared for the injured, and kept Morelos's financial records. She gave birth to her first child on the campaign trail (see Document 5). Of course, many women were also active on the other side in this war; some two thousand women belonged to the Patriotas Marianas, a royalist organization.

With hindsight we may conclude that Morelos's biggest mistake was that he did not move on the capital when he could have done so. Despite the urgings of Mexico City partisans, Morelos spent the entire summer of 1813 besieging the fortress city of Acapulco—apparently in a quixotic determination to carry out instructions received from Hidalgo three years earlier—while the Spanish army gathered strength and eventually smashed the strongholds of his allies, leaving him isolated. That was not how the Spanish general pessimistically understood things at the time, however (see Document 6). Opponents of independence did, it is true, eventually mount a vigorous and successful counterinsurgency program in the south. General Calleja provided all propertied Creoles with arms on the gamble that most would not be used against the government. By the end of the year Morelos began to suffer major defeats that continued for the next two years, even though in many places local insurgents remained strong and guerrilla war continued. Spaniards finally encircled his unit, overran his fortifications, and then executed him on December 22, 1815.

With Morelos gone (and Ferdinand VII returned to his throne), the independence movement in Mexico lost its vigor. The bulk of the Creole upper class had never joined the revolutionary movement, and Creole militias in Mexico preferred to enforce law and order rather than engage in a risky war. Now royalist forces searched out and emptied many of the remaining pockets of rebellion. Those whose loyalty to Spain was in doubt were at first persecuted and severely punished. Later they received an amnesty on condition of not taking up arms. Revolutionary leaders were either captured and executed or retired to private life, accepting pardons or disguising their identity. Others fought among themselves. A few bandits remained at large, cloaking their activity with the banner of independence, but only two men of genuine patriotism continued in rebellion. Holed up in the hills, Vicente Guerrero (1782–1831) in the west and Guadalupe Victoria (1786–1843) in the east still dreamed of independence for Mexico.

Through them Morelos's memory lived on, for he had given the movement definition, institutionalized an independent government with its own constitution, and laid out a social agenda. Although his social reforms would triumph only decades — even a century — later, they reflected the steady pressure exerted by the oppressed. Nevertheless, by the end of 1816 nearly the entire country was at peace or at least ready to recognize that a stalemate had been reached. Perhaps 10 percent of Mexico's population had died during the wars, although many of them perished in an epidemic that raged during 1813, especially in the cities controlled by loyalist forces. Mexico City alone lost twenty thousand people, and seven thousand died in Puebla. It was a sad condition for the once-prosperous colony.

BRAZIL

The complete independence of Brazil was secured gradually and almost imperceptibly over a period of twenty-three years beginning in 1808. During this time events in Europe overtook Brazilians and impelled them along a course that they had hardly considered on their own. We can confidently say that Brazil was independent by 1815, although 1822 is the acknowledged and celebrated date of independence, and in some ways the process did not end until 1831.

As noted earlier, the arrival of the Portuguese court and government in Rio de Janeiro in early 1808 transformed Brazil's status from an obscure colony to

FIGURE 4.7. *João VI*

a seat of imperial rule. This step inadvertently eroded the localistic loyalties within each province, creating for the first time a sense among many of their Brazilianness. The new administration immediately opened the country's ports to the trade of friendly nations—namely, England—securing for Brazil through a king's signature what the rest of Latin America struggled for years to achieve. This measure legally marking the economic independence of Brazil was soon followed, however, by another kind of colonialism when the British insisted that the import duty of 24 percent be lowered to 15 percent for all goods from England. Dependent as Prince Regent João was on them for military support to drive the French out of Portugal, he had no recourse but to agree.

The new government fostered agricultural innovations, encouraged industries, established a national bank, and instituted a new judicial system (a step toward a single court system). Prince Regent João gave Rio de Janeiro a sophistication that it had not known, bringing with him the pomp and ceremony of a genuine European court. He directed the founding of medical schools, a national museum, a national library, and a botanical garden. The royal press became Brazil's first legal printing establishment and in 1811 published a Portuguese translation of Adam Smith's *Wealth of Nations*, which so thoroughly presented the case for freeing trade from government control. Brazilian Creoles welcomed all these changes, but they also resented the interference of the newly arrived royal bureaucrats in matters they had always managed on their own.

When Portugal was liberated from Napoleonic rule, the court was naturally expected to return to Europe, but João (crowned João VI in 1816 at the death of his mother) preferred to stay in Brazil. To solve this awkward problem, he elevated Brazil to the legal status of kingdom, making Rio de Janeiro its capital. As the king of two kingdoms he could reside in only one — and he chose Brazil. Thus by 1815 the country achieved another goal that several Spanish American countries dreamed of but never realized, namely, bringing their king to rule among them. A revolution from above, tried so fleetingly and unsuccessfully in Mexico in 1808, succeeded easily in Brazil. Of course, the assumption of power by a viceroy (as happened in Mexico) cannot compare in significance with the arrival of a legitimate king and his court, and indeed this disparity suggests that if the Spanish king had fled to Mexico that nation's history might have been much more like Brazil's. There was no constitutional crisis in Brazil because the king had not abandoned his throne, so whatever dissatisfactions were brewing, they had no occasion to surface.

COMMONALITIES AND DIFFERENCES

In all these wars, in Chile and Argentina, in Venezuela and Colombia, in Peru and Mexico, many actors played a part besides political leaders and military commanders, even if these inevitably occupy the bulk of attention in any summary of the events. Whether struggling to secure independence or defending the royalist cause, common soldiers bore the brunt of the fighting, suffering the stress of battle and enduring the boredom of inactivity during long stretches, far from home. Other people made war making possible — farmers and millers who produced the food and muleteers and carters who transported it and all the equipment, as well as smelter workers, gunsmiths, leather workers, and cartwrights to make the gear. Others had to endure the depredations of marauding armies in search of food or shelter. Given the low level of literacy, a priest's weekly sermons formed a major channel of communication, while others organized public ceremonies and theatrical performances, drew caricatures or painted walls, and knowingly or unknowingly spread false rumors to undermine the other side. Even those far from the fighting experienced shortages and high prices, in addition to disruptions in their normal day-to-day activities. Everyone — ranchers, farmers, overseers, peasants, artisans, middlemen, professionals, or street sweepers — was affected in one way or another.

Women fed the troops and carried their water, made their uniforms, tended the wounded, prepared bandages, and buried the dead. It was common in those times for women and children to follow their husbands in long marches over hundreds, even thousands of miles or travel all the way across the Atlantic from Spain and Portugal with royal armies. When women stayed home, they faced the challenge of tending their families alone, taking care of their absent husbands' businesses, or coping with widowhood and poverty. Some upper-class women, following the tradition begun with prewar soirées, also raised funds and acted as couriers, spies, and propagandists. In Bogotá a seamstress named Policarpa Salvarieta gathered information in the houses of wealthy royalists where she went to sew. She was caught in 1817 and died before a firing squad in the city's main square. Others were arrested, exiled, or sentenced to hard labor. Indian women sharpened animal bones to make knives or constructed the slings their men used in battle, while white women smuggled firearms across hostile lines. In an era of authentic religious belief, women prayed for those they loved or for the success of the cause, keeping up morale.

And everyone made hard choices. During the first independence war, social revolution and political independence came to be seen as antagonistic goals. In Mexico violent conflict pointed the way toward major social change but failed to produce political independence, even hampered its emergence. In Brazil social relationships remained virtually unchanged, but a kind of political independence was achieved without the use of force. One tentative conclusion to be derived from this juxtaposition is that it was precisely the crisis of legitimacy in Mexico that provided the opportunity for the eruption of social violence. If so, one would have to add that although a necessary cause, such a political crisis was not a sufficient one to provoke social upheaval. In Venezuela at this time, during the first independence war, revolutionary leaders like Bolívar failed to expand the social base of the movement, ensuring its failure. In contrast to Mexico, it was the lower-class fear of Creole dominance that halted political independence in Venezuela. But in both places social tension played a crucial role.

Juxtaposing Venezuela and Argentina shows that despite their common interest in establishing closer ties with European markets and the important presence of Enlightenment ideas in both places, these countries did not follow a common track. Venezuela, being closer than Argentina to the Spanish military bases in the Caribbean, was more easily subdued. Venezuelan leaders, unlike Argentine ones, made the error of declaring independence rather than insisting on continued loyalty to an absent monarch, alienating many who might have supported the more limited goal of a local council ruling on his behalf. Most important, though, the preexisting class hatred in Venezuela far exceeded the animosities between gauchos and urban residents in Argentina. Mobilizing the gauchos to oppose the Argentine upper-class advocates of independence would have been much harder than was true with the llaneros, even if Spanish forces had been present to do so.

In both Argentina and Chile Creole militia officers forced the formation of local councils and the deposition of weak and demoralized Spanish administrators. Creole intellectuals—Moreno, Belgrano, and Rivadavia in Buenos Aires and O'Higgins, Martínez de Rozas, and Salas in Santiago—played a prominent role in the initial proceedings. In both areas conservative forces then eased out the liberals. Since the liberals did not hesitate to use force to regain their earlier position, civil war ensued. Out of this chaos arose a new phenomenon: *caudillismo*, the appeal of the man on horseback, the man of deeds who establishes himself as dictator or regional chief. Artigas on the east coast and the Carrera brothers on the west personify the point. In both Chile and Argentina the revolutionaries were divided, but Spanish armies could more easily reach Chile than Argentina, so here too location played an important part in explaining the result.

Throughout Spanish America the struggles during the first war for independence were civil wars, with Creoles, mestizos, Indians, blacks, pardos, and even Spaniards on both sides. The divisions were not between these groups but between reformists and traditionalists, between republicans and monarchists, between centralists and federalists, and between those who sought only local or national autonomy under a common constitution and those who insisted on outright independence from Spain. Some even sought to bring about social change. The fact that Spaniards were more powerfully present in Mexico than in any other Spanish American colony may explain why Creoles there at first saw their only option as the mobilization of the oppressed masses—a decision they soon came to regret. But everywhere some Creoles sided with Spain.

In 1816 only the relatively isolated Argentina and Paraguay were free of outside control. Elsewhere, regional rivalry, class hatreds, and divided leadership so weakened the revolutionary cause that by using small military contingents already in America in 1810 and limited reinforcements from Europe after 1814 Spanish troops succeeded in crushing the revolutionary forces, and did so with the help of some loyalist Creoles and revengeful lower-class elements.

Outside Mexico and Peru the most important result of the first War of Independence was the Creole taste of power. Creole militias had been crucial agents of revolution at first in Caracas and then in Bogotá, Buenos Aires, and Santiago. Just how important they were is demonstrated by the exception: In Mexico they sided with the royalists and crushed the movement. Elsewhere the Creoles gained a sharpened awareness of the differences between their interests and those of Spain. Whenever and wherever they gained power, they exercised it to advance their distinct interests, especially to facilitate commerce with northern Europe; among their first acts, nearly every revolutionary council opened the ports to non-Spanish vessels. The restoration of Spanish power reversed Creole gains and consequently sharpened the distinction between Americans and Spaniards.

Creole intellectuals advanced some aspect of Enlightenment thinking in all areas of Spanish America. In Chile and Argentina specific reform legislation was enacted. In Venezuela and Colombia the fighting, either with Spaniards or with other Creoles, was too intense to allow much time for the application of a reform program, although various constitutions spoke to it. Reformers in Mexico, with the exception of Morelos, alienated the very groups that might otherwise have cooperated in more modest goals. In Brazil the presence of king and court encouraged learning, scientific thought, and the notion that reason could lead Brazil toward economic development.

Although independence in Latin America was far from being won by 1816, it was now widely recognized as possible and accepted as an ideal toward which many aspired. Only the second war would demonstrate how far this change had already gone.

CHAPTER FIVE

The Second War of Independence, 1815–1825

T HERE WERE TWO PRINCIPAL CAUSES OF THE SECOND
War of Independence. One was the first war. It provided the experience of autonomy in both Spanish America and Brazil and created deep divisions between the former colonials and the mother countries. The other cause, and the decisive one, was the harshness of Spanish rule once it was restored and the threat of such a restoration in Brazil. Never again could there be doubt about the differences of sentiment, outlook, and goals between the Americans and the peninsulars. But to discover the origins of Spanish and Portuguese repressiveness we must first look to Europe.

REPERCUSSION OF EUROPEAN EVENTS

Much as the first War of Independence had been provoked by developments outside America, so did European events directly affect the course of the second one. With the defeat of Napoleon in 1814 a great conservative reaction swept across Europe. Years of revolution and war had left people weary, and many sought a return to the stability of the old regime. Others were willing to accept some but definitely not all of the changes in social organization wrought by the cataclysmic events of the previous quarter century. Elites everywhere worried that a resurgence of revolutionary fervor would further threaten their dominance and plunge Europe once again into war. An economic depression in the postwar years exacerbated their fears. Even in England habeas corpus was suspended, public meetings forbidden, and freedom of the press circumscribed. In France the restored Bourbon king issued a constitution that maintained a chamber of deputies, but its ultraconservative legislators, who were now in the majority, moved to restrict individual freedoms while the courts mercilessly condemned former revolutionaries and Bonapartists. Rulers of several small German states granted their people constitutions, but none was drafted by elected bodies. Frederick William III of Prussia and Alexander I of Russia did not even do that much. Prince Klemens von Metternich, Europe's strongest advocate of dynastic legitimacy and social order, not only dominated Austria completely as prime minister but also extended his influence over the Italian states, where, with his backing, rulers firmly squelched any effort to achieve individual liberty or popular sovereignty. In this context Spain's swing toward conservatism is not surprising.

When Ferdinand VII regained the throne of Spain after the Napoleonic period, there was much rejoicing both in Spain and in Spanish America. At last the French were gone! But the joy was short-lived. Ferdinand totally lacked statesmanship and vision. He began by throwing out the Constitution of 1812, insisting on absolute power, with no congress to make the laws. He ignored all the liberal advances of the previous years and even reversed reforms instituted by his grandfather, Charles III. He readmitted the Jesuits, restored the ancient rights of the nobility, and reinstituted the Inquisition. Although Ferdinand's conservative reaction won the support of the landed nobility, the morality of the court and the morale of the country remained as low as in the days of Godoy.

A number of factors contributed to the eventual weakening of Ferdinand's rule. Since the king distrusted anyone with ideas, only the most fawning adventurers rose at his court. Political persecution became ever more intense. As well, no longer did Spain receive rich revenues from the colonies. On the contrary they represented a constant drain on state finances and Spanish manpower. The merchants who depended on monopoly trade to the colonies saw their wealth visibly decline, although they continued to lend money for the colonial war, hoping for the best. Insurrections and revolts became increasingly frequent in Spain and brigandage widespread. Authority inspired little respect. Many army officers who had encountered and taken up liberal ideas during the war were out of sympathy with Ferdinand's conservative direction.

On one thing absolutists and their liberal opponents were in agreement: the ports of Spanish America must remain legally closed to all except Spanish trade. As one adviser to the king put it in 1817, "I would look upon the decree of free commerce as the same as the emancipation of America."[1] Where Spanish forces successfully reestablished colonial rule, monopoly trade was reimposed. In Caracas, for example, British imports, having amounted to over £85,000 in 1812, fell to just over £5,000 in 1815.

In most of Spanish America the years of Ferdinand's absolute rule were unhappy ones. Ferdinand was obsessed with the idea of returning the colonies to the position they had occupied before 1808. He turned a deaf ear to the entreaties even of the conservative monarchs in France and Russia who urged him to grant more autonomy to the colonies in order to preserve them. Ferdinand preferred a military solution.

He dispatched General Pablo Morillo with an army of ten thousand veterans to Venezuela and Colombia in early 1815. After first occupying Caracas, Morillo turned his attention to Cartagena — gateway to Colombia and center of its commercial life. He lay siege to it from August to December, causing the death from starvation of about a third of the city's population. Those who survived considered the malaria epidemic that ravaged Morillo's troops (and the desertions it stimulated) a just, even divine retribution. At the same time the restored royalist government in Bogotá executed five hundred patriots, including the scientist Francisco José de Caldas. The result of all this savagery was to discredit the royalists and encourage others to follow Bolívar. The fact that Morillo's troops lived off the land, paying nothing for what they consumed, and openly expressed their contempt and distrust of Creoles and the rest of the Colombian population led to disillusionment and disgust even among those who previously were pro-Spanish. Meanwhile, in Chile a Spanish military commander, exercising his despotic and arbitrary will, proceeded to punish the Creoles harshly, driving more and more of them into the camp of those who would eventually reassert independence. Whereas during the first War of Independence many could believe that constitutionalism and autonomy were consistent with loyalty to a king, such a belief was no longer possible.

In Mexico the first reaction to the restoration of absolutist rule in Spain was to intensify repression, which simply fostered more resistance, although with troops newly arrived from Spain the viceroy was able to solidify royalist control of most cities. When a new viceroy arrived in 1816 he decreed a general amnesty for those insurgents who surrendered, but guerrillas continued unabated in large sections of the country, interdicting roads and setting up new settlements not too far outside ostensibly royalist cities. Still, since large armies no longer confronted each other as they had during Morelos's ascendancy, Mexico enjoyed the appearance of peace and a semblance of unity. This was a welcome respite from the horrible bloodshed and destruction of the preceding years, and the more radical Mexican intellectuals now found no audience when they spoke of independence. The Indians seemed cowed militarily by the presence of superior Spanish forces, and the wealthy Creoles were reinforced in their conviction that Spanish rule spelled security. Yet they could not help resenting the increased taxation and the constant presence of undisciplined Spanish soldiers.

Then European events gave another spin to the wheel. During January 1820 in Cádiz a mutiny broke out within an army as it prepared to depart for the American war theater. The mutiny soon became a widespread insurrection, and

SPANISH MEN-OF-WAR WATCHING THE PERUVIAN PRIVATEER "R. R. CUYLER."—[SKETCHED BY W. S. DUMONT.]

CITY AND BAY OF CARTAGENA, UNITED STATES OF COLOMBIA, AS SEEN FROM LA POPA.—[SKETCHED BY W. S DUMONT.]

FIGURE 5.1. *Cartagena, a City Besieged*

by March Ferdinand was forced to restore the Constitution of 1812. The liberals were once again in control in Spain and sent out orders to put the constitution's provisions back into effect in Spanish America. And, of course, the army did not sail off to the colonies. The hope, however, of winning back the loyalty of Spanish Americans with liberal blandishments — which in any case did not include free trade — was doomed to failure.

What the Spanish liberals failed to understand was that the ties between America and Spain had become frayed in 1808 when Napoleon usurped the Spanish throne; that many strands had been entirely broken in 1810, when the Central Junta disbanded, Spain appeared to be lost, and Spanish administrators nevertheless failed to allow even temporary self-rule in America; and that the remaining threads had been severed in the years after 1815, when Ferdinand, instead of establishing a commonwealth with autonomy for each region, initiated his reactionary policies. Only massive force could have restored the old forms of Spanish power in America, and then only temporarily, but the Spanish liberals lacked the will to use such force even if they had been able to marshal it. The result was the rapid disintegration of what remained of the Spanish empire as those of its agents who struggled to maintain it now lost their support at home and were in fact instructed to find an accommodation with the very Americans against whom they had been fighting.

Then, in 1823, with the help of the French army, Ferdinand again assumed absolute rule, a move other continental powers endorsed. For a while it looked as if the next step would be to reassert colonial authority in Spanish America. These hopes of reimposing imperial rule over the former colonies by relying on the military force of Ferdinand's allies were frustrated, however, by the British, who, having succeeded at last in opening Latin America's ports to their direct trade, were not about to allow the Spaniards or their allies to close them once again. When Ferdinand issued an invitation for an international conference to consider allied help to restore colonial rule, George Canning, the British foreign minister, replied that the British would not attend any conference in which free trade was in dispute. Aware of this British commitment, the United States rushed to issue the Monroe Doctrine in late 1823, declaring that European intervention in the Americas would be considered an attack on the United States, thus gaining credit for a policy that only England could enforce. Without fresh troops from Europe, Spanish forces in America were unable to hold out against the revolutionaries. As Canning later put it with just a bit of ethnocentric exaggeration, "I resolved that if France had Spain, it should not be Spain 'with the Indies.' I called the New World into existence to redress the balance of the Old."[2]

The Portuguese empire reached the same result by a somewhat different path. When the court fled Portugal for Rio de Janeiro in late 1807, Napoleon's troops fully occupied Portugal. The arrival of a British army and the effort of many valiant Portuguese volunteers led to victories against the French, who were forced out by mid-1811. A regency was set up, although real power rested in the hands of the British general William Carr Beresford, whom we earlier encountered in Buenos Aires. Prosperity, however, did not return. With Brazil now economically independent, Portugal's trade suffered sharp decline.

With the final defeat of Napoleon in 1814 people expected the return of the royal court. Instead, Brazil was raised to the level of a kingdom, and King João VI decided to remain in Rio de Janeiro. In Portugal dissatisfaction with this state of affairs began to spread. Portuguese army officers who had fought to expel the French found it galling to be ruled from Brazil and to have to take orders from an Englishman. And the king's decision sorely disappointed the merchants who had expected a restoration of their former monopolies.

Meanwhile in Brazil during the period from 1815 to 1820 friction between the Creoles and the Portuguese intensified. The king's presence in Brazil solved old problems but created new ones. Fifteen thousand courtiers had flooded the small city of Rio de Janeiro in 1808 just when the Creole landowners began to find the city attractive for the first time. Many of the planters' town houses, perhaps rough-hewn by European standards, were turned over to the newcomers. Instead of gratitude, the courtiers expressed only spiteful and complaining scorn for the accommodations. Furthermore, the king gave all the best jobs in the administration to the Portuguese, which made a real point out of what had previously been a somewhat exaggerated rivalry between the Creoles and Portuguese. He also issued edicts and instructions on matters that the members of the câmaras had long considered their exclusive concern. At the Congress of Vienna in 1815 the Portuguese had been forced to join in forbidding the slave trade north of the equator and to promise to end it altogether eventually. But if this displeased planters, the agents in Brazil of Lisbon merchant houses were made equally unhappy by the ending of Brazil's colonial status, for now lesser Creole merchants and foreign merchants, especially British ones, competed with them openly and directly. Despite the prosperity that accompanied the reopening of European ports to Brazilian exports of sugar and cotton, dissatisfaction with the government grew. Separation from Portugal was no longer unthinkable because the king himself had made Brazil independent de facto and because many Spanish Americans, most notably those in neighboring Argentina, had already declared their independence.

If the presence of the king in Rio de Janeiro fostered the notion of Brazil as one unit, it also exacerbated regional rivalries within Brazil. Previously each province had thought of itself as one colony among equals, but now Rio de Janeiro and its neighboring provinces wielded more influence than the more distant northeastern ones, and these felt forgotten. In 1817 a short-lived, abortive republican revolution began in Recife and spread to several neighboring provinces. Its leaders were especially inspired by the French Revolution, despite their commitment to slavery. The immediate effect of this unfinished revolt was to lead the king to doubt the loyalty of Brazilians in general, even though those who defeated that movement were almost entirely Brazilian-born. The harshness with which authorities treated revolutionaries after their capture further alienated and alarmed many Creoles. The king then ordered several Portuguese battalions, veterans of the Peninsular War in Europe, transferred to various Brazilian cities, where their presence signaled the gap between the Portuguese and the colonials.

In August 1820 an army contingent in northern Portugal revolted, and soon towns throughout the country joined in. A new constitution was rapidly drafted, modeled on the Spanish one of 1812, seen everywhere as the fullest expression of liberalism. An elected Côrtes reflected the liberal impulse of the merchant class in the port cities. The result was that the king would be circumscribed by the Côrtes, and it ordered his return to Portugal. João VI now faced a dilemma. If he did not return to Portugal, Portugal would declare its own independence from Brazil and he would obviously lose that throne. Yet, with Brazilians fiercely jealous of their new proximity to the king, he would probably lose Brazil if he went back to Portugal. He compromised. He sailed for Portugal in April 1821 but left his eldest son, Pedro (1798–1834), as prince regent in Brazil with instructions, Pedro later said, to make himself king if formal independence should come. The Côrtes, like its Spanish counterpart, then attempted to reimpose colonial rule on Brazil, and the result was much the same. Brazilians now accustomed to running their own affairs would not tolerate a return to colonial status.

VENEZUELA AND COLOMBIA

The towering figure in northern South America during the second War of Independence was Simón Bolívar. After his flight from the chaos of Colombia in 1815, he remained undaunted and clear-eyed. From his haven in Jamaica he wrote one of the most famous documents of Spanish American history (his "Letter from Jamaica") in which he first surveyed the origin and course of the revolution by region, analyzing the problems and prospects for the future. He then outlined his political philosophy, reasserting his commitment to establish freedom in South America but declaring his belief that the people were unprepared for democratic procedures because the Spaniards had deprived them of governmental experience. He reasoned that a strong central government controlled by a powerful executive was the only alternative to anarchy (see Document 7).

At the end of 1816, enraged by the news of Morillo's atrocities in Colombia, Bolívar landed on the northeastern coast of Venezuela about halfway between Caracas and the mouth of the Orinoco River. He came from Jamaica via Haiti, where he had secured supplies in exchange for a promise to free the slaves of the mainland (Haitians hoped to secure allies against French interference). Two other developments ensured Bolívar's military victories over the next few years. The first was even greater foreign aid. The United States recognized Bolívar's belligerency, making it legal for American privateers, operating under various Spanish American flags, to sweep the seas of Spanish shipping and isolate the Spanish armies. Then English merchants, anxious to invade Spanish colonies with their goods, lent Bolívar more than £1 million, part of which he used to contract unemployed English, Irish, and Scottish veterans of the Napoleonic wars. Despite losing some battles, Bolívar, with this new support, defeated Spanish troops in the eastern llanos by the end of 1817. But what about the western llanos?

The second reason for his success was the changing nature of the support he garnered in Venezuela. By this time the llaneros had a new caudillo, José Antonio Páez (1790–1873), Boves having died in battle. Páez came from a poor background and had been forced to flee to the llanos at the age of seventeen after having killed a man in his hometown, apparently in self-defense. At first a greenhorn, he had been hardened by the rough conditions and tough companions and gradually emerged as the leader of all the llaneros in the west. At the end of January 1818 Páez met Bolívar and was attracted to Bolívar's force of character, his vitality, and his daring. He placed his followers under Bolívar's command. But Bolívar had to offer more to Páez's followers. They demanded property, and Bolívar issued a decree that national lands — that is, land seized from the royalists — would be divided up among the loyal troops. They joined up. With his now-augmented forces, Bolívar had complete control of the llanos, both east and west, within a year.

Even earlier Bolívar had begun a systematic policy of incorporating pardo troops into his forces, promoting their leaders equally with whites according to their performance, in effect imitating Boves. At this very time Spanish commanders, wherever they were victorious, restored the old hierarchical society and reenslaved blacks. Morillo, the Spanish general, even demoted pardo officers whom Boves, the ally of Spain, had rewarded with promotions. Bolívar now promised to free any slave who joined his army, although by this same step he legitimized the continuing enslavement of those who did not. Surely few thought military discipline and a soldier's harsh existence a great improvement over slavery, but at least they no longer fought against him. In short, Bolívar had come to terms with some of Venezuela's social realities.

Although the war in Venezuela was far from completely won and no attempt had been made to retake Caracas, Bolívar turned west into Colombia. At mid-year 1819, just when the llanos were supposedly impassable because of seasonal rains and military activity should have been at a standstill, his forces began a six-hundred-mile march from central Venezuela toward Colombia, wading in water up to the waist or swimming the horses. They then proceeded from the steaming lowlands up the narrow passes of the eastern slope of the Andes into bitter cold. They slept in snow, covered only with tattered rags. At twelve thousand feet, many died from altitude sickness, combined with their exhaustion, and their horses perished from lack of food. But, having crossed the range, Bolívar took the Spaniards completely by surprise, winning a series of battles culminating in a decisive victory on the plains near Bogotá in early August 1819. Although not a battle involving many troops, this defeat shattered Spanish morale. The viceroy in Bogotá fled ignominiously, and Bolívar marched along an open road into the viceregal capital to be welcomed by wildly cheering crowds.

Because of the 1820 revolution in Spain, the reinforcements that had been preparing to leave Spain did not come, and Morillo received orders to strike a truce instead. This he did and then resigned. He could not continue to maintain a colonial government if the armies at home did not back him. After the truce expired, Bolívar mopped up most of the Spanish entrenchments, entering Caracas in June 1821, where he left Páez in charge militarily.

Bolívar, trying now to build a nation, declared a general amnesty for all opponents. He summoned delegates to a single congress for both Venezuela

FIGURE 5.2. *Bolívar's Forces Crossing the Andes in 1819*

and Colombia, with the hope of making this one country. The delegates elected him president and, following his wishes, set up a centralized government with a powerful executive to administer all of this "Gran Colombia." The conservatism of this constitution stood in sharp contrast to the 1812 Spanish charter.

Bolívar understood that until Spaniards were driven out of Peru, independence was not assured anywhere in South America. He immediately sought a leave of absence from the presidency of Gran Colombia in order to pursue the war to the south, leaving Vice President Francisco de Paula Santander (1792–

FIGURE 5.3. *Bolívar's Residence Just Outside Bogotá*

1840) in charge in Bogotá. Santander's government revamped educational institutions to conform to British pedagogical principles, redesigned the tax code in accordance with the latest economic theories, and replaced the colonial judicial structure and its corporate and class divisions with a single national and uniform system. But Bolívar turned all his attention to Ecuador, for he wanted to include it in his Gran Colombia. Successful battles, especially those led by his chief lieutenant, Antonio José de Sucre (1795–1830), culminated in Bolívar's entry into Quito in 1822.

When he entered the city in his usual flamboyant manner at the head of a parade, a pretty woman threw him a bouquet from a balcony. Later that night they met at a fancy ball and soon became lovers. She was Manuela Sáenz (1797–1856), the illegitimate daughter of an elite Creole woman and an equally prominent but married Spaniard. Manuela's mother died either at childbirth or shortly thereafter, and her mother's family would have nothing to do with the girl. But her father, the owner of a textile mill, treated her more or less equally with his legitimate children, paid for her education, and gave her a substantial dowry, marrying her off in 1817 to James Thorne, a wealthy British merchant and shipping magnate in Lima. Thorne was twenty years older than Manuela and traveled frequently, usually to Ecuador, leaving his business affairs in her hands. In 1822 she returned to Quito for the first time in five years to see her father, who was about to retire to Spain, as other peninsulars were doing. It was there that she met Bolívar. Her half brother, who had once fought with the

Spanish army in Peru, had earlier switched sides and joined Bolívar, becoming his aide-de-camp. It may have been because of him that she was present at the ball where she danced with Bolívar. Manuela remained Bolívar's companion for the rest of his life, though he was far from faithful to her. As he moved southward into Peru she became his archivist and arranged for the transportation of his papers, releasing a document only on his written instruction. She followed him from military camp to camp, traveling always by a different route in order to protect this archive, riding astride and not sidesaddle as upper-class women did. One time when he appeared in danger of being captured, she smuggled the papers to a safe location. Later they lived together in Bogotá, where, as bitter political quarrels became ever more intense, she kept him informed of what was going on. When a small group of Bolívar's enemies stole into their house in the middle of the night she held them at bay with a gun while he escaped through a window. For this episode she came to be known as la Libertadora del Libertador (see Document 8). Beset by tuberculosis, Bolívar died in Cartagena

FIGURE 5.4. *Manuela Sáenz*

in 1830 on his way to self-imposed exile. Manuela, now scorned by the women of Bogotá who had once sought her favor, moved to a northern port in Peru where she set up a small shop. Having earlier come to terms with her maternal aunt, the executor of her mother's estate, Manuela inherited some property that she now sold. She reestablished a formal relationship with her husband, Thorne, but when he died the courts denied her any rights as his widow. She died impoverished.

ARGENTINA AND URUGUAY

The restoration of Ferdinand VII to the throne of Spain in 1814 brought long-postponed issues to a head in Argentina. Loyalty to the once-dispossessed king was no longer a tenable myth, now that he was firmly reinstalled on his throne. Argentina would either have to submit to Spanish rule or declare independence. If independent, should the new nation be a monarchy or a republic? If a monarchy, who should rule? If a republic, should the government be centralized or federal? These questions could no longer be avoided and were the chief ones placed before the constituent congress that gathered at Tucumán, in western Argentina, in May 1816.

The congress declared the independence of the "United Provinces in South America" but could not proceed further. Conservative delegates desired a monarchy, while the Buenos Aires liberals opted for a republic. In the meantime the congress appointed Juan Martín de Pueyrredón (1777–1850) supreme director. A monarchist and a man of influence, he had won fame in the 1806–1807 battles against the British. Being a porteño, he was uneasy in the isolated vastness of the interior at Tucumán and soon persuaded the congress to continue their proceedings in Buenos Aires. For the next three years the congress deliberated while he directed a vain search for a king and, in effect, became the government.

Pueyrredón believed, as did the congress, that the new nation should include all the territory that had formerly been part of the Viceroyalty of Río de la Plata, including Uruguay. But this area was under the rule of Artigas, as were the five provinces immediately to the north of Buenos Aires. Pursuing a course already begun by the preceding government, Pueyrredón negotiated with the Portuguese king in Brazil, in effect inviting him to invade Uruguay once again in order to put a stop to Artigas. The Portuguese moved in during August 1816 and occupied Montevideo by January 1817, thus reclaiming the province they had first entered in the seventeenth century. Artigas threw all his resources, both those in Uruguay and those from his allied provinces, against the invaders, but his forces were at a vast disadvantage when faced with veteran Portuguese troops. Still, Artigas did not capitulate but for three more years continued a guerrilla campaign against the Portuguese until finally forced to seek refuge in Paraguay, leaving the Portuguese in control of Uruguay. Uruguayan independence from Brazil was not secured until 1828, but at least Spain never regained a foothold there and could not use Uruguay as a landing point for a Spanish army.

Pueyrredón had only limited success establishing unity among the other Argentine provinces, and in 1819 an alliance of northern and western leaders unseated him. Now practically every Argentine province — and sometimes a portion of a province — declared its independence as a sovereign republic. The nation plunged into a ten-year period of recurring anarchy and unstable government that ended only when Juan Manuel de Rosas (1793–1877) came to power in the early 1830s and forced regionalists to yield to centralized authority, all in the name of federalism.

During the last half of the 1810s Argentine leaders were less interested in legislative programs of social reform than had been true earlier. The country nevertheless entered a period of social flux and mobility even in the more conservative west, and the power of those conservatives in Buenos Aires who wished to maintain the old social order was undercut by the frequent onslaught of ranchers and their rough cowboys. By 1820 the traditional society of more or less fixed relationships had been significantly weakened, and many considered a monarchy an anachronism. The liberal reformers in Buenos Aires, although unable to enforce their leadership in the country as a whole, could claim significant power in the city.

A major player who emerged at this time was José de San Martín (1778–1850). The son of a middle-ranking Spanish soldier in Argentina who had returned to Spain with his family when he was a young boy, San Martín entered the Spanish army at age eleven, eventually rising to a position of some responsibility. Disgusted with events in Spain in 1811, he went to London, where he met Miranda, and then offered his services to the government of Buenos Aires, harboring a romantic attachment to the cause of independence. Argentine leaders quickly perceived his abilities, and his influence grew steadily. He became acquainted with the intellectuals of Buenos Aires, although he did not share their passion to transform society. He was a friend of Pueyrredón and, from 1816, had considerable influence on the Tucumán proceedings. As a monarchist he endorsed Pueyrredón's search for a European king.

But San Martín focused his attention on organizing an Argentine army with the goal of attacking the Spanish seat of power in Peru. Already in 1814 he had moved his headquarters first to Tucumán and then to Mendoza. He promoted a guerrilla effort to ward off Spanish invasion from Bolivia but concentrated his

FIGURE 5.5. *José de San Martín*

full energies on equipping, supplying, and training a professional force. He took little interest in the squabbles among Argentine regions.

CHILE, PERU, AND BOLIVIA

San Martín soon perceived, as Bolívar saw later, that until the Spanish forces in Peru were crushed, no independent Argentine province would be safe. And he had a new plan for how to achieve this. Instead of heading directly across the Andes to Lima through Bolivia, he would cross the Andes into Chile at a point where the ranges were relatively narrow, go to the coast, and move by sea to Lima in order to occupy the seat of Spanish power right away. Mopping up the highlands would come later.

For three years in western Argentina San Martín prepared for the execution of his plan with the greatest care, attending to every detail while gathering his forces. As a professional soldier he believed in training and more training for his troops, inculcating professional discipline. He also insisted that they be paid on time and receive food and uniforms, persuading cadres of patriotic women to help him in these tasks. Meanwhile he personally scouted the passes through the Andes to Chile and decided which units should go through which pass. Finally in midsummer (January) 1817 he led his fully equipped army of five thousand men — 30 percent of whom were freed slaves — through the towering Andes into Chile. Many soldiers died on the way. His main moves were preceded by elaborate feinting maneuvers, so the Spanish army, caught unprepared, suffered a swift defeat. Then San Martín marched unhampered on to Santiago. With another major battle the next year he gained full control of Chile's central valley. Chile obtained its independence, and O'Higgins, who had joined San Martín in Argentina, was placed in charge of a government bent on progressive programs. O'Higgins also set to work marshaling resources for the next stage of San Martín's scheme.

Two years elapsed before San Martín was ready for the next move. For this part of the plan he needed a navy and a naval commander. The flood of unemployed British military personnel caused by Napoleon's defeat was a boon. Few men in Europe had established a greater reputation for daring exploits than the naval officer Thomas Cochrane, and he was ready to leave England because of a threatened trial for perpetrating a stock swindle, his unpopularity because of rash political stands, and his need of money. San Martín sent an offer to Cochrane, who accepted, arrived in Chile, and put together a navy and a transport fleet of twenty-three vessels, including several Spanish ships he captured. By 1820 all was ready. The army boarded the ships and set sail toward Peru. San Martín did not strike directly at Lima but landed well to the south, for he hoped to allow its citizens to rebel on their own. He did not want independence to be imposed on an unwilling people. This also gave him the chance to expand his forces with local recruits, many of whom were blacks or mulattos anxious to escape forced labor on haciendas. San Martín then sent some of his forces by sea to land north of Lima, leaving the city nearly surrounded, although not closed off from the interior.

By this time news about the events in Spain of 1820 and the new constitutional government there had arrived in Peru. Liberal Spanish officers who had fought in the Peninsular War were already dissatisfied with the lack of imaginative leadership demonstrated by the ultraconservative Peruvian viceroy. Now, encouraged by the revolution in Spain, these officers deposed him and chose one of their own as his replacement, titled captain-general, an action speedily approved by the liberal government in Spain. He tried to reach a modus vivendi

FIGURE 5.6. *Thomas Cochrane*

with San Martín, but San Martín was determined on complete independence, and the negotiations came to naught. The Spanish army and most of the Spanish merchants then departed Lima for the interior, choosing as their new base the city of Cuzco and its rich hinterland with its silver mines and food-producing highland valleys, leaving Lima for San Martín. The city's cabildo, aware of its precarious position, ostensibly welcomed him in July 1821.

In a series of much-acclaimed proclamations, issued formally by a cabildo abierto he summoned, San Martín declared Peru's independence, transformed all Indians into citizens, determined that all children subsequently born to slave women would be free, offered freedom to any slave who joined his army, and ended the slave trade. He created a new military unit made up of former slaves whose uniforms were distinguished by their bright red caps. But he also proposed maintaining the political privileges of the upper class and did not for a moment encourage social unrest from below. He sponsored the organization of an honorific society for the upper- and middle-class patriotic women of Lima, many of whom had kept him informed on Spanish actions while he was still camped outside the city. But the limeños were far from unified in their reaction to San Martín. Of those who thought about such matters, some were republicans and others monarchists, and of these some were absolutists and others constitutionalists. San Martín could count only on that portion of this last group who also supported independence.

San Martín's flaw now became apparent. He would not undertake any operation unless entirely sure of success. The experienced Spanish army of some eleven thousand men in the interior easily outnumbered his, which included many new recruits. So he awaited developments. Without silver from the mines he could not pay his troops, finance his administration, or afford imports. Cochrane, claiming back pay and ever an opportunist, departed with the remaining war chest and sold his services to Brazil. The Argentines and Chileans became restless and demoralized by the enforced inactivity far from home. San Martín himself suffered repeated asthma attacks and was wracked with acute pain caused by stomach ulcers, for which he took opium as a painkiller. His popularity waned, especially among people of property.

In late July 1822 San Martín met Bolívar at a secret interview at Guayaquil, Ecuador. What transpired has never become known to anyone except these two, but San Martín decided to leave the field and allow Bolívar to complete what San Martín had started. Back in Buenos Aires, despite his great achievements, San Martín was disowned by the liberals because of his conservatism and by the conservatives for his failure to rescue Pueyrredón's government when it was overthrown in 1819. Disillusioned, the man who had freed all of southern South America retired to Europe, where many years later he suffered a lonely death.

It was more than a year before Bolívar himself, already suffering from tuberculosis, took over in Lima. He soon left, however, choosing a northern highland city as his headquarters, thus taking the war to the enemy, but it was almost another year before he was prepared to move south to face the Spanish army. With Sucre's energetic aid, Bolívar built up a new and effective force, persuading local Creole entrepreneurs and miners to provide funds, recruiting soldiers, preparing supplies, hammering out weapons, getting uniforms, reconnoitering the land, and drawing up maps. Also important was the willing or unwilling support secured from noncombatant Indians in the agricultural valleys who sacrificed a significant part of their crops to feed the fighters, though they generally preferred to remain aloof from the struggle.

During this time the Spanish captain-general in the highlands had troubles of his own. Spanish forces in southern Bolivia were commanded by an archconservative and idiosyncratic general. When he learned in 1823 that Ferdinand VII had once again disavowed the constitution and reestablished an abso-

FIGURE 5.7. *Antonio José de Sucre*

lutist monarchy, this general declared that the area under his control would take orders only from the king directly. The captain-general, finding entreaties useless, was forced to dispatch a desperately needed portion of his troops southward to overpower the general. So only a part of the Spanish army could confront Bolívar's forces.

As result Bolívar won a clear victory in the interior of Peru in August 1824, and his troops, now commanded by Sucre, went on to defeat the Spanish army in the final battle of Ayacucho in December. Sucre next marched southward to clean up the remaining Spanish garrisons. A new nation emerged there in 1825, named Bolivia in honor of Bolívar. Sucre became its first president and attempted, valiantly but unsuccessfully, to create a modern nation tied into the

European economic system. There is some evidence that Indians here viewed Bolívar and Sucre as redeemers who would restore an older, imagined peaceful and just society. If this is the case, it is doubtful such a belief lasted for long. Bolívar in the meantime returned to faction-torn Lima to become chief executive of Peru and attempt to establish a stable government.

Bickering, however, had also become the norm in Gran Colombia, and Bolívar returned there to try to maintain national unity and stability. But the forces of regionalism overwhelmed him at the same time that tuberculosis was sapping his energies. As noted above, he died in December 1830 on his way into exile. Three months before his death Venezuela and Ecuador both declared their independence, shattering Gran Colombia. If Bolívar died sorrowfully, he is now remembered as much for his unflagging devotion to the cause of independence and his perceptive political theories as for his military role as the liberator of Venezuela, Colombia, Ecuador, and Peru.

MEXICO

After the capture and death of Morelos in 1815, many Mexicans despaired of ever winning independence from Spain. But not Vicente Guerrero, one of Morelos's allies in the southwestern lowland region near Acapulco, where the population of mixed race outnumbered whites four to one. Here the cotton producers, mostly mulatto sharecroppers, had long felt cheated by Spanish merchants who paid them little for their crop, charged them high prices for what they bought, lent money at usurious rates, and were always backed up by Spanish bureaucrats. The peasants found allies among larger landowners, muleteers, artisans, and some priests who shared their hostility to Spaniards. Morelos had attracted their support with a constitution that provided local autonomy and full citizenship for mulattos. He had encouraged them to become guerrilla fighters and fully backed Guerrero, a light-skinned mulatto, as their leader. After 1814 the royalists never succeeded in truly "pacifying" this region, or several other rural areas, especially around Veracruz. Although the guerrillas' political program was vague, they knew they did not want Spaniards in control. When they took over a district they set up local governments, levied taxes, and pardoned the smugglers who supplied them with arms. Drawing food and information from the population at large wherever they were, guerrillas invariably reemerged the moment the royalist military presence diminished. This continued year after year. In 1820 Guerrero saw a chance to form an alliance with other Mexican groups as the way to achieve most of his ends.

Perhaps in no other place in Spanish America did news of the Spanish revolution of 1820 have a more explosive impact than in Mexico. Conservatives still

FIGURE 5.8. *Vicente Guerrero*

believed that the liberal promise of a modern secular state with individual freedom and mobility threatened both religion and hierarchy. But now that the revolution in Spain had reestablished the ultraliberal Constitution of 1812, there was little reason for them to resist independence, especially if it could be established under the aegis of a European king and without abandoning their religion. At the same time, Mexican liberals had come to the inescapable conclusion that without the support of the local Creole aristocrats independence was a pipe dream. They welcomed the 1812 constitution, but they wanted to make it their own. No longer would they be dependent on the legislative measures of a Spanish parliament, the vagaries of royal fortune, or the whim of a Spanish viceroy. If support from conservatives for independence could be enlisted now, no matter what their reason for such support, liberals must seize the day. Furthermore, neither conservatives nor liberals among Americans were happy with the Spanish Cortes's refusal to end the monopoly of trade in Spanish hands, grant control over revenues to locally elected officials, or allow more than minority representation at the Cortes to the millions of Americans. Spain no longer appeared trustworthy to either group. Nevertheless, following the new instructions received from Spain and the provisions of the 1812 constitution, elections of representatives to the Cortes were held in most of Mexico.

At this time Agustín de Iturbide (1783–1824) emerged as a new leader. The son of a prosperous Basque immigrant, he had been an officer in the Creole militia when Hidalgo's revolt broke out. Despite Hidalgo's entreaties, Iturbide scorned that movement and devoted his energies to quelling it. For his efforts the viceroy had rewarded him with appointment as military commander of Guanajuato in 1813. There he had proceeded to pacify the region forcefully by such tactics as imprisoning the wife and children of those men suspected of being away in the guerrilla war and putting them into a kind of concentration camp. But his harsh means were inappropriate to the purposes of the new viceroy who arrived in 1816, determined to win over the opposition and create an enduring peace. This

FIGURE 5.9. *Agustín de Iturbide*

viceroy removed Iturbide from his command, granted amnesty and some authority to those insurgents who laid down their arms, incorporating them into the legal militia, and could reasonably claim that he had brought peace to most of Mexico. Iturbide, having been eventually readmitted to army service, was gradually restored to a position of authority over all remaining anti-insurgent efforts. Despite the fact that his forces suffered repeated defeats, in late 1820 he was charged with leading an expeditionary force assigned to eradicate the last major focus of continuing subversive activity—the Guerrero-led insurgency.

Iturbide now sensed that both conservatives and liberals were ready for a compromise. As he slowly moved closer to the rebel chieftain and doubtless considered the probability of suffering another defeat if a battle ensued, he embarked on an extensive correspondence with various Mexican factions. Even before he left Mexico City he had been in touch with a group of Creole conservatives who met in soirées organized by the upper-class and well-read María Ignacia Rodríguez de Velasco, to discuss the country's crises and consider how independence could be secured without social upheaval. These Creoles had become increasingly aware that the continued survival of the Spanish-led regime depended on them. But was that what they wanted? They now had doubts.

Iturbide also wrote to Guerrero. At first he offered only amnesty, arguing that under the Spanish Cortes many of the characteristics of the old colonial regime that everyone detested would be ended. In reply Guerrero pointed out that he had already rejected any such deals in the past and especially that he did not trust the Spanish Cortes, seeing how it had behaved in 1810–1814 (see Document 9). Guerrero then insisted that Mexico declare its total independence and that any new constitution must include full citizenship for everyone regardless of race, meaning specifically the descendants of Africans, making them eligible for any office. He also stressed that the regime must be a federal one, making room for the exercise of substantial home rule for every region, that is, that Guerrero's own bailiwick should be protected from centralized interference.

Iturbide quickly acquiesced, saying the two men shared the same goals. After further exchanges with the Mexico City Creoles, there emerged a manifesto, issued on February 24, 1821, that called for three basic provisions: independence under a constitutional monarch, preferably Ferdinand VII himself if he would come to America; citizenship for "all the inhabitants of New Spain, without any distinction between Europeans, Africans, or Indians"; and a guarantee that the Catholic religion would be the religion of the state, "without tolerance for any other," with the clergy retaining their fueros.[3] In this program there was something for almost everyone, although little for those who wished to see the enactment of Enlightenment principles. Guerrero's forces then joined Iturbide's, and together—as the Army of the Three Guarantees—they set out for Mexico City.

A few battles still had to be fought, but in most places the potential opponents, led by Creole militia and army officers, were beguiled by Iturbide's adroit use of propaganda and deserted to the revolutionaries. Even churchmen now announced that the war for independence would be a religious war to defend the old order against the liberal Spanish Constitution of 1812, and the conservative city of Puebla, led by the bishop himself, offered support. Many Spanish soldiers in Mexico were as disheartened by the thought of a colonial war, as were the troops who had rebelled in Cádiz. When Iturbide promised them safe conduct back to Spain they accepted eagerly. One by one most of the cabildos voted to yield their allegiance to the new state.

In July 1821 a new viceroy, Juan O'Donojú, landed in Veracruz, which, along with Mexico City, had not yet joined the revolution. He quickly informed himself of the situation, recognized the hopelessness of the Spanish cause, and signed a convention with Iturbide agreeing to Mexican independence, although under the protective wing of Spain (indeed, despite all objections, the Cádiz Constitution of 1812 would be Mexico's at first). In September he entered Mexico City and together with Iturbide organized a provisional government. It would be headed by a council on which O'Donojú would sit while Iturbide became its president, but there would be little if any representation of true revolutionaries. Spain, not surprisingly, refused to sanction the actions of O'Donojú but could do little about it, for only one or two Mexican forts were still controlled by Spaniards. Mexico was at last independent, and the Mexican constitution, finally promulgated in 1824, in addition to creating a federalist, decentralized republic, determined the equality of all men regardless of race—victories for Guerrero. When the Mexicans were meanwhile unsuccessful in finding a European monarch who would accept the crown of Mexico, Iturbide seized it for himself in May 1822 as Agustín I. But his reign did not last long, for in March 1823 a coalition of federalists opposed to his centralizing tendency forced him to abdicate and yield to a republic.

CENTRAL AMERICA

The events of 1808–1810 in Europe had hardly sent a ripple through the established order in Central America. The Hidalgo revolt in Mexico City merely strengthened the resolve of conservative forces to guard against liberal doctrines. But there were not many liberals. The university faculty in Guatemala had long accepted the scientific approach of the Enlightenment, but few intellectuals followed the social and political theories of the French philosophes. Rebellions broke out in San Salvador and Nicaragua in 1811, but their only intent was to escape the control of the Guatemala City merchant guild. A small conspiracy was uncovered in Guatemala City itself in 1813. Nothing more.

With the restoration of Ferdinand VII in 1814, the particularly conservative captain-general became even more intransigent. He supported the merchant guild against the cabildo at every step and seemed to consider every Creole a subversive. He especially cracked down on the smugglers who had used British settlements in Belize as their base. Guatemalan weavers approved his steps to exclude cheap British textiles, but those involved in the export trade chafed at the restrictions. Another captain-general, appointed in 1818, was more easygoing; he actually authorized some trade with Belize and looked the other way when presented with evidence of smuggling. By then, however, the Creole aristocracy and the intellectuals of the professional middle class were forming an alliance that began to work out the lineaments of a reform program.

When Iturbide declared Mexico independent in 1821, he assumed that Central America, as part of the old viceroyalty, would come under his rule. Conservative Spaniards there, as represented by the merchant guild, thought otherwise, however, and declared Guatemala's independence from Mexico. Creoles retaliated, seizing power and leading Guatemala to vote for reannexation to Mexico in January 1822. The mestizos of San Salvador then objected because they saw this move as a way of continuing their subordination to Guatemala. Only the intervention of a Mexican army finally subdued their revolt. Its arrival changed the lineup in Central America: Now the Creoles, carrying the federalist impulse even further, saw the advantage of separation from Mexico and declared independence in July 1823 as the United Provinces of Central America. Only Chiapas opted to remain in Mexico.

The ensuing history of the region is a turbulent one, leading to the eventual creation of several independent states. The constitution adopted in 1824, like the Mexican one, created a federal nation with considerable autonomy for each region. It also enshrined many now-traditional liberal freedoms. The end of the Spanish trade monopoly meant that British cottons flooded the market and cochineal exports boomed. Weavers went out of business, but mestizo smallholders prospered. The government abolished slavery. The hacendados found the liberal trend unsettling, and the liberals unnecessarily created many enemies by feuding with the church, encouraging the immigration of British settlers, transferring public lands into private hands, and imposing unpopular taxes. Despite a series of coups d'état and civil wars, however, the liberals endured for a number of years, until finally, in 1837, the peasant leader Rafael Carrera emerged to demand an end to their reforms. Leading both Indians and poor mestizos, he marched on Guatemala City. Carrera came to dominate Guatemala, but the other provinces rejected him. It was at this point, in 1838, that Nicaragua, Honduras, and Costa Rica seceded. The separation of El Salvador from Guatemala had already been accomplished by default. This completed the process of independence in the area that had once been the Viceroyalty of New Spain (Texas having become independent in 1836).

BRAZIL

As was true in Spanish America, the 1820 liberal revolution in Portugal only intensified the awareness of the gulf that separated Brazilians from the metropolis. Those few Brazilians elected to the newly created Côrtes discovered, upon their arrival in Lisbon, the deep gulf that separated them from the Portuguese delegates, creating a Brazilian identity among them. Then João VI had no sooner arrived in Lisbon in 1821 than the Côrtes majority deliberately set out to reduce Brazil back to colonial status. First, it made each Brazilian province depend directly on appointees sent out from Portugal. Next, it dispatched fresh troops to reinforce those in Salvador. Then, it abolished the courts and other national institutions that the king had created in Brazil. The Brazilian delegates who were present argued forcefully against these steps, but they were overruled. The final straw was the Côrtes's act of ordering Prince Pedro back to Europe.

The result in Brazil was almost inevitable, given the thirteen years of independent status Brazil had already enjoyed. Creoles insisted that Pedro remain in Brazil, and he acceded to their wishes in January 1822, defying the authority of the Cortes. As Portuguese troops in Rio de Janeiro prepared to force him to leave, they found themselves unexpectedly surrounded by as many as ten thousand militiamen and other hastily armed civilians who had managed to secure several artillery pieces. The Portuguese troops, numbering almost two thousand, well trained and disciplined, could probably have won any battle against the Brazilians but at an enormous cost in lives and goodwill. Instead they surrendered and departed Rio de Janeiro within a month.

Pedro soon sought support from elsewhere in Brazil. Acting on the advice of his chief minister and steady adviser, the Creole José Bonifácio de Andrada e Silva (1763–1838), Pedro convoked a constituent congress for Brazil itself, clearly understanding that such a measure would win over those who, even if wanting to be ruled from within Brazil, had been attracted to the constitutionalism of the Portuguese revolution. The Côrtes in Lisbon then played into Pedro's hands in March and April 1822 by considering a proposal that would once again require Brazilians to trade only with Portugal and close Brazilian ports to commerce with other nations. Pedro pointed out that those in the Côrtes who would legislate in this way for Brazil "knew it only in maps."[4] When news came back that the Côrtes had canceled the validity of his every measure, the positions of Pedro and the Côrtes were joined. On September 7, 1822, he

FIGURE 5.10. *José Bonifácio de Andrada e Silva*

declared Brazil fully independent. In December he accepted the crown as Emperor Pedro I of Brazil.

But the city of Salvador—as important a center as Rio de Janeiro—remained firmly in Portuguese hands. In August the Côrtes had already dispatched to it a veteran expeditionary force. When fighting broke out within the city between the Portuguese and Brazilian forces, some one hundred people died, including an abbess who vainly sought to deny entrance to Portuguese troops who claimed shots had been fired from her abbey. Whether because of such violence or their battle-tested experience in Europe or their greater discipline and organization or their advanced planning, the Portuguese won easily. In the aftermath a majority of the army's Brazilian soldiers and many black and mulatto militiamen left the city for the interior. A steady flow of Brazilian civilians followed them, seeking the protection of the rebels, so that virtually only Portuguese—especially merchants and soldiers—remained in the city.

A decidedly hostile mood toward the Côrtes took hold in the rural districts. Sugar exports had boomed in the previous years not only because competition from Haiti had been eliminated by its revolution while Cuban exports were only beginning but also because the opening of Brazilian ports to international trade had enabled direct exports to northern Europe, leading to higher profits for planters. The importation of machinery for their sugar mills and clothing for their slaves became cheaper. So now they strongly opposed the Côrtes's threat to reimpose the old colonial practice of awarding Portuguese merchant houses the exclusive right to control this export and import trade. They declared their loyalty to Prince Pedro and organized a provincial government of their own in an interior town.

Both sides in the ensuing struggle well understood the strategic importance of this region. The Portuguese saw it as a rich colony, understanding that if the province stayed on their side it would encourage the other northern provinces also to remain loyal and prevent easy communication between them and Rio de Janeiro. Pedro and his advisers recognized the same facts and determined to prevent that from happening. Without that central region the independence of any part of Brazil would have been in doubt, and without it the new country would certainly have lacked any semblance of unity unless much reduced in size. These perceptions resulted in an intensely fought confrontation, requiring a vast mobilization of Brazilian men and resources over a period of more than twelve months from late June 1822 to July 1823 and an equally determined effort

FIGURE 5.11. *Pedro I of Brazil*

FIGURE 5.12. *Maria Quitéria de Jesus*

by the Portuguese government to hold onto the area. Brazilian leaders put the militia of every interior town into service and launched a vigorous recruitment effort. One recruiter spoke with such eloquence that, unbeknownst to him, a young woman, Maria Quitéria de Jesus, decided to dress as a man and join up, eventually fighting with such valor that she won a field commission.

Meanwhile, the Portuguese forces in Salvador received more reinforcements. Each side launched attacks that were repulsed by the other. Given this stalemate, the Brazilian side decided to lay siege to the city, allowing no food to be delivered from the hinterland.

Salvador was especially susceptible to such a siege because it sits on a peninsula, and the immediately surrounding area did not produce much food. Supplies had to be brought across a very large bay or, in the case of cattle, driven over many miles from far inland. The immediate task of the insurgents was to block cattle drives, and in July 1822 the black militia occupied a strategic point on the road into the city, cutting off its supply of beef. Next, rebel forces stopped the boats that sailed across the bay with foodstuffs.

They could not, however, completely prevent boatmen based in towns along the coast of the province from surreptitiously reaching the city from the ocean to supply the Portuguese. What choices would be made by captains and crews, including slaves, who sailed from all these points? Their numbers roughly measure their importance. Although we have no numerical data for that specific date, we know that some 8,513 crewmen sailed in and out from the port of Salvador in 1856, of whom nearly three quarters were black or mulatto and roughly a quarter were slaves (thirty years earlier these proportions would likely have been still higher). The success of the siege would depend on men like these and their cooperation with the Brazilian forces.

What is startling is how many boats avoided Salvador, obeying the revolutionaries. Despite powerful monetary incentives offered by the Portuguese, those who were willing to supply the city proved more the exception than the rule, as most boat people supported the insurgents. By denying food to the Portuguese they eventually forced their withdrawal. If they had done the opposite the war might have had a very different outcome.

FIGURE 5.13. *Salvador as Seen from Its Bay*

Slaves played a critical part. Captains who considered helping the Portuguese must have weighed advantage against risk as would any businessman. Insurgents routinely seized vessels found trading with Salvador, along with their slave crews. What was the risk of being caught? In weighing the danger of being denounced to the revolutionaries, a major factor was the size and nature of the crew. The more numerous and less reliable they were, the more likely a boat violating the Brazilian-imposed embargo would be exposed. A canoe that could be manned by one person or maybe two could easily get away with it. But for a boat to trade successfully with Salvador from any Atlantic coast town required that several people on board participate in the subterfuge, a complication further escalated for anyone in charge of a still larger craft. Slaves aboard consequently gained bargaining power. If the captain traded with the enemy, could slaves be counted on to keep their mouths shut? At the same time, captains crucially depended on slave skills, knowledge, and experience to transport their goods.

Slave sailors were surely aware not only of the general instability of the times, but of circumstances specifically affecting them. The general who commanded the Brazilian troops on land sought to form a battalion made up of former slaves, freed by planters for the sake of the cause, and had ventured the idea of actively persuading masters to voluntarily free them for this purpose. Although such a step was vigorously opposed by planters, he had proposed it publicly, stirring rumors among slaves that those who volunteered would be freed; it was said they "speak of nothing else."[5] And slaves could expect to be warmly welcomed in the rebel army, with the clearly implied promise of eventual freedom. In these circumstances, if a boat and crew were seized by the revolutionaries, the sailor-slaves would at least find themselves in an ambiguous position, for who was their legal master now? They could logically conclude they were closer to freedom. So, as they sailed to and from Salvador, it seems likely they would consider throwing a spanner in the works — or that a captain would fear as much. This may account for the large number of captains who sided with the insurgents and the consequent straits that Salvador found itself in.

Of course the real solution for the Brazilians would be to truly blockade the port, but at first they had no navy to do so. Prince Pedro in Rio de Janeiro and his advisers recognized this need almost as soon as he defied the Portuguese Côrtes, and had set about acquiring ships and organizing a navy. To head it they recruited Thomas Cochrane, just "retired" from Chilean service in Peru. When the navy he organized finally blockaded the port of Salvador, the Portuguese had no recourse but to surrender. They left for Portugal at the beginning of July 1823. The same fate soon befell the remaining Portuguese garrisons in other northern ports, and Brazil was now entirely in Brazilian hands. Some measure of how slave owners now felt endangered was the immediate order of the new postrevolutionary government in Salvador to all officials to search out runaway slaves and to all landowners to verify that none hid on their properties, reversing the effect of their earlier attempts to recruit slaves as combatants.

Yet in some ways Brazil was still not truly independent. For Pedro I was Portuguese, was still the legitimate heir to the Portuguese throne, and had many Portuguese advisers with him in Rio de Janeiro. Despite his liberal protestations, Pedro did not accept the principle that the people, and thus the people's elected delegates, were sovereign. As he once declared, "I will do anything for the people, but nothing by the people."[6] When the constituent congress undertook legislative measures that he opposed, adopted steps designed to exclude all Portuguese from positions of power (which by implication cast doubt about his own rule), and began drafting a constitution that, he thought, unduly circumscribed the monarch's power, he arbitrarily dissolved it. He then, in 1824, issued his own constitution, more conservative in tone than the one the congress had been discussing, although maintaining many of the same provisions and even expanding the list of individual rights. Many of these provisions echoed the Cádiz Constitution of 1812.

Brazilian Creoles then found many other reasons to criticize Pedro I's rule. One of them was that he used Brazilian revenues to defend his dynastic interests in Portugal, once his father, João VI, died in 1826. Another was Brazil's defeat in Uruguay. After the success of the Portuguese armies in 1820 Uruguay had been given all the trappings of a Brazilian provincial government, although the real power resided with the army of occupation. Even after the bulk of this army departed for Portugal and Brazil became formally independent, the remaining Brazilian contingent—that is, soldiers of whatever origin but loyal to Pedro I—was still able to maintain Uruguay under Brazilian control. In 1825, however, thirty-three Uruguayan patriots landed from Argentina, and local dissidents rose up in revolt to greet them. Some locals formed councils that declared their willingness to join Argentina, giving it an excuse to send in its troops to help their cause. The Brazilians suffered repeated defeats, and within two years only Montevideo remained in Brazilian hands; Argentina controlled the rest. The British, whose trading interests suffered from the warfare, stepped in to moderate the quarrel and in 1828 forced both contenders to grant Uruguay independence, creating a buffer state between them. Both the Argentine and the Brazilian governments lost prestige at home, and Pedro was discredited as a military leader. Finally, as the price of British diplomatic recognition, Pedro was compelled to end the slave trade altogether. Creole planters, who formed the dominant economic class, believed that the basis of the country's prosperity would be destroyed if no more slaves could be brought in from Africa. They blamed him rather than the British. So, after Pedro's declaration of independence, nearly all his subsequent policies had turned the Creole upper and middle classes against him. Finally, in April 1831, a huge and angry crowd, backed by the Creole militia, marched on the royal palace; Pedro I had no other choice but to give in and sail for Europe.

Elite Creoles also feared republican anarchy, however, so they arranged for Pedro I to abdicate in the name of his five-year-old Brazilian-born son (also named Pedro) and leave him behind. The monarchy would be maintained under the same constitution that Pedro I had drafted. His son would be brought up according to notions suitable for this American empire, and the prominent Brazilian moderate and elder statesman José Bonifácio de Andrada e Silva would be his tutor. Regents chosen by the Brazilian parliament would rule during the boy's minority. Young Pedro would thoroughly understand that the landowning class must be treated with the greatest circumspection, a lesson that stood him in good stead, for he ruled until 1889. By 1831 Brazil was being run entirely by Brazilians with a Brazilian emperor as constitutional monarch. Only then was independence in Brazil complete.

COMMONALITIES AND DIFFERENCES

Leadership

During the second War of Independence, insurgent leadership across Latin America revealed marked contrasts as well as some similarities. Historians have traditionally attributed a great deal of importance to unique personalities, but it may be that it was not the individuals who produced the events but the other way around. When similar events occur despite differing leaders, the importance of the person is at least thrown into question.

Bolívar comes to mind immediately, for he was both a thinker and a man of action. His early education under the tutelage of Rousseau's disciple, his experience in the stimulating environment of revolutionary France, his acquaintance with books—all made him optimistic about the possibilities of social change. As a consequence he naively sought at first to impose liberalism on Venezuela. But when he failed—and he failed more than once—he pondered the reasons for his lack of success. He wrote the "Letter from Jamaica" perhaps as much to clarify his own views as to communicate them to others. Nothing in his background or training prepared him for war, yet here again he learned speedily from his mistakes and became skilled at both strategy and tactics. And as a leader it was not so much his eloquence as his charisma and sheer force of will that gained him loyalty. The attraction felt for him by the equally strong-willed Manuela Sáenz exemplifies his power.

San Martín, unlike Bolívar, was reserved and unemotional, even cold, and womanizing was never attributed to him. In his campaigns he relied on careful planning rather than on improvisation. Like Bolívar, however, he had great will-power and a firm belief in the justice and virtue of the independence struggle, making this his life project. He got along well with all classes of people and could inspire his troops with an optimistic nationalism, regardless of their regional background. He was not enamored of Enlightenment reforms but limited himself to winning battles. He was not a great soldier-statesman like Bolívar, but his virtues are nevertheless noteworthy.

Instead of a colorful statesman like Bolívar or an austere military planner like San Martín, Mexico in 1820 had the self-seeking Iturbide to lead it finally toward independence. Perhaps this deficiency in leadership was related to the bitterness of the earlier social protest. As the cause of independence had been discredited by the earlier threat of upheaval, it became the device of opportunists rather than the creation of broad-minded statesmen.

In Brazil two men together combined the qualities of Simón Bolívar: José Bonifácio de Andrada e Silva, known simply as José Bonifácio, and the prince regent, later Emperor Pedro I. José Bonifácio was born into a wealthy family in São Paulo and was dispatched to Europe at an early age to complete his studies first in law and then as a mineralogist, a field to which he contributed several scholarly papers. He was greatly influenced by the Enlightenment, but like many European intellectuals he was shocked by the so-called excesses of the French Revolution. After thirty years in Europe he returned to Brazil, becoming Pedro's closest adviser in 1820. Recognizing that power must be restrained and fearing that the Brazilian people were not ready for an idealized republic, he sought the middle ground: a constitutional monarchy with restrictions on the power of the king. He believed, rightly as it turned out, that these qualities would preserve the monarchy. As a true statesman, Bonifácio fully deserves the title "Patriarch of Independence."

Pedro had an overwhelmingly strong personality. He subdued opponents by a mere look and impressed a nation of horsemen with his superior horsemanship. Despite having had little formal education, he was competent at languages, quickly grasped the intricacies of constitutional structure, and immediately perceived political advantage. He liked to think of himself as a liberal, and indeed was at ease with the masses, having been brought up among stable boys and palace servants, but he was an autocrat by temperament. Like Bolívar, Pedro was deeply affected by an illicit love affair. Pedro was smitten with Domitila de Castro (1797–1867), a strong-willed married woman. He made her a marchioness and asked her to sit in at meetings of the Council of State. Pedro and Bonifácio together provided the leadership for independence.

Monarchism

Monarchism had a strong appeal throughout Latin America even as the independence wars were winding down. The unity of Brazil was ensured then and later by the legitimacy bestowed on the central government by the royal presence. Whether in the person of João VI, Pedro I, or the younger Pedro, Brazil had a king. The fact that the majority among the elite accepted a king's right to rule—combined with the fear of a civil war in a society so dependent on slaves—largely explains why this huge country remained one. Of course, not just any king would do. Mexico, like Brazil, adopted a monarchical form of government, but the emperor of Brazil was a legitimate heir of an ancient dynasty, whereas the Mexicans were unsuccessful in attracting Ferdinand VII or any of his relatives and had to settle for Iturbide, who could make no such claim. Pueyrredón tried for three long years to find a royal heir to rule in Argentina. Some Colombians and Bolivians also hoped, at one time or another, for a European monarch.

If the king of Spain had come to America, it is doubtful that he could have maintained the allegiance of all the Spanish colonies in one unit. Although Brazil is huge and there were several regional separatist efforts there after independence, it forms a single landmass, whereas Spanish America encompassed an area stretching from California to southern Chile. In any case, a king would have had to choose a seat of government, and, whatever choice he made, that would probably have alienated people in other major capitals. As a Spaniard put it in 1821, "Mexico would not accept the laws which might be sanctioned in Lima; nor would Lima accept the laws which might be sanctioned in Mexico."[7] Moreover, the fact that the intellectuals of Brazil, or at least its lawyer-jurists, had by necessity all received their training at the same university in Portugal encouraged a common outlook on power and loyalty to the state together with personal acquaintance with their counterparts from other regions. In contrast, the Spanish Americans had by 1810 eight major universities and more than twenty institutions of higher learning in some eighteen cities, so they did not form many connections with the future leaders of other places. Some of them would doubtless oppose the rule of a king based in another region, no matter how authentic were his dynastic claims.

Everywhere in Spanish and Portuguese America the prime movers leading to political independence—as distinct from social change—were the Creole landowners, miners, and merchants. Their desire for power impelled them increasingly to reject peninsular authority. By 1815 or so Creoles had had several years of experience governing themselves from a capital within their own borders. After that, the insensitive behavior of both the Spanish and the Portuguese Côrtes increased tensions between these European countries and their colonies. Independence resulted.

CHAPTER SIX

What Changed?

AT THE END OF THE INDEPENDENCE WARS BOLÍVAR concluded that he had "ploughed the seas."[1] Other participants probably felt the same disillusionment. But were they right? How should we evaluate the results of this long struggle? Did things get better or worse—and for whom? What assumptions do we make about the right and the good in answering these questions? Yet there is no doubt that for better or worse, independence signified a profound alteration in direction.

THE COST OF WAR

Once the war ended, how did most people remember it? Thousands and thousands had died, leaving many more bereaved and other thousands physically maimed or mentally wounded by horrors witnessed and felt. The sources are almost silent about these tragedies, and historians usually avoid discussing them. Geographic dislocation also characterized the war. Imagine a young man who had left his family near Buenos Aires in 1815 and years later ended up hundreds of miles away in northern Peru. Did he retrace his steps through Chile or go across Bolivia? Did he have funds to pay his way? Or did he settle down where he was decommissioned, marry, and have Peruvian children? Was he literate enough to write to his family back home, or were they left to wonder about his fate while plunged into poverty by the absence of a breadwinner? Such questions remain unanswered.

We can speculate that the common experience of armed service away from home must have changed these soldiers. Not only did they learn to handle weapons, but moving from a familiar to an unfamiliar world perhaps widened their perspective, challenged their usual expectations, and altered how they saw themselves and others. Some no doubt rose to become leaders in a way that might not have happened if the war had not swept them into its vortex, and, for all of them, their circles of personal connections certainly expanded. Because so many soldiers belonged to the laboring classes—slaves, free blacks, mulattos, Indians, mestizos, and poor whites—these experiences would have been particularly life-changing.

Yet the violence of war left a devastating heritage. All too often the cruelty exercised by one side in these protracted conflicts led to bloody vengeance when opponents had their turn. Bolívar's "war to the death" comes to mind. It may have won him victories in Venezuela in 1813, but it left an ugly example for his successors. As violence spread on both sides, it became expected. Mexico and northern South America were the locales of the most prolonged warfare during the independence period. These regions were also most often wracked by prolonged civil war in the decades that followed, compared to, say, Argentina and Chile where military rule was more the exception than the rule. This is not to minimize the daily violence of interpersonal relations across class lines that had characterized the colonial order throughout the region as those above oppressed those below, but now the inhumanity pitted Creoles against Creoles, rich against rich, in a more generalized way than before. The old rules crumpled. Brazil confronted several moments of political instability during the first half of the nineteenth century, but collective intraclass violence and wanton cruelty did not become generalized. Was this because the entire war lasted only a year and the fabric of society had not been so deeply torn as in Spanish America?

In another way, however, violence meant incorporation into the new era. For those subsequently excluded from voting who felt cheated, electoral violence was a way of asserting their citizenship and participating in the political life of the nation. Violence opened new spaces of sociability through which solidarity was established with some as they struggled against others. Through it, groups solidified their union and passed on political traditions to new generations. But we must ask, was it worth it?

The war's devastating destruction of productive property certainly stymied efforts at recovery. Silver mines in Mexico and Peru had been neglected, pumps destroyed, machinery vandalized, and shafts flooded. Textile mills in Colombia and Mexico were neglected. Herds of cattle in Uruguay and Argentina were seriously depleted. And, on a different plane, in Venezuela, where so many slaves had been freed to fight or had fled their masters, planters had to reorganize their labor system, starting from scratch. Everywhere new investment drastically diminished as lenders were few and banks nonexistent. The Catholic Church had once been a major banker, but even before the war the Spanish government had taken over its receivables in exchange for public bonds, now worthless. In turn those who wished to start anew found it much harder to secure the necessary funding.

AN ALTERED CULTURAL REALITY

The notion that corporate entities were essential parts of the larger body politic persisted after the war but in an attenuated fashion. The removal of the king threatened the order of the old society as much as the death of a father can undermine a family's cohesiveness. The complex interlayering of craft guilds, church bodies, cabildos, sodalities, and Indian "republics" had been shaken up and would never be the same. When in 1810 the Central Junta in Spain summoned a Cortes, the method for choosing the delegates was still based on the idea that they would be chosen by the old corporate entities, either directly or through the cabildos. But the 1812 constitution, drawn up by this very Cortes, called for individuals to participate in elections as equals, albeit still indirectly through one of the many newly created cabildos because a vague conception of a society of orders still persisted. But by the 1820s people in Spanish America took it for granted that a national congress and even a president could be elected by the people acting severally, not through any other body, even if in most cases "the people" were narrowly defined by their gender and, eventually, by their property and/or literacy. How individuals identified themselves to themselves and to others may still have had strong vestiges of the earlier corporate categories, but they had added another overarching definition of themselves as citizens. It was a major cultural shift.

Another and related change has to do with notions of sovereignty. With the king gone, sovereignty reverted to the cities and then to the people. True, this way of thinking had roots that went back beyond the sixteenth century, but independence brought the issue front and center for ordinary folk. Now that rulers themselves were chosen by them, where did sovereignty lie? Surely with the people.

Such a change in the way they thought about politics had ramifications for how they identified with place. Earlier, aside from their corporate memberships, people linked themselves first of all to their place of residence and work or the place where their parents were buried. In the absence of the king or queen only the ties that bound people to their home territory, to their immediate locality, to their *patria*, remained as a compelling emotional commitment. Bogotá, once the seat of a viceroyalty, found itself for a while ruling over only its immediate hinterland. Not only did the Viceroyalty of Río de la Plata eventually divide into several separate countries, but "Argentina" itself consisted of many provinces that battled each other for years, each seeking its own independence. Independence provoked a struggle to define the boundaries of the nation, a line on a map that separated "us" from "them" and it is sometimes unclear why national borders ended up where they did. In some places local loyalties continued to trump "national" ones far into the nineteenth century, which explains the frequent pitched battles between federalists and centralists.

It follows, however, that in the end the war fostered an overarching loyalty to culturally defined nations that substituted for, or at least subsumed, the multiple loyalties to corporations and localities. Whereas empires joined disparate nations, republics tended to separate them. Although Creoles had already forged some sense of their difference from and opposition to the European-born, only the independence struggle drove home the difference between Colombians and Venezuelans, Uruguayans and Argentinians. Could it be because of these wars and the large-scale mobilization they entailed that the development of national feeling in Latin America predated similar experiences in most of continental Europe? The proliferation of newspapers after the war was noticeable, but widespread illiteracy limited their reach. Did the impact of the war itself, experienced by so many, have a greater effect on political culture than the printing press? It can also be argued that in building this sense of common participation in a nation—this new unifying loyalty—the state played an important, even predominant part. Does that mean that states came first, nations later?

Liberalism, both in the Old World and the New, pivoted on the freedom of the individual, not on equality, yet elections suggested that every voter exercised equal weight in decision making. Freedom and equality were in constant tension. Every voter (but not every citizen and even less every person) now had a say in choosing representatives. Most electoral rules in the nineteenth century excluded domestic servants, for it was argued that they were too dependent on someone else to be able to exercise independent judgment. This was also true of sons if they still lived with their parents, as well as members of religious orders who took vows of obedience. Women were understood as similarly lacking in independence and subject to the commands of husbands or fathers. So, it was said, if women were to vote it would be as if a married man unfairly cast two votes. But such notions clearly benefited male property owners; so did these assertions have another, unspoken, rationale? Balloting was not secret. Each voter deposited a list of those he supported and, in some places, signed it. Candidates could prepare these lists ahead of time and give them to prospective voters. At the ballot box the ballot's color or size could signal which party the voter supported. Given the prevailing social rankings, even if universal suffrage had been the law everyone could expect the "good men," the socially dominant, to emerge victorious, carried along by their prestige and prominence—and there were many ways to punish any voter deemed insufficiently loyal to his patron. So equality before the ballot box was severely qualified. Still, political and economic liberalism did open the way for an individual to break free from his social origins and rise—or sink—according to other criteria. Did liberalism, then, force a certain kind of equality?

The failure to fully implement many liberal reforms stemmed from the objections raised by landowners and those who benefited from the previous system of corporate privilege. O'Higgins, for instance, showed himself to be a forceful executive in Chile who accepted the necessity of centralized power. He strengthened the police, captured bandits, encouraged trade, killed his opponents or sent them into exile, intervened in elections, and attempted to perpetuate himself in power. But he also abolished the practice of entail and so forced property to be divided equally among heirs. He attacked the privileges of the church, ignored titles of nobility, and chipped away at the ancient barriers between classes. In doing so, he threatened to cut the sinews of the old regime. Was this why, despite his forceful use of centralized executive power, his rule proved short-lived?

Other reformers met with similar resistance. In the province of Buenos Aires, for instance, Bernardino Rivadavia, as noted in chapter 4, was a committed liberal. A disciple of Jeremy Bentham who believed that the general good could be achieved principally by reducing the power of the state, he attempted to strengthen individual freedom through legislation. Rivadavia worked to encourage immigration from northern Europe, but the cattle ranchers of the region were not interested. He weakened the church by eliminating the compulsory tithe and controlling the movement of clergymen, becoming aware too late of how such measures offended common people over whom the clergy exercised much influence. He wanted to lessen import duties and rely instead on taxes on income and land in a society dominated by wealthy landowners, already tired of financing the wars. Like most liberals at the time, he did not champion the cause of the lower classes. He advocated giving ranchers clear title to previously public lands and saw gauchos who were being closed out of the open range as lazy vagabonds who should be drafted into the army or assigned to compulsory public works. Freedom was for the successful. Nevertheless, his tenure as a kind of prime minister in the provincial government lasted only from July 1821 to April 1824 and that as president of a chimerical United Provinces of the Río de la Plata from February 1826 to July 1827, when the union broke into its various component parts. Had he threatened the position of too many powerful people?

Valentín Gómez Farías, president of Mexico from 1832 to 1834, also attempted to impose the values of the Enlightenment on his reluctant countrymen. Society, he believed, consisted of atomistic individuals who should be free to prosper or fall according to their abilities, and the state's responsibility was principally to ensure that freedom. A physician by training, he believed that every problem had a rational answer. He abolished state monopolies, ended all the fueros (once again) of corporate groups, revoked the compulsory payment of church tithes, and stripped the church of its educational responsibilities, creating secular institutions of higher education. The devout common people were bewildered by his anticlericalism, the army and clergy resented the loss of their privileges, and those with vested economic interests felt disinherited. He was overthrown by a coup after two years in office.

Bolívar proved to be a perceptive political thinker. "The excellence of a government is not in its theory, its form, or its mechanism," he reiterated, "but in being appropriate to the nature and character of the nation to which it is applied."[2] Many of Bolívar's contemporaries believed that the rights of the individual could best be defended from the arbitrary action of the state if the central government were kept weak, the executive power curtailed, and provincial or local government exalted, while he believed in a powerful executive within a strong central government. Weak government, he thought, would lead to anarchy and anarchy to dictatorship. It was better to have a strong government to begin with, placed within the legal structure, than to end up with a strong government anyway but under a tyrant. A powerful executive, he said, would suit the Spanish American experience. He sought a middle way between liberalism and corporatism. Many of his proposals later became commonplace within the Latin American political class.

The major contribution of this generation—despite or rather because of their differences—was to identify a set of issues to be debated. As they considered enacting specific measures, their controversies passed from the theoretical to the practical. Some leaders wished to expand educational facilities because only in this way could human beings control nature and society; others saw this a low priority. One sector argued for the separation of church and state because they saw that union as a major bulwark of a hierarchical society, opposed to liberty. But by eliminating the king, the "Lord's Anointed," the independence movement had already brought about a secularist notion of government in thought if not in legal fact. Freedom to speak, write, and assemble was now recognized at least as an option. And by the mid-1820s even conservatives accepted written constitutions as a bulwark of state legitimacy. Change had been visualized concretely, even if not effected.

Still, it is easy to exaggerate the degree to which Latin Americans adopted new notions about government, when in fact older political theories persisted in many constitutions. Analyzing them suggests that for many writers the common good was to be achieved not by the satisfaction of conflicting interests through compromise and the balancing of legislative, executive, and judicial powers but through the morality of leaders, religious education, divine guidance, and control of speech and press. Several constitutions even embodied a board of censors to watch over the virtue of officials and specified moral qualifications for office. But in correcting one exaggeration should we conclude that the new political system could not be differentiated from the old? Or had things changed?

SOCIAL TENSIONS

The war brought to the surface social tensions that had earlier remained largely invisible. On the whole, those groups whom the well-off had feared in the eighteenth century made few tangible gains as a result of independence, and many of them actually lost ground. Certainly the Indians suffered under the new regimes. Although steadily exploited for three hundred years, they had also been somewhat protected by the paternalism embedded in Spanish rule. The limited corporate rights, privileges, and exemptions that Indians had previously enjoyed, new Latin American leaders now wished to remove. The notion of an "Indian Republic" disappeared from the language of legal documents, although the proliferation of cabildos meant that Indians might constitute a majority in some of them. Instead of customary rules limiting leadership among Indians to the elderly or those with a service record, a seat on a cabildo depended on an election in which all males of a certain age could vote. Electioneering was a real possibility, and for some this meant an improvement in their lot. Although in most places the tribute on Indian villages based on their adult male population ended, Indians now paid other taxes from which they had once been exempt. The legal systems instituted over the next several decades in Spanish America emphasized private property rather than communal landholdings, which many whites thought should be completely undone. The reformers' rationale was that if the Indians were forced to sink or swim as a result of their own initiative and hard work, they would shake off their alleged lethargy and participate more fully in national life. But instead of the promised results the individualism of the new era exacerbated the exploitation of Indians by those with more wealth, more connections, and more knowledge of how to handle competitive struggle within a capitalist society.

In most of Spanish America, leaders were willing to risk arming the lower classes in general and even slaves to pursue their fight for independence. This despite the earlier occurrence of Indian rebellions, especially in Mexico and Peru, and of slave revolts in Haiti and Venezuela. It could be argued that Spanish American elites, as they confronted the alternatives posed by Napoleon's usurpation of the throne, had no alternative but to mobilize the lower classes if they were to secure national autonomy. Through these wars they learned that they could cope well enough with a politically restive population. With mestizos (and some mulattos as in Venezuela) placed in command of military force and often rewarded with the ownership of lands taken from royalists, Creoles discovered that they were not as endangered by these working people as their counterparts in Brazil and Cuba apparently feared they would be. Resistance from below or *at least its perception* must have been less intense in Spanish America than in Brazil. Is this why so many Spanish Americans who held sway in various provinces continued to fight against each other well after securing independence? Did they feel confident that they could do so without provoking a social upheaval that would endanger their own social and economic position?

As for freeing slaves, the most common proposal at first was to offer freedom in exchange for military service, as had long been the traditional practice for those who defended the state. In Argentina, where approximately thirty thousand people, or about 8 percent of the population, had been enslaved when the independence movement began, revolutionary governments often required slave owners to sell their human property to governments for use in their armies. If the draftees fought for five years and survived the war, they would be free. San Martín relied heavily on this expedient, and his reputation went before him. In Peru the viceroy reported in 1818 that slaves had "openly decided for the rebels, from whose hands they expect liberty."[3] Bolívar, after his visit to Haiti, pursued the same policy in Venezuela, arguing that it would be unfair that free men should risk death to achieve freedom from Spain while slaves facing the same risks continued as slaves.

Yet, although he later urged the legislatures of Venezuela and Colombia to abolish slavery altogether, Bolívar had his doubts about Peru, where he thought that "if the principles of liberty are too rapidly introduced, anarchy and destruction of the white inhabitants will be the inevitable consequence."[4] A not uncommon expedient was to promise the abolition of slavery for a future, unspecified date. In 1820 Venezuelan congressmen, referring to black slaves, declared that "given the ignorant and morally degraded state to which this unfortunate portion of humanity has been reduced, it is necessary to make them men before making them citizens."[5] Although they went on to recommend the creation of schools and the education of children to prepare them for eventual emancipation, this congress did not take any effective steps to create such institutions. The booming prosperity of postindependence slave-based economies in Brazil and Cuba and the end of the slave trade tended to exacerbate the exploitation of those slaves already in place, lessening opportunities pointing toward emancipation. And it should be remembered that nowhere in Spanish or Portuguese America did one hear the phrase "free and equal," for freedom was not assumed to mean equality and did not signify citizenship or even social acceptance. Was it precisely the perpetuation of racial inequality that made it possible for dominant groups to accept the freedom of former slaves?

Recruiting slaves in exchange for their freedom not only decreased their number but encouraged measures to free the remainder. Slave numbers shrank dramatically. In Lima and its environs the slave population dropped by 60 percent during the course of the war. Liberal intellectuals in Spanish America, being ideologically committed to emancipation, continued to argue against anything that restricted the initiative of the individual. And, aside from Brazil, the gradual end of slavery was almost invariably one of the aims of leaders in the newly independent countries, even if this goal was only vaguely envisioned or laxly pursued. First, most Spanish American countries declared that all children born after a certain date would be free, although they all required that such a child should continue to serve the mother's master for a fixed term of years. Next, they all ended the African trade in slaves. Slave owners, predictably, objected to the outright abolition of slavery and prevented it from occurring in Argentina, Venezuela, Colombia, and Peru—all with substantial numbers of slaves—until the 1850s. By contrast, Chile declared the end of slavery in 1823, and Mexico ended it in 1829. It is suggestive that Brazil, the major slave-owning country, took no steps like these until 1871, and slavery was not abolished there until 1888, the last country in the western hemisphere to do so. Is it coincidental that Cuba, another place where slave labor formed the backbone of the economy, did not even attempt independence during the period examined in this book? Would it be safe to conclude that the need to control slaves militated against any political upheaval risking social disturbance?

Latin American societies continued to be characterized by the presence of the few very rich and a great mass of poor people, with only a fledgling middle class. For a free enterprise system to really work, it requires a more or less equitable distribution of wealth. Lifting price controls on food, for instance, would hypothetically encourage competition and lead suppliers to increase production, keeping prices down automatically. If, however, only a few own all the land the end of price controls merely encourages hoarding and price gouging. Where there are a limited number of employers labor is helpless to bargain. In this sense, did independence and economic liberalization simply mean that a privileged few increased their power and control?

Finally, the status of women may well have worsened as a result of independence. After the disruptions of the war there was a general effort to return middle- and upper-class women to "their place." Women encountered a heightened emphasis on "morality" and the insistence that a woman's role was in the home. It is important to note, however, that the civil codes drawn up by the newly independent republics tended to perpetuate colonial laws on the family that were generally more favorable to women and female children than that in Britain or the United States. Property was jointly held by wife and husband, daughters inherited equally with sons, and last wills could not be used to pass all property on to a favorite child.

INSTABILITY AND THE CAUDILLO

Independence meant the end of a government long considered legitimate in Spanish America. This result is obvious, yet at the same time of profound significance. In fifteen years the insurgents swept aside a system that had ruled virtually unchallenged for three hundred. During all that time there had been no coups d'état and no barrack revolts. Despite moments of latent anarchy, practically no one had seriously questioned the right of kings to rule or the right of the Bourbons and Braganzas to rule Latin America. At the head of a corporate society, a sovereign's continued reign ensured the legitimacy of the entire social edifice. Now Spanish kings were gone.

The result was like that of removing the flywheel of a machine. Moving at a faster and faster speed, it began to break up: bolts, nuts, springs, and gears flying in all directions. "This is chaos," wrote Bolívar. "Nothing can be done because the good people have disappeared and the bad ones have multiplied. . . . Everything is in a state of ferment and no men can be found for anything."[6] That's because everyone thought they could do it better than anyone else. And for a long time in most Spanish American countries rule by a dictator appeared as the only alternative to anarchy. Forty political revolutions occurred in Peru during the half century following San Martín's arrival, and eight different governments ruled there during 1834 alone. From the death of Bolívar to the end of the nineteenth century, Colombia had an average of one revolution per year and one constitution per decade. The temporary compromise worked out by Iturbide in 1821 between divergent Mexican groups lasted only a few months. Revolts and coups d'état dotted the country's subsequent history until 1854, while constitutions were regularly written, ignored, and rewritten. Throughout Latin America the independence wars threw into question whether the ruled would accept any government's right to rule.

It is also notable that whereas at the beginning of the movement toward independence its leaders were drawn from the professions (lawyers, doctors, priests), by the end almost all were military men. One result was the rule of dictators or caudillos. Generally military leaders — either in the army (greatly enlarged by the wars) or at the head of irregular forces — they came to power by force. They exerted power through personal authority and charisma, counting on personal loyalties to maintain themselves in power, displaying dynamism and shrewdness.

Yet is it not highly significant that virtually all these dictators claimed to be responding to the popular will? They did so by pointing to the support they received from traditional cabildo leaders or newly formed councils in cities or Indian caciques or, more vaguely, "the people." Nor were these dictators, despite their backgrounds, merely military chiefs. Once in power they took pains to fit into the existing legal framework and institute measures to legitimize their actions. They usually appealed to constitutional provisions that granted the executive extraordinary authority in times of danger and threats to public peace. They frequently made sure that legislative bodies endorsed their actions, trying to assert that their rule resulted from the consent of the governed. When they suspended individual rights, they did so, they said, to protect the nation and preserve the whole. They called for elections. These could be and often were rigged, but it was now important to stage this political theater as proof of their right to rule. Theirs was the new political lexicon. And, finally, these strong men did not impose their will single-handedly. They drew on material support from persons or groups who desired a remedy for their grievances or from some particular region that felt neglected, and only rarely on military force alone. In these ways were they not firmly linked to the transformational political culture that characterized this postindependence period?

Caudillos were not typically landowners. With a few exceptions such as Juan Manuel de Rosas of Argentina, they were landless mestizos, dissatisfied with their position and ambitious to rise. With land in the hands of aristocrats, mines owned by foreign investors, commercial activity still controlled by foreigners, and industrial prospects nonexistent, the quickest way to change one's status was to control the government. This had already become a pattern during the wars of independence. Páez, a man of humble background, acquired immense properties as he became the major political figure of Venezuela and remained so until 1863. Can we blame others for following his example?

Diego Portales (1797–1837), who ruled Chile as virtual prime minister during the 1830s until his death, deviated from the general pattern. Portales was no less a caudillo for being a successful businessman. He possessed both the qualities to attract loyalty and the strength of personality to enforce his will. He readily violated what liberals called "individual rights," and exile or imprisonment was the fate of those who opposed him. But not only was he genuinely concerned for the welfare of his country, he managed to institutionalize his power in such a way that stability endured after him. His secret seems to have been to involve the oligarchy directly in power rather than allow them to observe political deal-ings from afar. He virtually replaced the army, for instance, with a nationwide militia commanded by the landowners themselves. Order and progress were the catchwords of his regime. His police put down brigands, enabling entre-preneurs to develop heretofore untouched mineral resources. And conservative intellectuals obligingly wrote a new constitution that called for an exceedingly strong chief executive. As he had earlier put it, his ideal republic would have "a strong centralizing Government, whose members are genuine examples of virtue and patriotism, and [who] thus set the citizens on the straight path of order and the virtues."[7] Eventually liberalism and democracy might have their place, but for now he preferred discipline and hierarchy. In his view the end of the Spanish empire had meant the end of a legitimate order that could be re-constructed only by carefully entwining the interests of the state with those of Creole property owners.

This painful, uncertain search for legitimacy was almost unnecessary in Brazil, where the Braganza dynasty remained in power. When, in 1831, Pedro I abdicated on behalf of his five-year-old son, the Brazilian parliament chose regents who would rule on his behalf, bringing Brazil close to republicanism. Even so, the centrifugal forces of regionalism, the restiveness of the dispossessed, and the breakdown of authority were so great that the boy was hastily crowned as soon as he turned fifteen, in 1840. Subsequently, the regime preserved many of the characteristics of the corporate, hierarchical society and the landed oligarchy found full opportunity to express its political will. Could we say that once a wing of a long-reigning dynasty accepted its "Brazilianness" and came to terms with the Creoles, instability was eliminated and no caudillo found a vacuum of legitimate power into which to move?

INCLUSION IN THE WORLD ECONOMY

Independence, after a period of recovery from the wars, fostered a closer integration of all Latin America into the world economy. Imports from northern Europe and exports sent there multiplied rapidly. This kind of change concomitantly produced an expansion of plantation agriculture and cattle raising to supply the expanding consumption of Europe that accompanied its manufacturing development and urbanization. At the same time the onslaught of cheap imported European manufactured goods destroyed ancient craft industries in many parts of Latin America. Plantations drew more workers into the wage-earning sector, weakening communal village life. The areas that were more closely tied to overseas trade emerged to prominence while old ones declined still further. Argentina and Brazil became the economically dominant areas of South America, ousting Peru from a position it had long held and has never regained.

The opening of the ports was the most concrete example of the new regime. As a British businessman in Buenos Aires recalled in the 1820s:

> On free trade being tolerated by the viceroy in 1808, it was at once seen that the country was in every respect fitted for great commercial improvement; and on being thrown open altogether in 1810, it was very soon carried to an extent altogether unknown in former times: for the barriers of exclusive privilege and monopoly being once thrown down, the commerce of the country advanced at a pace beyond all example.[8]

In Brazil the value of British goods imported directly went from just a little over £1,000 in 1806 to over £3 million in 1818; in Mexico it jumped from £21,000 in

1819 to more than £1 million in 1825; and in Chile it went up ten times between 1817 and 1822. Or, measured another way, the importation of English textiles into Buenos Aires jumped from 3 million yards in 1814 to 15 million ten years later.

As a result of the new direction of the economy, some people gained while others lost out. Monopoly merchants were gone, opening up room for Creoles and foreigners to engage more successfully in trade. The creation of a unified judicial system ended the exclusive power of merchant guilds. And in some places, such as in Buenos Aires province, the dominance of merchants was now replaced by that of ranchers. Argentine governments granted public lands in huge tracts through long-term leases (eventually converted to private property). The gaucho, who had once roamed free, was soon reduced to the status of a peon, circumscribed by laws against vagabondage and forced into a position of deference and humility before the ranch owner.

The new trading relationships with overseas nations deeply affected commercial patterns, for exports were no longer funneled through a parasitic mother country. In 1820 Mexico shipped practically all its exports to Spain, while three years later only a tenth of its exports went there. Independence ruptured the old family connections between the Iberian merchants in the colonies and their relatives in Spain and Portugal. Overseas trade quickly became the specialty of the British, who had the necessary contacts with suppliers of manufactured goods and relied on a large merchant marine. Just eight months after the opening of Brazilian ports, 150 British traders had installed themselves in Rio de Janeiro. As well, many Spanish and Portuguese merchants were driven out of Latin America by sporadic and violent mobs that targeted their counting houses, as happened in Chile as early as 1812, in Brazil beginning in 1824, and in Mexico in 1827 and 1829. Evidently, the new nationalism had its drawbacks.

The news of the final defeat of Spanish armies in 1824–1825 led London investors immediately to speculate in fly-by-night mining companies designed to exploit the fabled riches of Spanish America from Mexico to Bolivia. Some £3 million were invested in such ventures during this bubble. But neither the welcoming governments nor the investing community was mature enough at that time to overcome the challenges presented by Latin American terrain, climate, and precarious transportation networks, and investors lost their shirts. Almost every new government in Latin America managed to float large loans in Britain, on which they later defaulted. It was only later in the nineteenth century that British investors in mines, plantations, and railroad companies came to play a large role in Latin American economies. British merchants, however, formed a highly visible and continuous presence from the 1820s on. Was this better than the previous pattern when Spanish merchant houses were in control?

Liberal principles, imported from Europe, undergirded many changes in economic life. The simplification of the tax structure is a good example. Instead of monopoly contracts, Indian tributes, internal trade barriers, special taxes to finance the operation of various corporations like the merchant guild, and multiple rates on different articles of trade, the tendency was now toward the creation of relatively uniform duties on imported goods, intended not as protective tariffs but as sources of revenue. This became the principal financial basis for government. The simultaneous but more gradual adoption of laissez-faire practices, that is, the removal of government restrictions on economic activity, also resulted from the new ideology. Much later such practices came to be identified with conservatism since they ignored the needs of the mass of people, who seldom benefited from them, but in the first half of the nineteenth century they were seen as radical innovations and hailed by those who fostered change. Could reformers have been expected to understand that when superimposed on the still remaining hierarchical and elitist traditions these policies could mean merciless exploitation? Should historical actors in general be judged according to what we now know but they did not?

The cost was high. Fifteen years of warfare with its human and material losses left a taste for revenge and a heritage of violence. But as wars do, securing independence created a changed political culture, in this case more focused on individuals and less on the corporate bodies to which people once belonged. Despite sharpened class divisions and the erosion of ancient protections for the disadvantaged, politics was now the people's business. It was possible to envision personal empowerment and to see oneself as someone with rights. Although women—even those who participated in the struggle—gained little and Indians lost out overall, for everyone there was now an altered mentality. Slaves in Spanish America had emancipation firmly in their sights, albeit delayed for so many. Governments struggled to assert their right to rule, but even caudillos seemed to acknowledge in words if not in deeds that they did so on behalf of the people. And certainly Latin America had been swept more firmly into the vortex of the world economy. Indeed some of the subsequent adversities faced by Latin Americans emerged precisely from this fact, as well as from the incompatibility of Enlightenment principles with older, entrenched values, and from the unresolved social tensions that surfaced at the time of independence. But is there any doubt that this had been an epoch of major and extremely rapid change in aspirations, coalitions, and outcomes?

Documents

DOCUMENT 1: MARIANO MORENO ADVOCATES FREEDOM OF
TRADE, 1809 (SEE PP. 35, 74)

(SEE PP. 35, 74)

A Petition From Ranchers: . . . There are truths so obvious that it insults the intelligence to attempt to prove them. Such is the proposition that this country should freely import the goods which it does not produce or possess and export its own abundant products which are being wasted for lack of outlet. Those who believe that an abundance of foreign goods is bad for a country are ignorant of the first principles of political economy. Nothing is more advantageous for a country than an abundance of the goods which it does not itself produce, for this lowers value and price, to the benefit of the consumers, and is harmful only to the importers. If an excessive importation of English cloth were to produce oversupply in this line of goods, these prices would fall and the trade would turn to other lines. Is it not better for the country that its inhabitants can buy for three pesos a cloth which previously cost eight or obtain two pairs of pants for the price of one?

To the advantage of importing foreign goods may be added the benefit the country will derive from exporting its own produce. This province is fortunate in having agricultural products which are much esteemed, reliable, and essential. How rapidly our agriculture could grow if the ports were open to all our exportable products and the farmer could rely on a profitable sale! Those who now hesitate to undertake farming because of the uncertainty of the market would then work with a vigor inspired by certain profit, so increasing the wealth of the producers and the revenue of the royal treasury.

These plains produce annually a million hides, without counting other skins, tallow, and grains, all of which are valuable to the foreign merchant. But our warehouses are full, for there is no opportunity of an active export; the result is an immense stock which ties up the capital of our merchants and prevents them from making new purchases. So the landowners are left with produce which they cannot sell at a good price for lack of export or buyers; in this way they are reduced to their present sorry state and forced to abandon an occupation which does not repay them for their labor and costs. Freedom to export will generate a rapid turnover, activate production, and bring new products into the market; profits will improve, agriculture will flourish, and trade will pick up as the wealth of producers increases.

Freedom of trade in America has been proscribed not as a real evil but as a sacrifice that the metropolis demands of its colonies. Well known is the history of that exclusive commerce and its development until it degenerated into a total monopoly of the Cádiz merchants. Enlightened opinion denounced a system so weak, so ruinous, and so ill-judged. But deep-seated evils cannot be cured in an instant. Minor reforms were preparing the way for a new system founded on sounder principles when the recent extraordinary events undermined the political state of Spain and destroyed by unforeseen blows all the pretexts on which the prohibitory laws had been based. . . .

Is it just that the valuable products of our agriculture should perish and waste because the unfortunate provinces of Spain cannot consume them? Is it just that the abundant produce of the country should lie rotting in warehouses because we no longer have the ships to export them? . . . Is it right that when the subjects of a friendly and generous nation appear in our ports and offer at a cheap rate the goods that we need and which Spain cannot supply, we should reject that proposal and allow a few enterprising merchants to capture the market by means of a contraband trade? . . . It is one of the fatal consequences of contraband that the importer is compelled to take payment in cash. It is true that his real interest lies in taking the return in goods which can lead to further business, but the risks involved in ignoring so strict a prohibition force him to sacrifice these advantages in preference to the greater security which exports in money offer over the exports of bulky commodities. So the merchant is deprived of further profit and the country of opportunities to export its products. . . .

"The provinces of the interior will be ruined." The agent of the merchant guild makes this dire prediction, going so far as to suggest that their ties with us are at risk. . . . The textiles of our provinces will not decline through free trade, because the English will never supply cloth as cheap and as serviceable. Therefore, the demand that clothing, furniture, coaches, and other articles be prohibited is an unacceptable constraint. A country that is beginning to prosper cannot be deprived of fine and elegant furniture, for which there will be increasing demand. If our artisans were able to make articles as good, they ought to be preferred, even though the foreigner would be unable to compete. But it would not be right to deprive the consumer of choice of good furniture simply because our artisans are not committed to excellence. It is scandalous that in Buenos Aires a pair of well-made boots costs twenty pesos. Fine furniture and other manufactures should all be allowed importation. If they are inferior to local manufactures then no harm is done; if they are superior they will invite comparison and force our artisans to improve their work and offer competition. In any case prices will come down to the benefit of artisans as well as consumers.

The interests whom I represent make the following requests: That free trade be granted for a term of two years, with possibility of renewal by the supreme junta. That the right of export be open to anyone by the simple fact of being a native of the kingdom, together with free choice of sales methods. And that all importers be obliged to take half their return in agricultural products of the country.

From "Representación de los hacendados por el Apoderado de los Labradores y Hacendados de la Banda Oriental y Occidental del Río de la Plata," September 30, 1809. Originally abridged and translated by John Lynch in *Latin American Revolutions, 1808–1826: Old and New World Origins*, ed. John Lynch (Norman: University of Oklahoma Press, 1994), 138–142 (excerpts only).

DOCUMENT 2: RACE PREJUDICE AT A CITY COUNCIL, 1795 (SEE PP. 18, 42)

The pardos and mulattos . . . are descended from Negro slaves. . . . In addition to their infamous origin, they are also dishonored by their illegitimacy, for if they are not themselves bastards, their parents almost certainly are. And it is also likely that they have fathers, grandfathers, or near relatives who are slaves at the present time, in some cases with local white families. One can see in the streets a pardo or mulatto illegally dressed as a white and he has a brother who is still a slave. Another may put on a great show of wealth yet also have nephews and relatives who are slaves.

May it please Your Majesty to consider these questions: Is it acceptable that the white residents and native-born people of this country should admit into their class, to mix with them, a mulatto descended from their own slaves or from those of their parents, a mulatto whose relatives are still slaves, a mulatto whose birth is defaced by illegitimacy and related blemishes? Is it possible to ignore complaints when public order is threatened and Spanish rule itself is placed at risk? . . .

The basic requisite for retaining this part of Your Majesty's dominions is the loyalty of the resident and American-born Spaniards who, as they are married and have their property here, seek to live in peace and in the religion and obedience in which they were born. All they ask in return is that Your Majesty maintain them in the honor and tradition of their ancestors, saving them from the outrage of mixing with pardos, seeing them promoted, having them as equals, and experiencing the consequent disorder and corruption of society. . . .

The fact remains that pardos [because the king, in exchange for a very high fee, allows them to change their racial/social legal category], are now granted access to the education that they have hitherto lacked and ought to continue to lack, and this is accomplished simply by means of dispensation from their inferior status. Soon classes will be swarming with mulatto students; they will try to enter the seminary; they will succeed in obtaining city-council positions; they will gain public offices and treasury posts; and they will be involved in all the public and private business of the province. The result will be resentment and retreat on the part of white and decent people and, while the pardos will be encouraged by their greater numbers, the whites will face disappointment and contempt. Those families who conquered and settled this province and paid for it with their lives and labor will be finished. Loyal subjects who have preserved with their loyalty the rule of the kings of Spain will be forever forgotten. . . .

Is it really the intention of Your Majesty to place confidence and security in the hands of men who, far from looking to Spain as the center of their interests, keep their eyes on the [enslaved] dark people of Africa (which is where they come from) to patronize them and raise them against the Spaniards, the authors — so they say — of all their grievances? . . . Could people of African origin do better for Spain than those of Spanish origin? Who is so mistaken as to believe that the pardos do not favor the blacks, through whom they are flawed, and hate the whites, to whose class they aspire only to insult and slight them? The mulattos look to the blacks with affection, to the whites with disgust. . . .

These, then, are the pardos, some of them sunk in poverty and consequent idleness, others occupied as blacksmiths, carpenters, silversmiths, tailors, masons, shoemakers, butchers, slaughtermen, and other trades. These can work how and when they please, they can set their own prices, and they can deceive everyone. . . . The pardo artisans do not contribute the slightest amount from their earnings to the royal treasury, the city revenue, or any other institution. Nor are they assessed for any charge or tax because the whole weight of taxation falls on agriculture and commerce. In this way the mulattos and pardos of the province (except one or two rare cases who have farm lands and live honestly from agriculture or trade) live in the greatest comfort and freedom in their small houses, working only as long as necessary for that day's bread and declining other jobs because they consider it beneath themselves to farm the land or to work for landowners. . . . And even those who are not employees, but undertake to work for a day-wage are so dishonest, crooked, and arrogant that they abandon work, make off with the advances made to them by hacendados, and leave the crops to rot and agriculture and commerce to suffer. This is a daily occurrence. . . .

The mulattos of this province, then, enjoy the benefits of society without contributing a farthing to its revenues and finances or to its public and charitable institutions, in spite of the fact that they are twice as numerous as the whites. This has come about because the laws regulating the conduct of mulattos, making them contribute, and ordering them to pay a moderate tax to the treasury, are completely ignored, either because officials are unaware of their existence or indifferent to their application. . . . They should be obliged to work on the land, to abandon their life of idleness in the cities, to improve their trades and place an official price on their products, and on all occasions to curb their arrogance.

> From "Informe que el ayuntamiento de Caracas hace al rey de España referente a la real cédula de 10 de febrero de 1795," abridged and translated by John Lynch in *Latin American Revolutions, 1808–1826: Old and New World Origins*, ed. John Lynch (Norman: University of Oklahoma Press, 1994), 182–187 (excerpts, with minor changes for the sake of clarity in the present context).

DOCUMENT 3: LAND REFORM IN URUGUAY, 1815 (SEE P. 78)

(SEE P. 78)

José Gervasio Artigas: Provisional Regulation for Land Development and the Security of Landowners:

1. The Provincial Alcalde, in addition to his other duties is hereby authorized to dis-

tribute land and keep watch over the peace of the citizenry, being the judge of first instance in all issues raised by this regulation.

2. Given the vast extent of these lands he may appoint three provincial lieutenants determining their jurisdiction and granting them authority in accordance with this regulation. . . .

6. For now the Provincial Alcalde and his subordinates will dedicate themselves to peopling the countryside with active workers. To this end each one will, within their respective jurisdictions, examine the lands that are available [for distribution] and the men worthy of receiving this benefit, making sure that those who are most needy shall be the most privileged. Therefore, free blacks, mulattos, Indians, and poor creoles may all receive the benefit of land if, with their work and upright behavior, they contribute to their own well being and that of the Province.

7. Poor widows shall also be favored if they have children. As well, married men will be preferred over single Americans and these over any foreigner. . . .

11. Once in possession, the recipients shall be obliged by the Provincial Alcalde and his subordinates to set up a lean-to and two corrals within two months. Those who fail to do so shall be warned and given one more month. If the same failure occurs again, the land shall be given to another more industrious resident, to benefit the Province.

12. The lands that can be distributed are all those belonging to those who have left the country [and] to bad Europeans and worse Americans who by that date have not been pardoned by the Chief of the Province in order to secure their former properties.

13. Also available for distribution are all those lands that may have been sold or given away by the government of the province between 1810 and 1815 when Uruguayan forces entered Montevideo.

14. Within this class of lands [as specified in Art. 13] there shall be the following exception if they were given or sold to Uruguayans or foreigners: if lands were given or sold to the former they shall be entitled to keep one piece of land as specified [below] in this regulation; if to the latter, all their land is available [for distribution].

15. In dividing up the land of Europeans and bad Americans, take into account whether they are married or single. Of the latter, all their lands are available [for distribution]. Of the former, take into account the number of their children. So that these shall not be harmed, they shall be given enough so that they can maintain themselves hereafter. The remainder would be available, if they have still more land.

16. The pieces of land to be granted will be one and a half league [i.e., six miles] along a road and two leagues deep, with the understanding that these lands may be larger or smaller depending on their location. Every plot will share water and, if the place allows it, a permanent boundary. The effort of the commissioners will be to economize land as much as possible and avoid later animosities between residents.

17. The government, the Provincial Alcalde, and his subordinates shall be vigilant to make sure that the beneficiaries do not acquire more than one estancia; [except that] those who have only a garden plot may be granted another lot. Americans may also be granted another piece of land if they want to move and give up the one they have for the benefit of the Province. . . .

19. The recipients of estancias may not alienate or sell their land, nor contract loans

secured by it, which will be null and void, until formally authorized by the Province which will decide what is appropriate....

22. To facilitate the prosperity of the recipients, the Provincial Alcalde and his three subordinates are the only ones authorized to allow recipients within their jurisdictions to come together and remove animals—cows or horses—from the estancias of Europeans or bad Americans. Under no circumstances may they do so themselves: They will always be accompanied by an ordinary judge or another commissioned person so that the large estates not be destroyed in the rush and so that what is taken be distributed equally. As well, the Provincial Alcalde and his subordinates shall take care that the livestock so distributed not be used for any other purpose except to tame them, castrate them, and round them up.

> From "Reglamento provisorio de la Provincia Oriental para el fomento de su campaña y seguridad de sus hacendados," September 10, 1815, Archivo General de la Nación, Montevideo (ex Archivo General Administrativo), Livro 490, fols. 6 et seq., in Lucía Sala de Touron, Nelson de la Torre, and Julio C. Rodríguez, *Artigas y su revolución agraria, 1811–1820* (Mexico City: Siglo Veintiuno, 1978), 151–156. Translated by Richard Graham.

DOCUMENT 4: JOSÉ MARÍA MORELOS SETS OUT PRINCIPLES FOR GOOD GOVERNMENT, 1813 (SEE P. 97 [CH. IV, P. 25])

[Minutes of a Meeting:] In the town of Chilpancingo on September 14th 1813, at the parish [church], Captain-General José María Morelos, [other officials], and all the electors present having gathered for the purpose of choosing a representative for the province of Tecpan, ... and the Captain-General, having delivered a brief and energetic speech on the nation's need for a body of wise men who desire its well-being, ... I read a paper written by the General, the title of which is "The Sense of the Nation," in which are laid out his principal ideas for ending the war and the foundations of a future Constitution.... [signed] Juan Nepomuceno Rosáinz, Secretary.

The Sense of the Nation

1. That America is free and independent from Spain or any other nation, government, or monarchy and that it be so ratified, presenting its rights to the world.

2. That the Catholic religion will be the only one, without tolerance for any other....

5. That sovereignty springs directly from the people, who wish to entrust it to the Supreme National American Congress, made up of representatives of the provinces proportionally.

6. That the Legislative, Executive, and Judical powers shall be distributed to suitable agencies to exercise them....

9. That [public] employment be limited to Americans.

10. That no foreigners be admitted [to public employment] unless they are artisans who can teach and are under no suspicion [of disloyalty].

11. That . . . the homeland will not be fully free and ours until the Government is reformed, knocking down the tyrannical government, substituting a liberal one, and also expelling from our land the Spanish enemy who have so often declared themselves to be against our homeland.

12. That, as good laws are above every man, those enacted by our Congress ought to be those that call for perseverance and patriotism, lessen both opulence and indigence, and increase the daily wage of the poor in order to improve their habits, eliminating ignorance, stealing, and robbery. . . .

15. That slavery be abolished forever, as well as any distinctions between castes, making everyone equal, so that the only distinction among Americans will be their vice or virtue.

16. That our ports be opened to friendly foreign nations. . . .

17. That each person's property shall be protected, and in his house he shall be respected as in a sacred refuge. . . .

18. That torture shall not be tolerated in our new laws.

19. That our Constitution shall establish that December 12 be celebrated in all our towns and cities, as dedicated to the Patroness of our Liberty, Our Holy Lady María de Guadalupe. . . .

22. That the infinite number of head taxes, property taxes, and fees that oppress us be abolished and that there should be set for every individual [a charge of] 5 percent on his seeds or other possessions or another similar light charge, that would not be so oppressive as the sales tax, trade monopoly, head tax, and other [present-day] taxes. . . .

> From Acta de la sesión de apertura del Congreso and Versión original de los "Sentimientos de la Nación" . . . leído por su secretario en la apertura del Congreso, both dated September 14, 1813, in Ernesto Lemoine Villicaña, *Morelos: Su vida revolucionaria a través de sus escritos y de otros testimonios de la época* (Mexico City: Universidad Nacional Autónoma de México, 1965), 370–374 (excerpts). Translated by Richard Graham.

DOCUMENT 5: PRAISE FOR MARÍA LEONA VICARIO, 1813
(SEE P. 98 [CH. IV, P. 26])

December 22, 1813
Señora Doña María Leona Vicario
  In a report at today's session [of the National Assembly in the National Palace in Chilpancingo], the most excellent Sr. don Ignacio Rayón presented an official letter from the most serene Sr. don José María Morelos, Generalíssimo of the National Armies of Northern America, dated the 11th of this month from his camp at Necupétaro, conveying to you [María Leona Vicario], among other things, that it had been very satisfying for him to learn that the governor of Oaxaca, Coronel don Benito Rocha, had authorized the payment to you of five hundred pesos, and would have now granted a comparable monthly payment were he not completely unaware of matters that concern

the treasury, adding that he did not believe the Supreme Congress, which has oversight of such matters, would refuse to authorize such [a payment].

The statement of Sr. don Rayón was then distributed, referring to the actions which, in his judgment, make you well deserving of the country's recompense, and more so than anyone else. Then, speaking fully and with noble simplicity, he confirmed this judgment and extraordinarily aroused the sentiments of the other most excellent members [of the congress]. The account of your actions was not news to them, and they knew how much the nation owes to you for having sacrificed your valuable estate and your native soil for its liberty. You risked persecution, traveling on long and dangerous routes, facing misery, and [undertaking] imponderable labor with a perseverance that serves as a model not only to those of your sex but also to the most valiant men.

> From *El Ateneo Mexicano* (Mexico City: Imprenta de Vicente G. Torres, 1844), 406, in Ernesto Lemoine Villicaña, *Morelos: Su vida revolucionaria a través de sus escritos y de otros testimonios de la época* (Mexico City: Universidad Nacional Autónoma de México, 1965), 445–446. Translated by Richard Graham.

DOCUMENT 6: A SPANISH GENERAL BEMOANS INSURGENTS'
STRENGTH, 1813 (SEE P. 98 [CH. IV, P. 26])

To the Minister of War:

I told you in my last report dated the 5th of September . . . about the measures I had taken to begin the campaign against the rebel Morelos . . . to compel him to lift the siege of Acapulco. . . . The unexpected news that Acapulco had surrendered [to Morelos] . . . changed the look of things to the point that, if it does not frustrate all my measures, it at least leads to a long delay in their execution. The consequences of that surrender, together with the less than favorable [outcome] of military events in Puebla province, have led that rebel to go back to Chilpancingo, which is now his capital, reinforced with the weapons and artillery he took from Acapulco. There he has held a council of deputies from a number of towns that name him Supreme Chief of the American Nation. He has extended his front lines close to Puebla, a city which he threatens with the sizable troops that have joined him, having moved from Oaxaca province with their major leaders, and also [threatens] this capital city by way of Izúcar and Cuautla, towns not too far from it. He simultaneously maintains a respectable force in Chilpancingo, which he has fortified. . . . I find my plans for the present campaign foiled, consequently delaying the recovery of Oaxaca and Acapulco, which would have had a major impact on public opinion and the restoration of order in these lands.

I have said on another occasion, and I repeat, that in this kind of war, supported and sustained by the spirit and desires of six million inhabitants, all ready to defend their independence, where the king's few troops are scattered over hundreds of leagues, [we are] in the same situation and worse circumstances as the French armies in the [Iberian] Peninsula. . . . The troops coming from the Peninsula, now reduced to half strength by the unhealthful season in which they arrived in Veracruz and the long time that they were retained there, alongside those from here [Mexico], diminished by desertions, by the appeal [of the enemy], and by the perpetual fatigue of a campaign in which many die or are disabled, suffer losses that cannot be replaced by the measures available to me of relying on vagrants and convicts. . . .

Our enemies, meanwhile, everywhere increase and find voluntary and enthusiastic soldiers with which to fill their columns. They receive prompt and generous help from the towns that shelter and hide them when they suffer defeats, so they can once again form new corps with which they constantly wear out our divisions. The [tactics and strategy of] war that they learn from us are making them ever wiser and bolder. If one adds to this their number, it won't be long before the outcome of this contest will no longer be in doubt, being unfavorable to our cause. . . .

(signed) Félix María Calleja

From "Deprimente informe de Calleja al Ministro de la Guerra," October 5, 1813, in Ernesto Lemoine Villicaña, *Morelos: Su vida revolucionaria a través de sus escritos y de otros testimonios de la época* (Mexico City: Universidad Nacional Autónoma de México, 1965), 385–390 (excerpts). Translated by Richard Graham.

DOCUMENT 7: SIMÓN BOLÍVAR'S "LETTER FROM JAMAICA," 1815 (SEE P. 111 [CH. V, P. 7])

I have now the honor of replying to your letter . . . and feel most gratefully impressed by the lively interest you have been kind enough to take in the cause of my country, evidenced by the concern you express for the misfortunes with which she has been oppressed by the Spaniards from the period of her discovery even to the present day. . . . If justice be allowed to determine the contests of men, success will crown our efforts. Doubt it not: The destiny of America is irrevocably fixed. . . . More vast is our hatred for the Peninsula than the ocean which separates her from us; less difficult is it to join the two continents than to conciliate the two countries. . . . The veil is at length removed: Although she wished to keep us in darkness, we have seen light. We have been already free! Do our enemies then contemplate on reenslaving us? We are now contending for our liberty with enthusiasm. . . .

Let us cast our eyes around and we shall see, throughout the whole extent of this immense hemisphere, a simultaneous struggle. The warlike disposition of the Río [de la] Plata provinces has cleared that territory and their victorious arms have reached Peru and Cuzco, disturbed Arequipa, and put in alarm the royalists of Lima. . . . New Granada, which may be considered the heart of South America, obeys its [own] general government, excepting the kingdom of Quito which with difficulty restrains its enemies. . . . With respect to the heroic but unhappy Venezuela, her disasters have been so numerous and have occurred with such rapidity that she is now almost reduced to a state of absolute want and of dejected misery. . . . The islands of Puerto Rico and Cuba

... are the places of which the Spaniards keep possession with the smallest difficulty, as they are not within the immediate influence of the independents. But are they not American? Are they not wronged? Will they not desire their emancipation? ...

This momentous subject, presents an enormous military scene two thousand leagues in length and nine hundred in breadth in which sixteen millions of human creatures are either defending their rights or bowing under the oppression of the Spanish government which formerly possessed the most extensive empire in the universe, but is now, not only too impotent to rule the new world, but insufficient to maintain itself in the old! ... What madness it is for our enemy to suppose that we are to be reconquered by a nation without a navy, without money, without soldiery! ... Besides, can a nation like Spain ... monopolize to herself the exclusive trade of one-half of the world? ...

It is still more difficult to divine what will be the fate of the new world, to establish any principles with respect to its politics, and to predict what nature or kind of government it will ultimately adopt. ... Who has ventured to say, such a nation shall be a republic; another a monarchy; this shall be small; that great? ... I shall, however, make bold to offer some conjectures. ...

The Americans, under the Spanish system[,] ... occupy no other place in society than that of brutes for labor; at best, that of simple consumers, clogged with oppressive restrictions. For example, the prohibition of [manufacturing] all European productions; the forestalling of the articles which the King monopolizes; the nonadmission [even] of manufactures which the Peninsula herself does not possess; the exclusion of commerce, even to articles of the first necessity; the obstacles put between provinces, to keep them from intercourse and commerce. ... So negative is our condition that I can find nothing equal to it in any other civilized society: ... We are never governors nor viceroys; ... archbishops and bishops very seldom; diplomatists never; military officers only as subalterns; no magistrates, no financiers, and indeed scarcely merchants! From what I have said it is easy to infer that America was not prepared to separate from the mother country so suddenly as she did, owing to the effect of those illegitimate cessions [to Napoleon] at Bayonne ... and by the unprovoked war that the [Spanish] Regency unjustly declared against us.

The Americans have risen suddenly, without any previous knowledge and, what is still more remarkable, without any acquaintance with public business which is so essentially necessary for the accomplishment of all political undertaking. I say, they have suddenly advanced to the dignified eminence of representative legislators, magistrates, commissioners of the national treasury, diplomatists, generals, and all the authorities, both high and low, which are necessary to form the hierarchy of a state organized with regularity. ...

The occurrences in Terra Firma [northern South America] have proved to us that institutions [that are] purely representative are not adequate to our character, customs, and understandings. In Caracas the spirit of party took its origin in those societies, assemblies, and popular elections. And those parties advanced us to a state of servitude. And thus Venezuela, which has been the republic among us most advanced in its political establishments, affords us a striking example of the inefficacy of a democratical and federal system of government in our unsettled condition. In New Granada the excessive authority of the provincial governments and the want of vigor and capacity in the general officer have reduced that beautiful country to the state in which we now see her. For this reason civil war has always raged there and her enemies have maintained themselves against all probability. Until our patriots acquire those talents and political virtues which distinguish our North American brethren, I am very much afraid that our popular systems, far from being favorable to us, will occasion our ruin; for, unhappily for us, these good qualities appear to be very distant from us in their requisite perfection, whilst we are infected with the vices contracted under the dominion of the Spanish nation.

The inhabitants of this continent have shown a desire to form liberal and even perfect institutions, no doubt from the influence of that instinct which all men possess of aspiring to the greatest possible happiness and which can only be obtained in those civil societies founded on the grand basis of justice, liberty, and equality. But shall we be able to maintain on its true equilibrium the difficult charge of a republic? Is it to be conceived that a people but just released from their chains can fly at once into the sphere of liberty? . . . These American States require the care of paternal governments [so] that the sores and wounds inflicted by despotism and war may be healed. . . .

I am not favorable to the opinion of American monarchies, and I will give my reasons. The interest of a republic, when well understood, is confined to preservation, prosperity, and glory. . . . No stimulus excites republicans to extend their boundaries to the sacrifice of their means or for the sole purpose of inducing their neighbors to participate in a liberal constitution. They acquire no right, no advantage by conquests. . . . Very different is the policy of a king, whose constant attention is directed to the augmentation of his possessions, his riches, and his prerogatives. And rightly enough, for his authority increases with these acquisitions as much with respect to his neighbors as to his own subjects who fear in him a power as formidable as his empire which is preserved by war and conquests. For these reasons I think that the Americans, desirous of peace, sciences, arts, commerce, and agriculture, would prefer republics to monarchies. . . . I do not approve of a federal system between popularity and representation, as it is too perfect and requires virtues and political talents which we do not possess. For the same reason I disapprove of a monarchy composed of aristocracy and democracy which has raised England to fortune and splendor. Not being able, amongst republics and monarchies to select a perfect and accommodating system, we contented ourselves with not admitting any dogmatical anarchies or oppressive tyrannies, and sought a medium between the two extremes which would alike conduct us to dishonor and unhappiness. I will explain the result of my speculations as to the best fate which can attend America — not perhaps the best, but that which will be most acceptable to her. . . .

From the situation, riches, population and character of the Mexicans, I imagine they will first establish a representative republic, in which the executive branch will possess great power, which will be centered in an individual, who, if he discharge his functions with diligence and justice, it is natural to suppose will preserve a durable authority. If his incapacity or violent administration should excite any popular commotion that may prove successful, the very executive power will disperse. . . . If the more powerful party should be military or aristocratical they would probably found a monarchy, which at first might be constitutional and limited, but which would inevitably afterwards decline into an unlimited one. For it must be admitted that there is nothing more difficult in political order than the preservation of a mixed monarchy and it is equally true that none but a patriotic nation like the English can submit to the authority of a king and maintain the spirit of liberty under the dominion of a scepter and a crown.

New Granada will unite with Venezuela if they agree in the form of a central republic. . . . This government will imitate the English with this distinction, that in place of a king, they will have an executive power which will be elective, perhaps during life, but certainly not hereditary; an hereditary legislative senate or house which in tempestuous times may interpose between the commotions of the people and the acts of the government; and a legislative body called by the free elective franchise and without any other restrictions than those imposed on the English House of Commons. . . . As this is my native country, I have an incontestable right to wish her what, in my opinion, may be most to her advantage. It is possible that New Granada may not agree in the recognition of a central government, as she is extremely partial to federalism. In such case she may perhaps establish a state by herself. . . .

We know very little of the opinion which prevail in Buenos Aires, Chile, and Peru. . . . Peru . . . is afflicted with two things which are enemies to all just and liberal regimen: gold and slavery. The first corrupts everything, the second is corrupted by itself. . . . The higher classes in Lima would not tolerate democracy; nor the slaves and freedmen an aristocracy. . . . I am very much afraid that the Peruvians will scarcely succeed in their efforts to recover their independence.

From all that has been said, we may be led to the following conclusions: The American provinces are now struggling for emancipation. They will in the end be successful. Some will be constituted in a regular manner as federal or central republics. The extensive territories will undoubtedly found monarchies. . . .

Happily the promoters of Mexican independence have availed themselves of the current fanaticism with the greatest activity by proclaiming the celebrated virgin of Guadalupe as queen of the patriots, invoking her in all their sacred appeals, and representing her on their standards. By these means political enthusiasm has become united with religion, and has produced a most vehement ardor for the sacred cause of liberty. . . .

I will tell you what will enable us to expel the Spaniards and to found a free government. Unity to be sure; but that unity is not to be effected by supernatural prodigies, but by energetic measures and well-directed efforts. . . . We shall then follow that majestic march towards the grand state of prosperity which is destined for America. . . .

Such, Sir, are the observations and thoughts which I have the honor of submitting to you. . . .

> I am, &c, &c,
> Simón Bolívar

Excerpts from "General Bolívar's Letter to a Friend on the Subject of South-American Independence, Jamaica, September 6, 1815," in *Jamaica Quarterly Journal and Literary Gazette* 3, no. 1 (September 1819): 162–174 (with minor alterations in punctuation and the modernization or Americanization of spelling).

DOCUMENT 8: TWO LETTERS FROM MANUELA SÁENZ TO
BOLÍVAR, 1822 AND 1828 (SEE P. 115 [CH. V, P. 10])

(1) Quito, December 30, 1822

My incomparable friend:

In your welcome letter of the 22nd you reveal the interest you take in the tasks with which I am charged. I thank you for this, although you merit it even more because you have taken my present situation into account. If I have always been grateful when we were together, how much more now that you are more than sixty leagues from here.

The triumph of Yacuanquer [where Sucre won a battle, opening the way for a decisive victory over opponents in Pasto] cost me a lot. Now you will say that I am not a patriot, for what I am about to say: I would rather have triumphed with you than have ten such victories as that in Pasto.

I imagine you as being very bored in that village; but, no matter how anxious you are, you are not more so than is your best friend, namely,

Manuela

(2) Bogotá, March 28, 1828

Dear Sir,

In the last mail I said nothing to you about Cartagena so as not to speak of unpleasant things. Now I do it to congratulate you because it did not turn out as they wanted it to: another thing Santander has done, not believing it enough for us to execute him. God willing, all the ill-intentioned persons would die who are called Paula, Padilla, Páez [Paula Santander, José Prudencio Padilla, and José Antonio Páez] — and with regard to this last one I always suspect something. It would be a great day for Colombia the day in which these villains would die. It is these and others who are killing with their wickedness. . . . This is the more humane thought: That 10 may die to save millions.

I enclose these two letters from Quito, and I believe it my duty to tell you that this Sr. Torres is a very honorable man and our good friend. If you do it, I will be content, but also if you do not, because . . . you well know that I have never spoken to you except on behalf of deserters and those condemned to death. When you have pardoned them I have thanked you in my heart without making a big point of it; when you have not pardoned them I have forgiven it and felt it without complaint. And I know well how much I can do for a friend, and certainly never endanger the man whom I most idolize.

Goodbye. For five days I have been in bed with fever which I thought was *tabardillo*, but it has broken and I now am only a little warm but have a very sore throat. It is all I can do to write.

Yours,
Manuela

From Vicente Lecuna, ed., "Cartas de mujeres," *Boletín de la Academia Nacional de la Historia* 26, no. 62 (April–July 1933): 332, 335. Courtesy of Pamela S. Murray. Translated by Richard Graham.

DOCUMENT 9: VICENTE GUERRERO ON INDEPENDENCE, 1821
(SEE P. 126 [CH. V, P. 19])

[To Agustín de Iturbide, Dear Sir:] When we heard of the meeting of the
Cortes in Spain we believed they would end our misfortunes by granting us justice; but
our hopes were in vain because with painful disillusion we experienced effects which
were much opposed to what we had been promised. What can we say? When Spain was
in agony [in 1810–1812], when it was oppressed to the limit by a powerful enemy and at
the point of being lost forever, when it most needed our help for its regeneration . . . then
they unveiled all the damage and the disdain which they always felt toward the Americans. Then they declared their great pride and tyranny. Then they violently reproached
the humble and just requests of our Representatives. Then they laughed at us and completely committed themselves to their iniquity. They did not concede to us equal representation, nor stop referring to us by the infamous name of "colonists," even after having
declared that the Americas are an integral part of the Monarchy. This is horrifying conduct, so contrary to natural, divine, and human law.

And what's the remedy? It should be equal to so much evil. We lost our last hope
and, caught between ignominy and death, we chose the latter and shouted "Independence and eternal hate for that hard people." We declared it to the whole world in our
newspapers; and although unfortunate, the effects have corresponded to our desires. We
are animated by a noble resignation, and we have promised before the altar of the living
God to offer our existence in sacrifice — or triumph and give life to our brothers.

You are one of our brothers, and you are hardly ignorant of all that I have said. Do
you believe that those who in that epoch spoke of liberty and declared us slaves, will
help us now that they have achieved their own liberty and are no longer hampered by
the war? There is no reason to be persuaded that they are so humane. You have many
proofs in view, and although the passage of time may have made you forget the shame-
ful life [lived by] our elders, you cannot be ignorant of the events of these last days. You
know that the King identifies our cause with that of the Peninsula because the havoc of
war in both hemispheres has made him understand the general will of the people. But
see how the people's leaders are rewarded in this hemisphere, and the infamy to which
he wishes to reduce their leaders in that hemisphere. Do tell, what cause can justify the
disdain with which are seen the demands of the Americans on innumerable political
points, and in particular the lack of representation in the Cortes? What benefit results
for the People when being a "citizen" requires so many qualities that most Americans
cannot attain it?

And last, and this would be a lengthy subject, I could provide many facts which
would leave no doubt about it. But I do not want to be so bothersome, because you already know these truths and know that [at a time] when all the Nations of the Universe
are Independent from each other, governed by their own sons, only America depends
demeaningly on Spain, despite being worthy of occupying the best place in the universal
theater. Man's dignity is great, but the Europeans have not known how to respect it, nor
shown respect for whatever the Americans own. And what honor remains for us if we
let ourselves be insulted so scandalously? I become ashamed when I contemplate this

point, and I will eternally declare myself to be against any of my elders and peers who resign themselves to such an ominous yoke.

> Letter, Vicente Guerrero to Agustín de Iturbide, January 20, 1821, from *Cartas de los señores generales Don Agustín de Iturbide y Don Vicente Guerrero* (Puebla: Imprenta Liberal de Moreno Hermanos, 1821). Kindly selected, edited, and translated by Peter Guardino.

For Further Reading

Aside from the time of the discovery and conquest of America, no short period of Latin American history has received more attention from historians than the years during which the region secured its independence from Spain and Portugal. Rather than provide a bibliography on independence, I have here listed five engaging books, all of which are based on the authors' intimate knowledge of contemporary documents and a broad knowledge of other historians' work, which they carefully cite. Each deals with a different region and serves as a jumping-off point for further exploration of the literature, and each adds complexity to the broad outline I have presented here.

On Southern South America
Lynch, John. *San Martín: Argentine Soldier, American Hero*. New Haven: Yale University Press, 2009.

On Highland South America
Cahill, David. *From Rebellion to Independence in the Andes: Soundings from Southern Peru, 1750–1830*. Amsterdam: CEDLA, 2002.

On Brazil
Schultz, Kirsten. *Tropical Versailles: Empire, Monarchy, and the Portuguese Royal Court in Rio de Janeiro, 1808–1821*. New York: Routledge, 2001.

On Northern South America
Lynch, John. *Simón Bolívar: A Life*. New Haven: Yale University Press, 2006.

On Mexico
Guardino, Peter. *Peasants, Politics, and the Formation of Mexico's National State: Guerrero, 1800–1857*. Palo Alto, CA: Stanford University Press, 1996.

Chronology

Asterisks (*) indicate when Spain or Portugal finally lost control in each country and each portion of the former empires became independent.

1700–1713	The War of the Spanish Succession results in the Bourbon dynasty replacing the Hapsburgs on the throne of Spain.
1717	Viceroyalty of New Granada established, with its seat in Bogotá.
1759	Jesuits expelled from Brazil and Portugal.
1763	Capital of Brazil moved from Salvador to Rio de Janeiro.
1767	Jesuits expelled from Spanish America and Spain.
1776	Adam Smith publishes *The Wealth of Nations*. Viceroyalty of Río de la Plata established, with its seat in Buenos Aires. United States declares its independence.
1777	Captaincy-General of Venezuela established, with its seat in Caracas.
1778	"Decree of Free Trade" allows ports within Spanish America to trade with each other and with several ports in Spain. Captaincy-General of Chile established, with its seat in Santiago.
1780–1781	Rebellion of Tupac Amaru in Peru.
1781	Comunero revolt in Colombia.
1789	French Revolution begins. Whites and then mulattos rebel in Haiti. Conspiracy of Creoles in Ouro Preto, Brazil, discovered.
1791	Slaves successfully revolt in Haiti, eventually led by Toussaint l'Ouverture.
1795	Slave revolt in Venezuela put down.
1798	Conspiracy of blacks and mulattos discovered in Salvador, Brazil.

1802   Toussaint l'Ouverture imprisoned in Haiti and sent to France, where he dies.

1804   Haiti wins independence under Jean-Jacques Dessalines.
Spanish government requires amortization of debts previously owed to church entities.

1806   Miranda attempts to free Venezuela.
British suffer their first defeat in Buenos Aires, Argentina.

1807   British suffer their second defeat in Buenos Aires, Argentina.
Napoleon's forces invade Portugal as Portuguese court and government sail for Brazil.

1808   Joseph Bonaparte usurps Spanish throne, and Central Junta in Seville coordinates anti-French resistance.
Viceroy attempts to lead a revolution in Mexico himself, but Spaniards overthrow him.
Montevideo organizes a governing council loyal to the Central Junta in Seville.
Brazilian ports opened to British trade.

1809   Governing councils in Ecuador and Bolivia are crushed.
William Carr Beresford and Arthur Wellesley begin anti-French campaign in Portugal.

1810   Central Junta in Spain dissolves itself and is replaced by a five-man Regency, which then summons a Cortes to meet in Cádiz with some delegates to be elected in Spanish America.
Hidalgo launches revolt in Mexico.
Venezuelan governing council assumes power in Caracas, deposing captain-general.
A governing council assumes power in Bogotá, Colombia.
A governing council assumes power in Santiago, Chile.
* A governing council replaces viceroy in Buenos Aires, Argentina, in May.
* A governing council assumes power in Asunción, Paraguay, in July.

1811   Hidalgo captured and executed in Mexico.
Morelos emerges as Hidalgo's successor and wins several victories in southern Mexico.
Venezuelan congress declares independence.
United Provinces of New Granada set up in Colombia.
Carrera leads coup in Chile, closing national assembly.
A triumvirate assumes power in Buenos Aires, Argentina.
San Martín lands in Buenos Aires, offering his services to the independent government.
Artigas retreats from Uruguay under threat of Portuguese invasion.

1812 Spanish Cortes issues a liberal constitution.
Morelos captures Oaxaca and dominates southern Mexico.
Spanish forces from Puerto Rico smash first independence movement in Venezuela.

1813 Anglo-Portuguese-Spanish army drives French out of Spain.
Morelos convenes a national constituent congress, which declares Mexico independent.
Iturbide placed in charge of "pacifying" Guanajuato.
Bolívar, coming from Colombia, successfully reenters Caracas, after declaring a "war to the death."
Argentine army repulsed in Bolivia.
A congress convenes in Buenos Aires, Argentina.
Artigas reinvades Uruguay.

1814 Napoleon defeated and Ferdinand VII restored to throne of Spain, revoking the 1812 constitution.
Spanish forces begin retaking Venezuela and Colombia, and Bolívar flees to Jamaica.
Pamacahua joins rebel government in Cuzco, Peru, and launches massive Indian rebellion throughout southern Peru.
Belgrano's Argentine forces defeated in Bolivia by royalists.
Spanish forces victorious in Chile.
San Martín sets up headquarters in Mendoza, western Argentina.
Argentine insurgents occupy Montevideo, Uruguay.
Francia named dictator in Paraguay.

1815 Morelos captured and executed in Mexico.
Spain dispatches large army to northern South America.
Bolívar writes "Letter from Jamaica," outlining his political thought.
Pamacahua captured and executed in Peru.
Artigas liberates Montevideo from Argentine control.
Brazil designated an independent kingdom, albeit with the same king as Portugal.

1816 New, more moderate viceroy arrives to pacify Mexico.
Bolívar arrives once again in Venezuela and consolidates his position in the eastern llanos.
Spanish forces victorious in Colombia.
Congress of Tucumán convenes in Argentina and declares independence.
Portuguese once again invade Uruguay.

1817 San Martín crosses the Andes and enters Chile.
Republican revolution in northeast Brazil defeated.

1818 Bolívar and Páez join forces in the Venezuelan llanos.
* San Martín decisively defeats the Spaniards in Chile, and O'Higgins takes over.

1819   Bolívar enters Colombia by surprise and wins decisive battle before entering Bogotá.
Pueyrredón unseated in Argentina.

1820   Liberals in Spain and Portugal revolt, reinstituting constitutional rule.
Guerrero joins Iturbide to unify forces in Mexico within the "Army of the Three Guarantees."
Spanish general Morillo strikes a truce with insurgents in northern South America.
San Martín lands in Peru.

1821   * Mexico declares independence in August, with Central America in tow.
Bolívar enters Caracas, leaves Páez in charge there.
San Martín takes over in Lima.
João VI returns to Portugal, leaving Brazil in hands of his son Pedro as Prince Regent.

1822   Iturbide becomes king of Mexico.
* Bolívar declares "Gran Colombia" independent, then captures Ecuador and annexes it.
San Martín meets Bolívar in Guayaquil, then leaves the field to Bolívar.
* Pedro I declares Brazil independent.

1823   Ferdinand VII once again abrogates the Spanish constitution.
Iturbide overthrown in Mexico.
* Portuguese forces finally leave Brazil.
* The United Provinces of Central America separates from Mexico.

1824   * Battle of Ayacucho ends Spanish power in Peru.
Pedro I of Brazil promulgates a constitution for Brazil.

1825   * General Sucre frees Bolivia.
Uruguayans launch revolution against Brazilian rule.

1826   Rivadavia becomes president of Argentina.

1828   * Uruguay wins independence from both Brazil and Argentina.

1830   Bolívar dies on his way into exile.
* Venezuela separates from Colombia.
* Ecuador separates from Colombia.

1831   Pedro I abdicates throne of Brazil to his infant, Brazilian-born son.

1832   Gómez Farías becomes president of Mexico.

1836   * Texas becomes independent.

1838   * Nicaragua, Honduras, and Costa Rica declare independence from Guatemala.

Glossary

audiencia   A court of appeals and high council to a viceroy.

cabildo   A municipal or county council in Spanish America.

cabildo abierto   An emergency meeting of leading townspeople to discuss measures to be taken in a time of crisis.

câmara   A municipal or county council in Portuguese America.

caudillismo   A political system organized under the rule of a caudillo.

caudillo   A political leader at the local or national level who rules through force or charisma, not by virtue of democratic election or hereditary right.

Cortes (Sp.) or **Côrtes** (Port.)   A parliament.

Creole   A person born in Spanish America of European descent who, at least theoretically, has no Indian or African ancestors. In this book used also for such a person born in Portuguese America, even though it does not have this meaning in Brazil.

fueros   The special rights and privileges, especially to a separate court, pertaining to guilds, churchmen, military officers, and other corporate groups.

gaucho   A cowboy in Argentina or Uruguay, usually of mixed racial background.

hacendado   The owner of a large landed estate.

hacienda   A large landed estate, typically worked by debt peons. In this book the word is used particularly to signify an estate that supplies local rather than European demands for agricultural products. Cf. plantation.

intendant   A government administrator of a province in Spain and colonial Spanish America who reported on some matters directly to the king.

limeño   A resident of Lima, Peru.

llanero   A cowboy in Venezuela, usually of mixed racial background.

llanos   Plains, especially in Venezuela and Colombia.

mestizo   A person of mixed Indian and white ancestry.

mulatto   A person of mixed black and white ancestry.

pampas   Plains, especially in Argentina.

pardo   In Spanish America, a free mulatto. In Portuguese America it was just another word for mulatto.

peninsular   A person from the Iberian Peninsula, in contrast to someone born in America.

plantation   A large landed estate, typically worked by slaves or otherwise coerced laborers. In this book used particularly for those the products of which were exported to Europe. Cf. *hacienda*.

porteño   An inhabitant of the port city of Buenos Aires, Argentina.

senado da câmara   See *câmara*.

Notes

CHAPTER ONE

1. Quoted in John Lynch, *The Spanish American Revolutions, 1808–1826* (New York: Norton, 1973), 23.

2. Quoted in J. R. Fisher, *Government and Society in Colonial Peru: The Intendant System, 1784–1814* (London: Athlone, 1970), 154.

3. Governor of Bahia to Visconde de Anadia, Salvador, 27 August 1807, Arquivo Histórico Ultramarino, Lisbon, Cat. 29.985.

4. Fernando Antônio de Noronha, Governor of Pará, Ofício, 9 November 1795, quoted in Arno Wehling, *Administração portuguesa no Brasil de Pombal a D. João (1777–1808)* (Brasília: FUNCEP, 1986), 88.

5. Edmund S. Morgan, *American Slavery, American Freedom* (New York: Norton, 1975).

6. Quoted in Anthony Pagden, *Spanish Imperialism and the Political Imagination: Studies in European and Spanish-American Social and Political Theory, 1513–1830* (New Haven, CT: Yale University Press, 1990), 12.

7. Quoted in Kenneth Maxwell, "The Generation of the 1790s and the Idea of Luso-Brazilian Empire," in *Colonial Roots of Modern Brazil: Papers of the Newberry Library Conference*, ed. Dauril Alden (Berkeley: University of California Press, 1973), 117.

8. Quoted in Luiz Mott, "A escravatura: a propósito de uma representação a El-Rei sobre a escravatura no Brasil," *Revista do Instituto de Estudos Brasileiros* 14 (1973): 133n.

CHAPTER TWO

1. Quoted in John Lynch, *The Spanish American Revolutions, 1808–1826* (New York: Norton, 1973), 190.

2. Quoted in Lynch, *Spanish American Revolutions*, 193.

3. Quoted in Octávio Tarquínio de Sousa, *Fatos e personagens em tôrno de um regime*, vol. 9 of *História dos fundadores do Império do Brasil* (Rio de Janeiro: José Olympio, 1957), 13.

CHAPTER THREE

1. Quoted in William Spence Robertson, *The Life of Miranda*, 2 vols. (Chapel Hill: University of North Carolina Press, 1929), 1:318.

CHAPTER FOUR

1. Quoted in Lucía Sala de Touron, Nelson de la Torre, and Julio C. Rodríguez, *Artigas y su revolución agraria, 1811–1820* (Mexico City: Siglo Veintiuno, 1978), 152.

2. Quoted in Timothy E. Anna, *The Fall of the Royal Government in Mexico City* (Lincoln: University of Nebraska Press, 1978), 85.

3. Quoted in David A. Brading, *Miners and Merchants in Bourbon Mexico* (Cambridge: Cambridge University Press, 1971), 346.

4. Quoted in Wilbert H. Timmons, *Morelos: Priest, Soldier, Statesman of Mexico* (El Paso: Texas Western College Press, 1963), 86.

CHAPTER FIVE

1. Quoted in Timothy Anna, *Spain and the Loss of America* (Lincoln: University of Nebraska Press, 1990), 172.

2. Quoted in R. K. Webb, *Modern England: From the Eighteenth Century to the Present* (New York: Dodd, Mead, 1973), 167.

3. "Plan del señor coronel D. Agustín Iturbide," Articles 1, 2, 4, 12, and 14, http://scholarship.rice.edu.

4. Quoted in Francisco Adolfo de Varnhagen, *História da independência do Brasil até ao reconhecimento pela antiga metrópole, compreendendo, separadamente, a dos sucessos ocorridos em algumas províncias até essa data*, 3rd ed., ed. Baron of Rio Branco and Hélio Vianna (São Paulo: Melhoramentos, 1957), 269.

5. Quoted in Hendrik Kraay, "'Em outra coisa não falavam os pardos, cabras, e crioulos': O 'recrutamento' de escravos na guerra da Independência na Bahia," *Revista Brasileira de História* 22, no. 43 (2002): 109–126.

6. Quoted in Neill Macaulay, *Dom Pedro: The Struggle for Liberty in Brazil and Portugal, 1798–1834* (Durham: Duke University Press, 1986), 251.

7. A. L. Pereyra, quoted in William Spence Robertson, "The Policy of Spain toward Its Revolted Colonies, 1820–1823," *Hispanic American Historical Review* 6, no. 1–3 (February–August 1926): 22.

CHAPTER SIX

1. Quoted in Gerhard Masur, *Simón Bolívar* (Albuquerque: University of New Mexico Press, 1948), 687.

2. Quoted in Guillermo Morón, *A History of Venezuela*, ed. and trans. John Street (London: Allen & Unwin, 1964), 128.

3. Quoted in Timothy E. Anna, *The Fall of the Royal Government in Peru* (Lincoln: University of Nebraska Press, 1979), 151.

4. According to a British consul, April 25, 1826, quoted in Peter Blanchard, *Slavery and Abolition in Early Republican Peru* (Wilmington, DE: Scholarly Resources, 1992), 10.

5. "Decreto sobre la libertad de los esclavos," 1820, in *Documentos que hicieron historia: Vida republicana de Venezuela* (Caracas: Ediciones Presidencia de la República, 1989), 1:245.

6. Quoted in Masur, *Simón Bolívar*, 437.

7. Quoted in Simon Collier, *Ideas and Politics of Chilean Independence, 1808–1833* (Cambridge: Cambridge University Press, 1967), 339.

8. Quoted in R. A. Humphreys, ed., *British Consular Reports on the Trade and Politics of Latin America, 1824–1826* (London: Royal Historical Society, 1940), 31–32.

Illustration Credits

1.1. "Moulin a sucre." In Johann Moritz Rugendas, *Malerische Reise in Brasilien* (Paris: Engelmann & Cie., 1835), div. 4, pl. 9.

1.2. "Church of N. S. de Guadalupe, about a league from the capital." In H[enry] G[eorge] Ward, *Mexico in 1827* (London: Henry Colburn, 1828), 1:242.

1.3. Emile Antoine Bayard, "Revolt of African Slaves on San Domingo." Corbis Images.

2.1. "Buenos Aires from the Plaza de Toros." E[meric] E[ssex] Vidal, *Picturesque Illustrations of Buenos Ayres and Monte Video, Consisting of Twenty-Four Views: Accompanied with Descriptions of the Scenery, and of the Costumes, Manners, &c. of the Inhabitants of Those Cities and Their Environs* (London: R. Ackerman, 1820), facing p. 26.

2.2. "Valparaiso Bay." In Alexander Caldcleugh, *Travels in South America During the Years 1819–20–21, Containing an Account of the Present State of Brazil, Buenos Ayres, and Chile,* 2 vols. (London: John Murray, 1825), 2, facing p. 45.

2.3. "Mexico from the azotea of the house of H. M.'s Mission, San Cosme." In H[enry] G[eorge] Ward, *Mexico in 1827,* 2 vols. (London: Henry Colburn, 1828), 1:frontispiece.

2.4. "Lima with Bridge over the Rimac." In Alexander Caldcleugh, *Travels in South America During the Years 1819–20–21, Containing an Account of the Present State of Brazil, Buenos Ayres, and Chile,* 2 vols. (London: John Murray, 1825), 2:96.

2.5. "Brazilian Plantation House on Ilha Bela." Photo by Richard Graham, 1976.

2.6. "Rio from Gloria Hill." In Maria Graham [Lady Maria Calcott], *Journal of a Voyage to Brazil and Residence There during Part of the Years 1821, 1822, 1823* (London: Longman, Hurst, Rees, Orme, Brown, and Green, 1824), 168.

2.7. "Vue prise devant l'eglise de San-Bendo [*sic*]." In Johann Moritz Rugendas, *Malerische Reise in Brasilien* (Paris: Engelman, 1835), div. 3, pl. 12.

3.1. Francisco de Goya, "The Third of May 1808: Executions at the Montaña del Príncipe Pío, Madrid," 1814. Museo del Prado, Madrid. Corbis Images.

3.2. Francisco Goya, "The Duke of Wellington." Corbis Images.

4.1. "Bernardo O'Higgins." Courtesy of the Museo Histórico Nacional de Chile.

4.2. "Miranda and Bolívar Signing Venezuela's Declaration of Independence." Corbis Images.

4.3. José Gil de Castro, "Simón Bolívar, 1825." Salón Elíptico, Palacio Federal, Caracas.

4.4. "D. Miguel Hidalgo y Costilla y Gallaga." In Manuel Rivera Cambas, *Los gobernantes de México: Galería de biografías y retratos de los virreyes, emperadores, presidentes y otros gobernadores que ha tenido México desde don Hernando Cortés hasta el c. Benito Juárez*, 2 vols. (Mexico City: Imp. de J. M. Aguilar Ortiz, 1873), 2:6.

4.5. Juan O'Gorman, "Father Hidalgo's grito, 1810." Detail of mural, National Museum of History, Mexico City. Corbis Images.

4.6. "Father José María Morelos y Pavón." National Museum of History, Mexico City. Corbis Images.

4.7. "Le Roi Don João VI." In Jean Baptiste Debret, *Voyage pittoresque et historique au Brésil, sejour d'un artiste français au Brésil depuis 1816 jusqu'en 1831 inclusivement, epoque de l'avénement et de l'abdication de S. M. D. Pedro 1er, fondateur de l'Empire brésilien*, 3 vols. (Paris: Firmin Didot Fréres, 1834–1839), 3:pl. 9.

5.1. W. S. Dumon, "City and Bay of Cartagena." Corbis Images.

5.2. Tito Salas, "Bolívar and the Patriot Forces Crossing the Andes." Palacio Federal, Caracas.

5.3. "Quinta de Bolívar." Photo by Richard Graham, 1959.

5.4. "Manuela Sáenz," Quinta de Bolívar, Bogotá.

5.5. François Joseph Navez, "José de San Martín [1828]." Museo Histórico Nacional, Buenos Aires.

5.6. Peter E. Strehling, "Lord Cochrane." National Maritime Museum, Greenwich, England.

5.7. José R. Salas, "Antonio José de Sucre," painted ca. 1890 and based on a miniature made in Quito in 1828 by José Sáez. Courtesy of John Carter Brown Library.

5.8. "Vicente Guerrero." In Enrique Olavarría y Ferrari, *Episodios históricos mexicanos: Novelas históricas nacionales*, 2 vols. (Mexico City: Juan de la Fuente Parrés, 1887), tomo II, parte 1ª, p. 826.

5.9. "Agustín de Iturbide." Corbis Images.

5.10. "José Bonifácio." In Sebastião Augusto Sisson, *Galeria dos brasileiros ilustres*, 2 vols. (Rio de Janeiro: Lithographia de S. A. Sisson, 1861), 1:facing p. 39.

5.11. "L'Empereur Don Pedro I." In Jean-Baptiste Debret, *Voyage pittoresque et historique au Brésil, sejour d'un artiste français au Brésil depuis 1816 jusqu'en 1831 inclusivement, epoque de l'avénement et de l'abdication de S. M. D. Pedro 1er, fondateur de l'Empire brésilien*, 3 vols. (Paris: Firmin Didot Fréres, 1834–1839), 3:pl. 9.

5.12. "Dona Maria de Jesus." In Maria Graham [Lady Maria Calcott], *Journal of a Voyage to Brazil and Residence There during Part of the Years 1821, 1822, 1823* (London: Longman, Hurst, Rees, Orme, Brown, and Green, 1824), 293.

5.13. Lithograph made from a photograph by Victor Frond. In Charles Ribeyrolles, *Brazil pitoresco: album de vistas, panoramas, paisagens, monumentos, costumes, etc., com os retratos de Sua Magestade Imperador Don [sic] Pedro II et [sic] da familia imperial, photographia-dos por Victor Frond, lithographiados pelos primeiros artistas de Paris. . . e acompanhados de tres volumes . . . sobre a historia, as instituições, as cidades, as fazendas, a cultura, a coloniza-ção, etc., do Brazil [sic]* (Paris: Lemercier, 1861), pl. 35.